ZERO *to* O
Seventy-Five

How I Escaped the Kids' Table

THOMAS E. BYRON

Copyright © 2023 Thomas E. Byron
All rights reserved
First Edition

NEWMAN SPRINGS PUBLISHING
320 Broad Street
Red Bank, NJ 07701

First originally published by Newman Springs Publishing 2023

ISBN 978-1-68498-763-4 (Paperback)
ISBN 978-1-68498-764-1 (Digital)

Printed in the United States of America

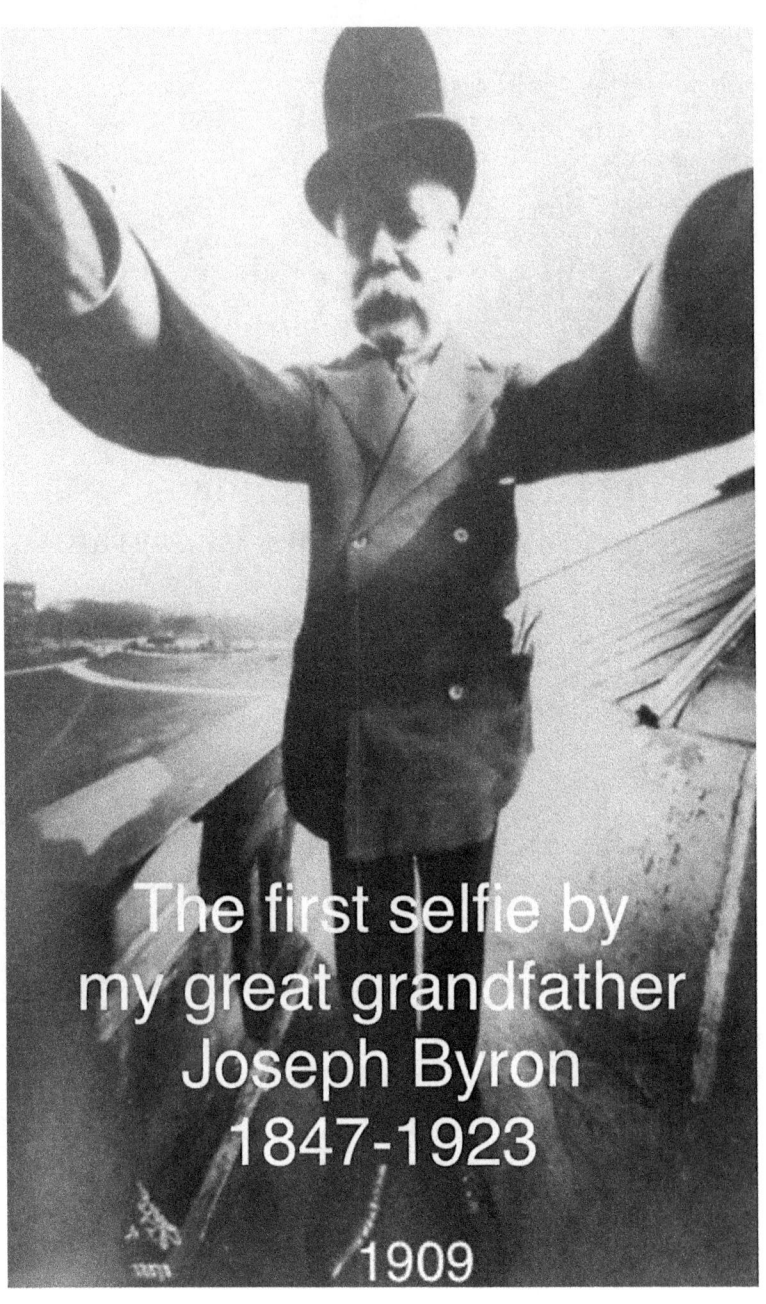

If you thought selfies were a new craze, think again: Amazing self-portraits taken by pioneering photographer in 1909 put Instagram to shame

By Snejana Farberov
14:59 EDT 08 Feb 2014 , updated 11:56 EDT 09 Feb 2014

My great-grandfather, left, and his friends (with your author in the lower right).

To my loving wife, Sheila
I never would've begun this journey you, dear reader, are about to experience. I would never have finished this epic piece of writing—my first!
Je t'aime

Contents

Preface xi
Introduction xix
Who Am I, or Who Was I? 1
1946–1949 11
Let's Introduce You to My Five Siblings 14
The World I Would Enter 24
Beginning My First Year in 1946 26
1948, 1949 28
1950 32
1951 35
1952 38
1953 40
1954 44
1955 49
1956 56
1957 60
1958 62
1959 69
1960 71
1961 75
Fall 1961: The Bay of Pigs Invasion, Cuba 76
1962 78
November 1963 83
1964: Post-Ricky Period Begins a Month after Graduation! ... 84
1964–1965: New Year's Eve 99
1965 100
Joined the US Air Force, 1966 101
Early Summer, 1966 104
1967, Winter 110
1968, Julie's Birth 113
1969, Lisa's Birth 118
Return to Civilian Life, 1970 124

1971	132
1974, Mark's Birth	135
My Three Children	138
1975	139
Early 1976	140
Winter '76/'77	146
February 1977	149
1978	154
1979	158
1980	161
1981	164
1982	165
1983	167
1984	170
1985	173
1986	174
1987	177
25 June 1988	183
1989	185
1990	188
1991	195
1992	197
The Long-Anticipated Elvis Stamp, Issued 08 January 1993	200
1995	207
1996	210
1997	214
01 December 1997	219
1998	220
1999	222
2000, Y2K	223
2001	224
2002	227
2003	228
2004	229
The Post-Judy Period of My Life Begins	233
2004	236

2005–2011: Some Lifetouch Adventures, Year by Year 239
2006 242
2007 243
2008 244
October 2009 246
2010 248
2012: Titanic Memorial Cruise (TMC) 249
2013 267
2014: Belfast and County Antrim Adventure and TMC
Reunion from Cruise 268
Post-Paul Period Begins and Last Visits Remembered: July
2015, New Mexico 283
05 September 2016 286
22 November 2016 288
2017 Travel Adventure: Abroad for a Fortnight in the UK 289
2018 304
2019 Southampton Adventure with Three Germans,
Two Frenchies, a Drunken Norwegian, and Two Yanks 305
13 April 2019 307
15 July 2019 309
Last Chapter 310
A Place for an Old Man to Mention Things He Forgot Page 311
A Few Moments to Remember as My Time to Complete
This Story Draws Near 314
17 August 2020 315
22 March 2021 317
Random Accidental Meetings 321
Pithy Byronisms 327
My Last Thought 333
Postscript 335
On My iPhone / Funeralmusic.jpeg 337

Your author's DNA https://www.ancestry.com/dna/origins/share/
023e68fc-3203-4ff4-a15c-b8e3e4bbcaca

Preface

In full disclosure, I have three cousins (*Clayton, Robert* Luce, and *Patricia* Murtaugh) who are living who would be surprised that they were omitted here. I am *not* the sole survivor of my great-grandfather, but I was the only descendant that is a professional photographer.

When I was a much younger man, life was even more different than it is now. As *you* read this adventure of mine, you'll see why I'm like I am (or was)!

- I will provide examples of how I have seen all of these changes. I will share every emotion as I talk to you about what followed. These are unnumbered because one is no more important than the other.
- Coins were desired to buy anything when I was young. Now fancy electronically accessible plastic is worth money you never see (which I rarely use), or you can borrow the cash you need (your *worst* option). Your bank's teller is a new machine. You put your card into it to get some money. No need to talk to anyone!
- People used to talk to other people (and it was face-to-face). Now you can speak to a piece of flickering plastic or a different color plastic device of your choice. Miracles (voice and moving images) happen.
- You could start a cooking fire with your morning (news) paper. Now you can read the information on an electronic device but can't start fires. Sad.
- We used to dress up when we flew somewhere. Now we dress *down* seat-mates if they annoy us (a custom your narrator refuses to accept as appropriate).
- "Pictures" used to come from film. Now they come from digital magic. Immediately! Everything is *now*! How sad. As an aside, my ancestral family photographers used "glass plates" soaked in photographic chemistry for their negatives. The

print was made, and the plate was washed clean of the image on it. Today, we take a digital image, print it, and delete the pixels. We reuse the same device repeatedly, just as *Joseph Byron* did when he created that selfie image of 1909 you just saw. Same steps but cleaner, less expensive, and a lot faster!

- We used to take hours to cook our food, but now we (many of us) microwave everything. *Zap!* In seconds! Now what are we doing with all that extra time?
- TV shows started at 8:00 p.m., and now we record (DVR) them. Now we can watch any time we please and fast-forward through any or all commercials!
- Our phones now connect us to the entire world, right in our hands. We can watch live events occurring anywhere on the planet or in orbit around our earth, but we have neighbors fifty feet away that we know *nothing* about.
- *Clockwise* and *counterclockwise* are meaningless words in a digital world.
- We used to write letters and mail them using postage stamps. Ick! Unsanitary. We solve that now by sending letters electronically and impersonally by electronic mail.
- If you run afoul of the law (the "long ago you"), you were punished based on the outcome of dealing with the blind, as in Lady Justice. If you break the law now, your political affiliation might determine where you exit the courthouse: to freedom or to prison. Robbery was against the law when I was a youth. Now, you pay nothing, or a minor fine, in various regions of America for many crimes, in addition to robbery, that you may commit.

Let's begin, but with a cautionary thought to keep in mind. This is *my* first piece of writing anything this long and this detailed. Please have patience. I completed this "auto" while typing this *with my left index finger!* This is an epic piece! It is NOT a Guinness World Record—as yet!

I will start with an introductory history of my family and me. I am fortunate to have access to various excellent sources, firsthand accounts from my Aunt Grace (we'll meet her later), and photographs going back further than anyone I know of and who has access to old photos!

While I'm mentioning photographs, they are *not* pictures; I remember my grandfather's words on that subject. I bring "receipts." The title of this autobiography refers to a "kids' table!" Here's that group of us outside with our grandfather. We all ate (we did not "dine") in a separate area from the primary adults' dining room. We were fairly well-behaved.

This photograph was captured by our grandfather, *Percy* Byron, with a long cable release. These are the kids' table children, except *Paul*, *Judy*, *Lou Ann* (Louise L.), and *Clayton*.

Thanks! Let's go! But first, a *note*. All links to video clips (turn on your sound), music, and online references cited are accentuated in grey. All family names are in *italicized* (for easier searching).

I will introduce you to the photographic talent of *Joseph* Byron, my great-grandfather: https://www.mcny.org/collections/prints-photographs. It is the backstory as to why I chose that specific selfie as my cover page. It is my favorite selfie, but it's the direct result of my ancestor's PNA, or photographic natural ability. (Please credit your author with creating that gem of an abbreviation.) It is not to be confused but similar to your DNA, which my son *Mark* and I possess. Thinking about ancestry is prominent in my mind because I've recently met *my* (first) great-grandson this year! What a blessing. And when you, my great-grandson, read this, welcome, *Chapman* Scott Whisenant (born on 03 May 2021)!

Advice from the Older Me to the Younger Me

There will always be second-guessing episodes in everyone's life, but they are not written nor long remembered. The following is my list, *not yours!* Sorry.

1. You (I'm talking to *me* again) should have tried going to college sooner. It was a burden. My defense is that I graduated twice (with two different marketable degrees), owing $0.00, which, looking back, is an accomplishment. These additional degrees were in studies heavy on math, I'm proud to say!
2. You (I'm talking to me) would have been wiser to have turned down at least one of those multiple company transfers since you never got a promotion. You did meet *Sheila* because of that, and Lisa met her husband, *Tim*, and brought two great children into the world. *Mark* ended up back in his birth city and began a photography career, also earning a degree. Now he has a son in college (my grandson *Zach*), and I hope he will have a career as a major league pitcher! He has that athletic talent for sure!
3. My daughter *Julie* met *Ron* Fecteau in 1998 and has been with him longer than many of us have been with our mates. To all that, I say, "Dwell on the present, not the future!"

Special thanks to my *sweet* wife, *Sheila*, for all your help during my many years (between five and ten years, I was never keeping track) putting this autobiography together! I'm a slow one-finger typist.

Thanks, Beth G., for reviewing my manuscript, pointing out my mistakes, and giving insights into my efforts! *Sheila* and your author, with our friend Lyn M. for their opinions! Thank you to my youngest daughter, Lisa, for all your welcomed corrections!

This is dedicated to Mrs. Faulkensten, my junior and senior high school English teacher, for your excellent lessons on the finer points of the English language! Those lessons were from 1963 to 1964 (eleventh and twelfth grades), and they are recalled here fondly! I also owe much of my writing skills to my sister *Judy*, also in your teaching, five years before me. I noticed that her artwork was in your classroom as my reminder of who I followed! I thank you sincerely, Mrs. Faulkensten, my high school English teacher, "par excellence," your influence is commemorated here. It will continue long (fifty-eight years, as I publish these words) beyond those years I spent in your classroom. Thank you. Photograph on the next page is the author's work.

Dedicated to my "little" sisters, *Laura* and *Debbie*; my daughters *Julie* and *Lisa* and my son *Mark*; his son, *Zachary*; my granddaughter, *Lauren* Whisenant, and her husband, *Bryan*; and my grandson, Alex Chapman. Special separate dedication to my great-grandson, *Chapman* Scott Whisenant. As a great-grandson, you have a handwritten letter from me that I gave to your mom on 6 June 2021, to hold on to until you can read.

My Siblings and My Children

My sisters *Laura* and *Debbie* are quoted here in a few places along my journey, and I thank them for allowing me to repeat them and include a few of their insights. My older sister *Judy* raised me since my birth mother had *Ricky, Laura,* and *Debbie* to raise! *Julie, Lisa,* and *Mark* are my pride and joy children. You are unique, and I couldn't imagine my life without your help.

THOMAS E. BYRON

Russell Buchanan, seen here, paying rapt attention to a great teacher.

ZERO TO SEVENTY-FIVE

I was taking photographs and might not have been as focused on my lessons. Notice my sister's artwork adorns the front wall of her classroom five years after she was her student. That's an honor for something to stay in a school for five years after leaving that school. Her artwork might have lasted well beyond my graduation in 1964.

There will be some random accomplishments in my life, in no particular order, and details as we travel along my life's path. Be careful, and I bumped around a lot on this road. Watch your step and keep an open mind, and take a strange journey with me.

1. I've rebuilt automotive engines and drove one (*once*) far beyond ~~142 mph~~ any legal speed. Test purposes!
2. I've rebuilt military aircraft in the Air Force, and I've voluntarily flown (as a passenger) nearly Mach 1 in that same plane immediately after working on it.
3. I've lived in Ohio, Pennsylvania, Kentucky, Tennessee, Alabama, Louisiana, Georgia, and Michigan, including Texas, for six weeks of basic GI training, and Illinois for ninety days of training. A total of ten states.
4. I've been married twice, first for twenty years, then my second marriage thirty-five years to date in 2022.
5. I have three grown children, four grandchildren, and one great-grandson! *Sheila* has three grown children, seven grandchildren, and one great-granddaughter!
6. I owned several houses and even more different cars.
7. I attended formal education for twenty-nine years, but I took a six-year break after the first twelve years of K-12 and then entered the military. I married and had *Julie* and *Lisa* in the Air Force and then went to seventeen more years of night school. During my fourth year of college, my third child, a son, was born, and then I graduated when *Mark* was thirteen. Do! Not! Attempt! This!
8. I took piano lessons briefly. Ms. Heinz was my teacher, and she was good at her teaching, but I was not good at learning! I got past learning E-G-B-D-F, "every good boy does fine," and F-A-C-E, as in your "face." Then there were the sharps and

flats, which I never grasped. I love piano music. I can't play it, but my youthfulness at age eight to focus wasn't that good! That was a Freudian slip and a sideways reference to my photographic talent.
9. Sheila and I built a photography business and photographed five hundred weddings in twelve states and internationally: Kentucky, Tennessee, Indiana, Pennsylvania, California, Arizona, Georgia, Missouri, Mississippi, Colorado, Ohio, Vermont, and the Turks and Caicos.

Welcome, and thanks for buying my book, or finding a copy as a gift, or another unusual way (a thrift store or a yard sale?). Either way, I hope you enjoy my many years of effort putting this together and experiencing, secondhand, my few successes and my many foibles! This autobiography is your author's first and last book! For those skimming through this, I am writing this entire book *with my left-hand index finger!* You read that correctly. I am a one-finger typist. It's not a Guinness Record breaker as yet, as I mentioned! I have laid my marker down though! (Just in case.) I will choose that as my life's moniker.

You may be interested or bored. You may know me, or you may not know me. Either way, you arrived at our brief meeting here is just great. Know this: what you're about to read is true! Some will be funny. I know several paragraphs will be sad. What I talk about is my side of the event and sounds one-sided. *It is!* This autobiography is *my version* of events, Your Honor.

From time to time, along our journey here, pay attention and know that I'm trying to tell you what *my* life was like. Why I am (or *was*) considered strange—or at least a tick off. This essay, as I said, is my first and is my only chance to make my case to you, members of the jury. "Draw near, be attentive as I make my case!"

(https://youtu.be/vAOVRkSCWmg)

As I've already demonstrated here, my humor is a bit off. Relax, get a cuppa or a drink or a bottle and enjoy! No names have been changed, and no one's convicted *or* innocent here! Thanks!

Introduction

Guinness Book of World Records (GBWR) application applied on 4 August 2021, for the longest (ninety thousand words) autobiography typed with merely one finger.

Dear Thomas Byron

Thank you for sending us the details of your proposed record attempt for "longest autobiography one finger typed."

Unfortunately, after thoroughly reviewing your application with our research team members, we are afraid to say that we cannot accept your proposal as a Guinness World Records title.

Our team of expert Records Managers receive thousands of new record proposals every year from worldwide. Each of these proposals is carefully analyzed to determine whether they meet a stringent set of criteria. Every record verified by Guinness World Records must reflect a level of existing competition in a particular field, be measurable by a single superlative, be verifiable, standardizable, breakable, and present an element of skill. Therefore record titles are not created to suit an individual proposal but rather due to competition in a particular field. As we have not established any specific competition in this instance, we are not currently considering a record title that fits your proposal.

For information on what makes a record, we would advise before applying to visit http://www.guinnessworldrecords.com/records/what-makes-a-guinness-world-records-record-title. This page will provide helpful information if you think about breaking or setting a record.

Once again, thank you for contacting Guinness World Records.

Allow me to introduce myself, your author, on the journey you are about to commence. I was, in my father's own words to me (*eek!*), a Christmas-pass-**conception**! You read that correctly!

A brief genealogy follows—those parts of my DNA (of whom I now treasure).

People change their names for many reasons. One might speculate at length as to why basket maker James Byron Clayton (1826–1880) abandoned his family name when opening a photographic studio in Nottingham in 1857. The most straightforward argument, and probably the closest to the truth, is described by Bernard and Pauline Heathcote in their booklet *Pioneers of Photography in Nottinghamshire* [1].

His younger brother, Walter Clayton (1833–1893), had already upstaged him by opening a studio in Greyhound Street, Nottingham, a year earlier. Perhaps it was to distinguish himself in a rapidly growing market with numerous competitors, and his baptismal middle name, Byron, seemed to have a little more cache. He dropped the Clayton surname and became James Byron, photographer of Ram Yard, Long Row East.

James Byron Clayton was baptized at St. Mary's, Nottingham, on 13 August 1826, one of four surviving children of James Clayton (d. 1863) and his wife, Ann née Soar (1798–1873), who operated a basket-making business at Greyhound Yard. He was married in 1845 to Mary Taylor, daughter of a coal miner from Underwood.

Joseph CLAYTON b. c. 1767 d. May 1835 m: 17 July 1799, St. Mary's Nottingham, NTT.
Eleanor BARKER d. c. 1835–1837.
James CLAYTON Bapt. 21 February 1802, Wesleyan Church, Nottingham, NTT, d. 1863 Nottingham, NTT, m: 14 February 1820, Radford, NTT.

Ann SOAR Bapt. 24 August 1798, St Mary, Nottingham, NTT (daughter of George SOAR and Sophia COX) d. c. May 1873, Nottingham, NTT.
Ann CLAYTON Bapt. 3 September 1820, St Mary, Nottingham, NTT.
James Barker CLAYTON Bapt. 16 December 1821, St Mary, Nottingham, NTT bur. 29 December 1824.
James Byron CLAYTON, a.k.a. James BYRON, Bapt. 13 August 1826, St Mary, Nottingham, NTT, d. 21 December 1880.
Chester CHS m: c. May 1845, Basford Rd., NTT.
Mary TAYLOR b. Underwood, NTT, Bapt. 8 June 1825, Greasley, NTT.
William CLAYTON b. c. November 1845, Nottingham, NTT, d. c. November 1858, Nottingham, NTT.
Joseph Byron CLAYTON, a.k.a. Joseph BYRON, b. 22 January 1847, Nottingham, NTT, d. 1923 New York, USA, m: 16 November 1875, Julia LEWIN b. June 1854, Leicester, LEI.
Maud M. Byron CLAYTON b. c. November 1876, Nottingham, NTT.
Percy Claude Byron CLAYTON, a.k.a. Percy C. BYRON, b. 21 September 1878, Nottingham NTT, d. 6 June 1959, m: Louise S. b. October 1884, NY.
Elizabeth L. BYRON b. Aug 1909 Edmonton, AB, CAN.
Grace J. BYRON b. c. 1914(?), CAN.
Joseph Marrin BYRON b. 4 October 1914, CAN, d. November 2006.
Jane A. BYRON b. c. Nov 1916, CAN.
Florence Mabel Byron CLAYTON b. Feb 1880, Nottingham, NTT, m: Joseph MAY.
Georgina Byron CLAYTON b. Dec 1882, Nottingham, NTT.
Louis Phillippe Byron CLAYTON b. c. February 1886, Nottingham, NTT.
Jane CLAYTON b. c. 1830, Nottingham, NTT.
Walter CLAYTON b. c. 1833 Nottingham, NTT, d. 1 June 1893, Babbacombe, DEV, m1: c. Aug 1863, Hull Rd. YKS Sarah Anne/Annie TOMLINSON b. c. 1840 d. c. November 1867, Nottingham NTT m2: c. Feb 1880 Leicester LEI, Jeannette Annie WRIXON b. c. 1853 Newcastle/Gateshead d. c. February 1925, Camberwell Rd., SRY.

Joseph CLAYTON b. 8 Feb 1804 Bapt. Wesleyan Church, Nottingham NTT.

Reminiscences preserved by Byron-Clayton family tradition have suggested that James Clayton Sr. founded the photographic business in 1844. Research by Heathcote & Heathcote (2001) has failed to find any hard evidence of this, although he has been artistically inclined and worked briefly as a portrait painter. It has also been suggested that he may have worked secretly in the mid-1840s, taking portraits at his basket-making workrooms on Greyhound Street. The daguerreotype patent holder in Nottinghamshire was a Hungarian emigré named George Popowitz, who operated from the Bromley House studio in Angel Row, Nottingham, and rigidly enforced his monopoly.
(https://photo-sleuth.blogspot.com/search?q=Byron-Clayton+)

Who Am I, or Who Was I?

I have been told that I am a psychoanalyst's nightmare or the best customer ever. I don't know which, or I will continue refusing to answer. When is it too late for a seventy-five-year-old? For a twenty-five-year-old, this is much easier to answer speaking for myself. I have been paying attention, and thus, I'm now (*almost?*) an elderly old curmudgeon. A few stories, a few thoughts on my past, and I will help you (from a distant time and place?) understand me better.

I was into this life for many decades before I realized that people can be born crooked and can't help it. A famous US president once said, "Trust but verify!" I was many years past my high school days when I realized I was pretending to be stupid and got lousy grades as my reward. "Stop paying attention to the opposite sex and keep your nose in a book," I finally said to myself! It took me seventeen years of night school (which began six years post-high school) to realize I was correct. I surprised my inner critic and did well in college. Was it me listening to my own opinion, or was I listening to the idea(s)? I was anonymously entered into the Omicron Delta Epsilon honor society in economics upon graduation. *Lesson number one:* listen to your inner voice. It won't lie to you! I learned at age sixty that smoking at age fourteen "ain't good for ya!" I quit smoking on 23 July 2012, shortly after retiring early in 2012. A chest x-ray and a follow-up MRI showed that my lungs were good.

That leads me to my next "what did you learn?" You can't change your DNA. Those strings of millions of information inside every part of you can significantly impact your life span, health, and mannerisms. Popeye, from the comic strip, taught me that in the 1950s, and I didn't heed his advice: "I yam what I yam!"

Lesson number two: take away "we are who we are!" Those are a few of my favorite things I've learned. Too late. But to quote myself, "Life is a series of mistakes and lessons learned as you move forward."

My childhood is blank except for the flashbacks I'll be recounting. This explains where the child in me went. He ran away! Mmm? What do you think? Is he hiding inside me? I'm aware of that ploy. The child in me was clever and sneaky (devious at times), if necessary. You might know he's dead, or you'll soon learn that he is. My brother took that option at age fourteen (see "1964"). I can't ask him now, *can* I? Yet again, I can't remember much about that event except the following pieces of memories I've put together over the years. *My two younger sisters are my primary supporting witnesses in this case, Your Honor.* Here's how it happened. My brother carried out his final thought. Or did he? We *shall* explore that angle in excruciating detail.

I came home on a Sunday afternoon from camping up in the mountains of Eastern Pennsylvania. Another escape, you say? When I came home that summer, on a *hot* July afternoon, I carried my pack into the house. It was rapidly becoming apparent to me, at this point, why our narrow street was crowded with parked cars. Not an everyday sight, and it was unnerving! My older brother, Paul, greeted me when I came inside. *That* never happened before! He said, looking like he'd seen a ghost, "*I thought you were dead!*" I was not, but I soon realized that my little brother had committed suicide.

The rest is a blank, as I have mentioned. Not that long ago, as this suicide story continues, my older brother, Paul, had left home when he graduated from high school in 1958. He never lived in his hometown again. None of us did, except my sister Judy for a brief time. I will mention that about her house and her husband's shooting gallery in their basement shortly. You read that correctly! Paul went to Washington state with his friend Tim, as far west as possible. They had both graduated from high school. It was always a long hot summer, we never had air-conditioning at home or in our cars. Paul asked me about his friend Tim (last name Hudson?) a few years before he died. He left me and I effectively became "the older brother." I never did resolve where Tim ever went. It's now a useless piece of trivia without involving Paul.

My inner child died on one of those hot summer days fifty years ago. Your own brother's death, a.k.a. "little buddy," creates a profound scar. I am here as his unauthorized substitute/replacement. I am the last male standing in our family. "The show must go on!"

This day of writing, Saturday, 24 September 2016, is my seventieth birthday. (*Nope!* There was no party.) I had written a preliminary copy of my autobiography, but it was panned, and it was an epic fail.

Fast-forwarding, by now, from 2018 to 2022, I'm refining, rewriting, editing, tweaking, and concluding this long effort! But now, fast-forward from my birthday above mentioned as I review my scribblings, it's 2019, and I've upgraded my tools and sped up my ability to finalize this autobiography on an iPod Air! Voilà! Efficiency! My speed has taken a quantum leap! I'm glad you are presently reading my story about never giving up! A final draft (or so I thought) on 17 June 2019, was first published to a limited audience online, with little feedback now. On my seventy-fifth birthday in 2021, I *thought* I was finished! But until I decide what to do with this writing, I'll rethink and refine what I've created. It's that engineer-brain in me, always pushing me!

The ancient and well-documented family photographic history I've inherited is a considerable source of pride! Other people have written about the Byrons/Claytons. That's where the information you read earlier here has come from. My family began photographing their world in 1844, and today, in 2019, my son Mark is a *great* professional and talented photographer, as I had hoped he would be! The history that I witnessed, or was told about by my father's sister, my Aunt Grace, was *sordid* and *colorful*. Details to follow as you and I continue to explore my life.

I would be incomplete if I failed to mention my seven years of writing thousands upon thousands of answers on Quora, which honed my writing style and skills. There are many emails in the file containing all my writings there. I left that site in 2018 to complete this autobiography. That volume of near daily paper has given me the idea to complete a task as this auto. I went to that site randomly in the summer of 2012 (see chapter "2012") after Sheila and I made our first trip abroad. *All* I wanted was to learn just a few writing tips and techniques to memorialize and share our unique *Titanic* experience (the ship that *you* know from the movies). It was an excellent place to begin my efforts to write a story that I would eventually include here. As you'll learn, steamships were Grandfather Percy's life. Ergo, I inherited that interest. I wanted those Quora readers to be as excited as we were! That effort on Quora has now exceeded eight years of writing and over eight thousand posts and twenty-four thousand followers. If you go to Quora, you may see that I have copied several of my sections of this autobiography from that site. Why should I rewrite what I had written? Quora has taught me a few things about writing.

THOMAS E. BYRON

https://www.quora.com/profile/Tom-Byron?ch=17&oid=4475792&share=760ca00e&srid=3JBw&target_type=user

ZERO TO SEVENTY-FIVE

I will be using all of these license plates, from 1966 to 2021, that were my license plates on my several cars. They will now be repurposed as the heading for that year I'm discussing as we travel through my story. There is no Pennsylvania plate because I was not the owner of *this* '57 Chevy seen in the above photo. After this car, I will use *every license plate I ever owned* as chapter headers, and they are my initial proof (year-by-year)! They all hang in my library today as a reminder of my path on my life's journey. They are the only tangible evidence to support (*the* year) the stories I'm about to relate. *You Are There* was an old TV show (1953–1972) from my youth. Yes, we are there, using these license plates. Yes, I will admit that is pretty clever. (*Thank you!*) Some years, I got new license plates, and some years, I paid more fees that year and only got a sticker to put on the old tag. Governments waste more money than they try to save by giving you a lousy new sticker.

I remember my times (the good, the bad, and the ugly exciting) in the military from 06 April 1966 to 02 February 1970. Aside: I prefer the military mode of time and dates. Dates are ordinal, not cardinal. Time is easier to add and subtract if you use a twenty-four-hour clock, which I learned. And many of my cohorts were given the "early-out" option from our C.I.C. (a.k.a. POTUS). Everyone who had worked for more than one enlistment (four years) told me, "You can't make it on the outside [that is, being a civilian]!" They were persistent and convinced of this. I wondered why.

Here's my reasoning. They worked for a large organization/group, the military, a.k.a. the government, who spent their time and the taxpayer's money in a closed system. No one competes with the government, but they do compete to win *contracts with* the government!. No one ever, or rarely, discussed the costs of anything—your time, the supplies used, or their time spent consuming those supplies. The pay wasn't that great. That's why I took a second job, but the bennies, a.k.a. benefits, were good. Free health care was good, and the doctors were not competing for patients since it was a closed group. It was an assembly line lifestyle. I was the product of the government spending *your* money on *other* people! It's the most *inefficient* way to spend money, and our government has that down pat! Bonus: the most efficient way to spend money is spending your money on yourself. The government spends *your* money on *other* people! Not efficient at all! Costs and quality are never considered.

I began to wonder. If you knew me, you know that I wonder about everything! What if I competed in a skill where I could learn and then take it into a larger and more competitive society for more pay and more benefits? Even more security. I decided to serve my country, and I soon became a civvy again. I firmly decided I would go to college, at night, and continue to support myself and my family. Going to college during the daytime was not an option! I went into a significantly competitive group—America and 197 million people, not the much smaller group of 750,000 people. Those numbers are exact, not guesses. (I always verify the numbers I use.)

Education in different fields could transfer to many other careers and companies. There weren't that many private companies (read that as zero) that needed military people who could repair the hydraulics of civilian jets. Note: the civilian aircraft mechanic's job required an expensive A&P (Aircraft and Power plant) license and a *major* test. Companies must not have trusted the military's way of doing things. I decided to study electronics, and I earned an associate degree with honors. This skill was more marketable. Then I decided to pursue a bachelor's degree in economics—even more marketable. I spent twenty-two years as an engineer in the Bell System during much of my journey in night school and again even after I graduated. The work was challenging, mentally and physically. There were a lot of mental gymnastics and outdoor physical labor. I was walking many miles every day as part of my work. I was outside designing where the cables needed to go, or where people and governments would *allow* you to go!

I had decided to be responsible for myself from the instant I decided to enlist in the USAF and not rely on a massive government bureaucracy or anyone but myself. Those I met in the military told me, you should "put in your twenty years and then at age forty retire with no marketable skills [and find yourself looking for a job]." I added the last part they never mentioned. No doubt that a job at a profit-driven company was interested in efficiency and marketing competition. Not the military lifestyle—sitting around too much. Not for my tastes. Being aggressive was not a trait I saw in the military group I worked with. I should add that my unit wasn't a combat group. We repaired broken planes, while the combat groups killed "broken people" who wanted to kill us! More to the point, what is the thing I want to be remembered for when I'm gone? I am creative (photography and writing), and I inherited great genetics. I was a sixth-generation photographer, and my son, Mark, is a seventh-generation photographer with even more skills than I had!

I never gave up on life's curveballs, and even I threw some *at* myself! I went to night school and earned an associate's degree as cum laude (electronics technology) and then a bachelor's degree (economics) with membership in Omicron Delta Epsilon, an honor group. I worked for forty-seven years and missed *one* paycheck! I served in the military during the Vietnam era. I was married twenty years the first time and now going past thirty-three years the second time. I got it right the second time!

Attention: There are a few, as in three, people who know this quote.
In summation and using phonetic spelling, as these words are extra Merriam-Webster:

> "I've had an elegant sufficiency, I am filled to my stenachtaceae, and I feel quite salaunchified!"
> (Joe Byron)

Here are some of my life mottos and thoughts on life and death for your amusement and consideration. In no particular order.

On life:

- Do no harm.
- Be the best version of yourself you can be.
- Life is our only tour, no encores and no retakes.

- Forgive others *and* yourself.
- Never blame anyone *but* yourself.
- Keep alert.
- Forget yesterday, work on today, and hope for tomorrow.
- Don't be lazy and then expect success.
- Respect yourself.
- Peace is better than hatred.

On death:

"The best preparation for death is early planning."

- First off, it is inevitable. Accept that. Be prepared for it.
- Make a will if you own anything. *(My belongings go to my kids. Sheila's belongings go to her kids.)*
- Never ignore your talents and abilities. Work on them as you are able.
- Remember your friends and cherish your family.
- Don't be afraid to fail. Have a dream? Go for it.
- Regrets need to be handled and dealt with before it is too late.
- Pay attention to your health. Know your body.
- Shun physical risks. Skydiving and bungee jumping look like fun, but you will rarely see an eighty-year-old who has done or is doing or might do this.
- Don't do stupid stuff!
- The best chance for the most extended life is impossible to accomplish, so choose your parents wisely.
- Genetics is a gift from all your forebears. Maximize what you are given.
- When you are on your deathbed, you will regret sleeping in on weekends, being lazy, and never traveling.
- You will never hear someone say, "I wished I spent more time." You fill in (…) instead of being with friends and loved ones!
- Avoid too much of everything, and you might face death more peacefully.

- As you get to the age I am (seventy-five), you will have seen more and more death. You will learn from that! Go to friends' funerals!
- You might defer this inevitability a little bit, but that's all.
- Don't dwell on it. Worry will shorten your life, but think about what you want to do during your time on this earth and *do it*!
- This is a summary, as is your time on earth. "It is not a dress rehearsal. It *is* the only act."
- Live well between the dash (1946–20xx). I was one of number 228. My wife was number 229 (or vice versa?) of Americans to participate in the hundredth-anniversary visit to the *Titanic* wreck site.
- I took up this Quora "*QUestion-OR-Answer*" on my website for *questions or answers*, and I used it to refine my writing abilities and lead discussions on a variety of topics. It is how and why I wrote this biography.
- I've seen most of the good and the bad that life has put before me.
- I've seen births (up close—*eek*—with my camera) and death as close without my camera.
- I've lived in eight states (Ohio, Pennsylvania, Kentucky, Michigan, Illinois, Texas [nine if you count Texas boot camp], Louisiana, Georgia, and Tennessee). Ten if you measure ninety days in training at Chanute AFB, Illinois. I did attend four different universities (UC-University of Cincinnati, McNeese State Louisiana, UT-University of Tennessee, and UAB-University of Alabama Birmingham) as "Ma Bell" always liked to move me around.
- Was I that talented, or did they want to get rid of me? I don't know or care. It's easier to roll with the punches!
- I've had several odd encounters, and I will explain them as I continue. See a list of thirty-four examples at the end of this autobiography.
- Life's been an enjoyable, fun, sad, confusing, and surprising experience. *"Been there, done that!"*

I do digress, but while you're here, let me welcome you to "your time inside my head." Let's continue. When we were young, my generation was told, "Do not hang around with those bad children. They'll ruin your reputation!" From a faraway place, I'm warning you. Yes, you, dear reader, proceed cautiously and don't linger here any longer than necessary! My story is true, perhaps a tick disturbing, but it's as close to how an old man dares to go. If you're old enough, pour yourself that tall drink I asked you to do earlier and return! Get comfortable. Follow me down a long road and through my journey called life!

1946–1949

We're almost to my introduction, Chapter 4, so let's begin with our trek! *"The yelling will never stop! Why can't you ever make up your mind? You're the most miserable person ever!"* Then more yelling, which I refused to listen to. Meanwhile, my poor mother never had a moment of peace. She was trapped in our house and did not even drive a car to escape, take one of us to a doctor, or buy any groceries. We did have milk and bread delivered regularly to the metal boxes sitting on the front steps of our house. Mom had six children to deal with for weeks while the bully, our father, was out of town. He was never referred to by the familial name Dad for justifiable reasons, as you will understand as we continue.

When "he who must be obeyed," to turn a phrase an old barrister (Horace "Rumpole [sic] of the Bailey") I saw on BBC TV always said when she, his wife, Hilda, is referred to. Our father barked orders like an obsessed drill sergeant! No one was happy! We preferred him to be "Our Father, who art the traveling salesman," which is the most accurate personification of that moniker! More on that as we travel along my journey. "Your Honor, I will show the jury my evidence when it's apropos!"

My father was a bit aggressive physically (and verbally) and thought he was a good boxer. He would remind you often! While he was a medical corpsman in the Navy (1942–1945?) in San Diego, California, he fought more than a few times, if the truth were known! He told me this tale about how many times he got knocked down, and he said his opponent asked him, "Do you know who I am?" Then he said, "I'm Joe Lewis's *sparring* partner! You should *stop* this foolishness!" That happened around 1942, or four years before my arrival.

I grew up in an exciting drama filled and an ancient house. The house in Cincinnati was old, as was the house I would grow up in (1955?–1966), and the place was built with stone quarried by Keasbey and Mattison Company (https://en.wikipedia.org/wiki/Keasbey_and_Mattison_Company?wprov=sfti1). It was an asbestos factory, so this little town stayed alive. I will have more to say about the town's train station when we arrive at the year that I worked near there. It will *surprise* you! We'll visit there in a few chapters. The house I lived in was built in the early twenties, and I know this because of the old newspapers used as insulation I found in a crawl space in the cellar (in the early sixties). The coal-fired "monster of a furnace" was in the far-left front corner as you got to the bottom of the wooden steps. From this vantage point, you could see many large pipes that branched out and upward like an old giant oak tree to heat this three-story house. Immediately behind this antiquated beast of a heating unit was the coal bin. Above it was the chute from the outside where the Ambler Coal Company delivered the fuel that heated this three-story, three-bathroom, five-bedroom house with four porches. Also, there was a large kitchen, dining room, and front hall on the first floor with a living room all along one side of the house, from the front to back of this old place.

There were two of the five bedrooms on the third floor. Mine was in the back of the house, which I shared with Ricky. Paul had the front bedroom to himself. Seniority, I suppose? Several old and decorative antique gaslight fixtures were cut off from the gas mains decades earlier. Yet they were idly standing by for gas to be turned back on and light up the night. That would never happen, *but* if you got close enough to these ancient lamps, l could *still* smell the gas. Faintly. Were we all living in a time bomb? The joint never blew up, but the old man did blow up physically and verbally (read that as emotionally) more than a few times!

To paint a better mental image of this house I've described, think of where Mrs. Bates lived in the movie *Psycho*! Both places were terrifying, like that 1960 horror movie! I had turned fourteen that September when I watched that movie alone in late October and then walked home alone. It was a dark, chilly, windy, and a late fall evening. My house was up at the top of the hill, many blocks from the theater in town! I remember how terrified I was! My dear mother said, "I'll never shower again!" after seeing that movie. That is a true story!

There was an old "cement pond" for goldfish in a seven-by-three-foot wide and three-foot deep pond in our backyard, most of the time! Otherwise, we had to walk to the nearby pet store and buy replacement fishes. They even stayed over the winter when the pond froze if they survived the summer.

    If this place could talk. In 2010, I visited the old house and the new owner, Bob, gave me a tour. I narrated as we moved from room-to-room to prove my bona-fides. It looked different from an oldster's perspective! Before we entered my old bedroom, I told him about a patch on the ceiling. He looked. He chuckled! There was the plaster patch my father repaired the hole my head made, *bouncing* on my bed! He laughed, realizing I was indeed the former occupant!

Let's Introduce You to My Five Siblings

As I go through my life events, I may flashback to my brother's final act of defiance. My younger brother, (*Ricky*) Richard Marrin, had his father's middle name. He was central to my life story and was an enigma to many, including me. I was too busy with life and myself to think any more profoundly than that. How could one kid ponder deeply enough with my years of experience? Our older brother, *Paul*, was named with his grandfather's initials (PC, or Percifal Claude) as Paul Carroll, a moniker he loathed vehemently. Paul had severe issues with his "old man", *his* word for him. I wouldn't understand much of this (if I ever did) until late in life. Very late! *Ricky* had a punching bag, like the ones boxers use, which he used in the basement. He talked about colors he'd seen in dreams, and he even had serial dreams (I remember him telling me they were about Superman). Those diverse activities using aggression and profoundly creative thought at other times—yes, he was moody—and that made him difficult to get close to. (Personal aside: *reader*, I know the rule about ending a sentence with a proposition. It's "something, up with which, I won't put.")

It was a hot July afternoon when Ricky ran away from home. No one said they knew what had triggered him (we never had family chats), though my opinion leaned toward our father as the issue. I was on a camping trip that weekend. Running away was a family tradition. My older brother, Paul, had done the same a few years earlier. In that same family tradition, he would never return home (his one exception was Ricky's suicide). I can't remember when Paul left home! I left home forever on 07 April 1966, when I went into the Air Force. Instead of fighting my demons as my two brothers did, I chose to help fight my country's enemies by repairing fighter jets in Michigan!

My older sister, *Judy* (Judith Ann), moved to Arizona after living for a few years in Vermont. She was, in her words, a "soul who bonded with the desert life," and she stayed there until she died suddenly (see chapter "Post-Judy"). My youngest sister, *Debbie* (Debra Jane), moved to Vermont after my older sister, Judy, got married in Ambler,

Pennsylvania; on the *same* day, I got married in Chicago, Illinois! How's *that* for family unity? My other sister *Laura* (Laura Lee), the second youngest of the clan, went to Vermont (in the sixties) and then on west to "Californie" (shout-out to *the Clampetts*. Look it up!), where she lives in 2022.

We are all spread out by now. My two younger sisters were in Vermont, and I was in Michigan and Paul was in Washington state and then went to sea as a cook. As I write this, he's been in Farmington, New Mexico, for several years. My memory of my time at our house (not a home) has been fried (i.e., erased). I stated that correctly, it was *never* a home. It was *always* just a house. Paul and I never returned. None of us did! Ever! My father ran away from *his* home back in the mid-1930s. Running away was a family tradition. My little fourteen-year-old brother, Ricky, couldn't stand it anymore in our house, driving home the point again that it was impossible to describe it as home, and he was too young to go! He hitchhiked westbound on the Pennsylvania Turnpike (formerly a train route), the same way and adventure I would take a few years later. We'll get to that in a moment.

Ricky came home from that adventure, and he came home to the terror of his father, who had gotten home much earlier than expected. All of us felt the same terror at times, but none more than poor Ricky. He was trapped! Fatally so, it would turn out. He was too young to be treated this way. Others knew this but couldn't (or we were afraid to) or wouldn't help. The bully (a.k.a. our father) was Ricky's ever present nemesis. He was always mean and always our detached father," never our Dad. I was, and I *am*, a seeker of balance, a.k.a. a good Libra. Some take drastic measures to reach stasis. I would go into the military and never live in that place that could have been home again. On my first nineteenth wedding anniversary (1986), the Challenger spacecraft blew up. On my first twentieth anniversary, my marriage blew up! On my second nineteenth wedding anniversary, in 2006, Sheila and I lived happily in Georgia!

I must digress here and briefly mention the wedding present our father gave my sister Judy in 1967. This is true, and I'm the last surviving party to what I'm about to tell you. On or around 1997, I visited my sister Judy in Tucson, and her (first) 1967 wedding came up.

"You know, Tom," she said. "I never opened my wedding present from Dad." Reaching down under the coffee table, she brought out an old and never opened gift box. *True* story! This is about thirty years post-ceremony. Do you see a stubborn streak in me, my sisters, in all of us Byrons? She opened it then and, well... I forgot what she found when she opened it. It was a vast "nothing burger!" That's how we cope. "We sublimate, cogitate, eliminate, and eradicate!" I am quoting myself!

My three sisters moved away. Vermont attracted Laura and Debbie, as it did Judy! It was a remote state, if ever there was one, and they loved the place! My older brother, Paul, traveled the world. The following is a book about that ship. I have a copy Paul gave me in my vast (500 books?) personal library, *On Almost Any Wind* by Susan Schlegel (https://www.goodreads.com/book/show/1099016.On_Almost_Any_Wind). He worked on this steel-hulled sailing vessel named *Atlantis* as a cook! The ship was operated by the Woods Hole Oceanographic Institute (WHOI), commonly spoken as *"Who*-whee," and our cousin on our mother's side, Val Worthington, worked there.

Paul lived out his final years in the lovely small town of Farmington, New Mexico, far, far away from any big city and any ocean, of which he sailed on most of them! I visited him twice there. He enjoyed being isolated and away from our old house, far away from his nemesis, and his name for our father, the old man! Our parents ended up living in Florida for many years. My grandfather, Percy, stayed close to his children, but my parents moved 1,015 miles away! That's a great way to say, "We don't care to see you very often!" After everyone left our house, we rarely got together lest one significant time, come to think about it! That time was in late 1987. We never got together ever again after that one-day reunion! As you will learn later, 1987 was the pivotal year in my life—and many others' lives, for that matter.

We all knew that my younger brother, Ricky, was "the younger smarter brother." He was a gentle soul compared to everyone else in our family. He was my more brilliant brother (IQ 160+, so I heard). He and I were a few years different in age (three), and we played outdoors together during those brief adventurous years. We built a fort. One could call it a hideout built from old lumber near our house. Our shack was only five feet high, six feet long, and three feet deep. The roof always leaked a little. It wasn't easy to scrounge up good roofing material even back then! Also, we weren't skilled builders either! We were naughty little buddies and could hide without leaving our backyard. More on our antics later.

When my older sister, Judy, and her partner, Cesare (pronounced *Chez*-ah-ray), lived a block away, Ricky was introduced to guns by the man who would have become his brother-in-law. He was an avid gun user. He practiced safe usage and proper handling of such a deadly weapon, a .38 caliber revolver. He and I once spent a noisy half hour shooting that .38 in his below-ground basement shooting gallery. Ear protectors were essential! Cesare didn't use and own guns to hunt with. They were for personal protection only. The note on their second-floor apartment door, a few years later, comes to mind when they lived on the third floor in the 2300(?) block of Delancey Street in central Philadelphia:

> If you haven't been let in up here, please leave.
> There is a loaded shotgun behind the front door.

The sign was correct, and I saw that weapon personally.

One afternoon, in the springtime of Ricky's short life, as I would be told later, he had asked Cesare, "What happens if I put this rifle to the ground and pull the trigger? Will it make a loud noise?"

Cesare explained the physics of gunshots in his typically attractive English/Italian/East Tennessean mangled speech he learned from a Southerner. With his accent, a mixture of hillbilly and a thick Roman accent, he replied, "No! Why do you ask a question like that?"

The reply Ricky gave or any further details have been lost to eternity. I forget, and Cesare and my sister are both gone now, so we'll leave it.

Judy mainly raised me and the three younger kids—Ricky, Laura, and Debbie. Our older brother, Paul, completed the sextet of the Byron Clan. (There is a group photo on page 55.) We all think we are unique, and at the same time, we realize that we are not. I have reviewed a few events here, and I'm afraid to put this together, being that I'm the worst procrastinator in recorded human history. I agree with the former and hope to disprove the latter. It is a monumental undertaking, reviewing one's life.

My parents' first child might have been conceived out of wedlock. Actually, all evidence, Your Honor, indicates he was. You know how family stories are, and in ours, there never was a lot of us as close-knit families go. This is key to understanding the family hostilities, which I am trying to discuss. I never took the psychiatric route, though I can still hear those words echoing.

Everyone was lied to about this sham date of their marriage for fifty years, and we were all the victims of this. It probably was the root of all their fighting. He didn't want to be married, and she knew he was a bum. I never saw them hug and kiss. I finally researched their marriage date and found my parents' original marriage license in a Tennessee courthouse. It took about five minutes at the archived records office to find that written record! Even in my father's poetical (written in the literal sense) autobiography, he reports "married in 1939." The very essence of *hubris* here is a "Sit up and take notice," a statement from Joe Byron's poetic autobiography! In a separate time and place, he told me, "We got married in Tennessee." Did he think I wouldn't follow up on his clue?

> My good wife Betty married me
> In 1939 –
> And then my days became more fun
> For she kept me in love

ZERO TO SEVENTY-FIVE

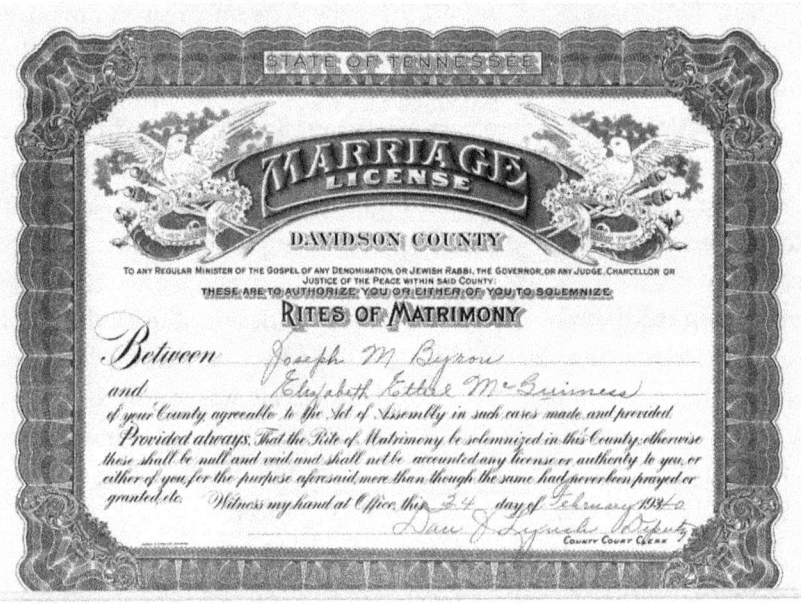

I confirmed the lie, and I never confronted him with this detail. Why should I? Still, my father stoically preached the same morality and honesty until his death. Common? Maybe. The only reason I mention this is that before my parents' wedding, my father's life was a tumultuous series of "incidents and more than a few accidents." He, too, had been a runaway and rode off on a 1930-era Indian motorcycle. Grace told me about this, and Patty reminded me to include the following gem. Grace used to have to visit morgues in and around New York City to ask if an unclaimed body was there as she inquired at each morgue, "I can't find my brother!" He was wild and reckless, and there were stories that I've heard about how he worried his poor dear mother, Lulu, nearly to death! His school teachers were nuns who smacked his left hand with a ruler every time he wrote left-handed. He was forced to become a "righty". His mother was just as strict and probably even more domineering! My father's younger sister, Grace, told me that on or around 1938 or 1939, he couldn't marry his then girlfriend (not the same girl who *did* become *my* mother). Her name is lost to history, and the memory of my Aunt Grace's telling me this is fuzzy, but *not* the following story about whoever she was. He was twenty-four or twenty-five when she was pregnant and then committed suicide upon receiving that startling news from my father-to-be that he wouldn't marry her! His sister Grace told me all about her brother Joe many different times when we discussed family history. I always got the idea she didn't want to die without telling me, or someone, the truth. Little did she, nor I, know that *I would write this autobiography!* This hopefully refines my unique history a little further. Another item is that my older brother was born in August, but our parents were only married in February of the year he was born. They lived in the New York City area and drove a long way (1,008 miles on two-lane roads) from New York City to Tennessee, where there is no waiting period for marriages. Did our father remember his phony wedding anniversary every year my older brother, Paul, had a birthday? No one alive anymore to ask that question. He gladly accepted the nice silver ice bucket I paid for, and gave them, as a twenty-fifth wedding anniversary gift. He kept the secret that their actual wedding date wasn't October 21 (her birth date). I'm sure he felt he'd be found out. I found out, but like the Libra I am, wanting balance over disharmony, I said nothing! Many years later, he gave me back the ice bucket when they moved from Florida to Bennington, Vermont. Who has ever heard of someone doing *that*?

Our father *was* the traveling salesman. See the note from my mother my sister Debbie gave me in 2003 (pp. 236–237) for solid evidence. He was the *proverbial type*. There was one comment addressed to me as a young man more than once or twice: "You sure look like Jimmy. Is he your cousin?" I would not have wondered along with the questioner. So why was I asked so often, or why do I think I was asked a lot? I will always wonder! My mother's *family* includes the Worthington family and the McGuinnesses, mom's maiden name. That side of (my) the family was not ever very friendly to the Byron side! As you travel along here in my autobiography, and my recalling my childhood, you'll understand why!

My maternal grandmother's maiden name was Ethel Dobbins, and she married Richard McGuinness. (This is my little brother's surname. I assume that's not a mere coincidence). Still, I rarely met but a few members of my mother's family! They were persona non gratis. Do you think they knew what I've heard about that infamous Nashville, Tennessee, wedding? My guess is *yes*! They must have known, resulting in them not being too keen on visiting the Byron side of the family. They were indeed perceptive. Consequently, most of what I might have know about the McGuinnesses is lost. I know from the ancestry web site that I'm 65 percent Irish, 14 percent Scottish, and 21 percent English and NW European. And who were the Secundas? I remember going to a reunion and meeting that group. I have nary a clue! I bet they weren't my father's side of my family either! I add that to say only their name. Someone will hopefully add the answer for future generations.

The Byron family is interred in Moravian Cemetery on Staten Island, New York City. The last family internment was Ricky's cremains. My father's cremains are located in an unknown place (to myself). I will mention later my dear sweet mother's cremains. My father grew up down the hill from this cemetery. In the late nineties, my wife, Sheila, and cousin Patty Murtaugh and I visited our family cemetery in Staten Island, New York.

"Why not swing by Uncle Joe's old home?" I asked my cousin Patty, who knew the address. After anxiously waiting as we three strangers stood nervously, and with high hopes, at the front door, we knocked. Was anyone home? Would they allow us entry?

We were lucky, and a lovely senior lady (whose name escapes me) welcomed us inside her home. It was amazing! It was like entering King Tut's tomb. You knew only what you'd seen in photographs, but at this moment, you were *actually* there! Wow! We looked around the first floor only. She was very gracious and put up with our story and our curiosity! Until you do something like this—going back fifty years plus—what could be more delightful? The photos that I'd seen of his home were brought to life! My father's parents are interred in the gated area of the same cemetery, uphill from this house, where the world-famous Vanderbilt family are interred (in a separate gated space). My brother Ricky (Richard) Marrin Byron's cremains are interred in the same grave as Percy. There are, for clarity, some Marrins on my father's side. How is that unique, you ask? And rightly so. My family, on the Byron side, was in a contentious battle for many years with the Vanderbilt over establishing a local ferry service in New York City harbor. I was told (by Aunt Grace) that a relative of mine worked alongside Robert Fulton to develop the steam engine on these ferries. Robert Fulton and the steamboat is an interesting history here, as well. See the "Steamboat Voyage, 1807" (http://www.eyewitnesstohistory.com/fulton.htm).

A little backstory is required here.

Cornelius Vanderbilt in the year 1834. Vanderbilt competed[1] on the Hudson River against a steamboat monopoly between New York City and Albany. Using the name "The People's Line," he used the populist language associated with Democratic president Andrew Jackson to get popular support. At the end of the year, the monopoly paid him a considerable amount to

---

[1] You know who won!

stop competing, and he switched his operations to Long Island Sound. [7]:99–104 Cornelius Vanderbilt. (ibid.) (https://en.wikipedia.org/wiki/Cornelius_Vanderbilt?wprov=sfti1)

They are together for eternity, laid to rest only a few hundred feet apart.

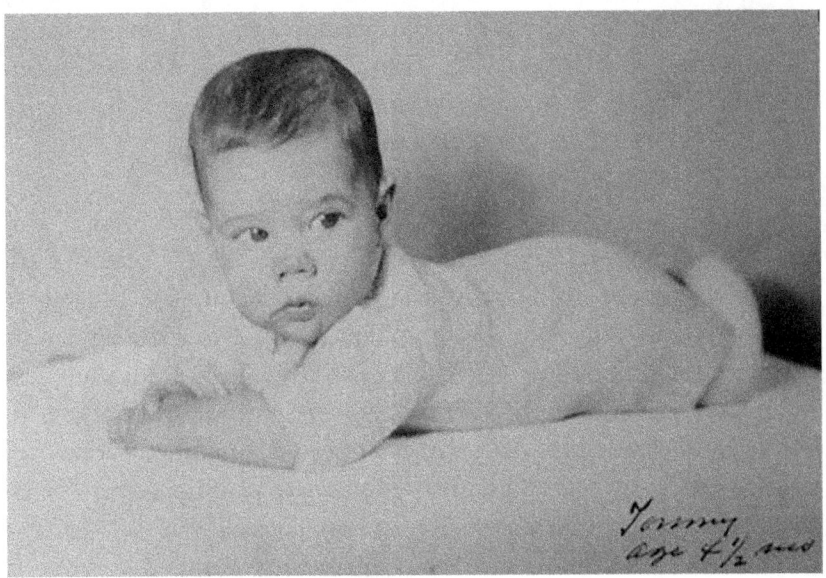

The World I Would Enter

1946

I lived my childhood amid hostility, lies, omissions, and anger, and I will relate detailed thoughts about these items and other events (year by year). I will describe opinions and experiences which I have observed along the way, year by year. This, after all, is my story! As Paul Simon's song said, "There were incidents and accidents" (https://youtu.be/uq-gYOrU8bA). There would be several events that meet those criteria, as I will relate.

How I got here, or when I was born. Here's a full disclosure as to why I think about life in specific ways. My degree is a bachelor of science in economics. My associate's degree is in electronic technology (I understand how stuff, not your humble narrator, is wired). Therefore, I would relate to how prices of everything when I was born were relatively low (see list below), as were wages, but postwar expectations for consumption were high. The wartime economy would transition into a peacetime economy, and there was plenty of pent-up demand from the GIs returning to their former jobs as civilians in 1945 to 1946. The production of cars, houses, and consumer goods increased, as were we boomers!

Our baby boomer generation was massive, and we received a lot of attention. There were 3.4 million of us, many of whom went (not me) to the most significant rock concert ever—Woodstock 1969. We are turning seventy this year as this is written, or we would have turned seventy. The Vietnam War would take the lives of sixty thousand of us. Boomers are the most plentiful births ever recorded in America for one year. I went through K to 12 schools in two different brand-new school buildings as I progressed through junior (7–9) and senior high (10–12). They are in use today, but still as crowded as they used to be since my former small town keeps growing. The World War, known by the initials WWII, was over, and our boomer generation would be in the next group to be in charge in a few decades. Gas prices were at 15¢/

gal. Average new car cost was $1,200.00. US postage for a letter was 2¢ ($0.02). Minimum wage was 25¢ in the US.

Sometime in *December 1945*, my father said, "I was home on a Christmas leave from the Navy, and you were conceived." I'm telling you this because I was told by my father nearly those exact words.

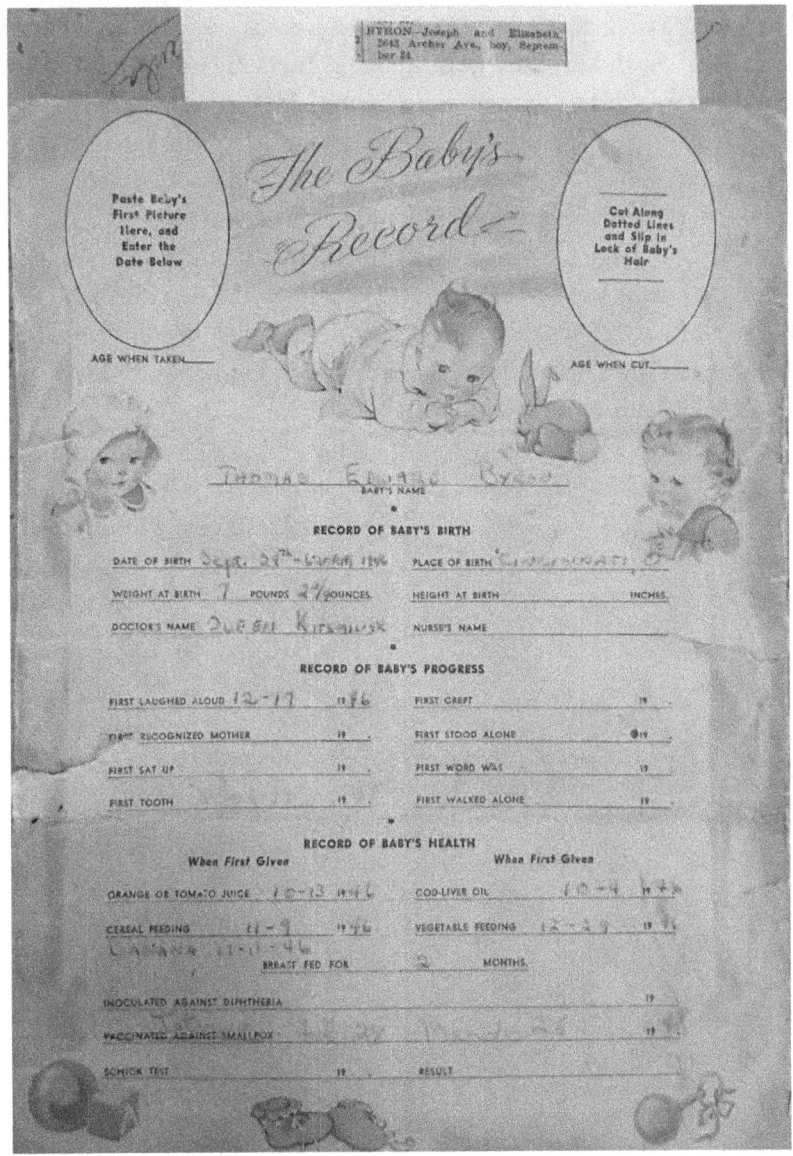

Beginning My First Year in 1946

I was conceived four months after the first nuclear weapons were used in World War Two, and I have been on a journey in America ever since. *I was conceived in 1945 on a US Navy Christmas leave.* How do I know this? And *why* did my father ever tell me? I will say to you, dear reader, that there were many strange things in my life from which I am now the way I am! Today! I cannot *un*-remember that bizarre conception tidbit! Truman was my first president (number 33), and politics were not yet in my blood. Follow me onto my older self as we proceed, and politics will loom large for me. My sister Judy, my pseudo mom, raised me! You didn't expect to remember much of the year I was born, did you? That's all I have to say here, but everything flowed outward from here. Nothing to report about my first birthday or what may have happened.

Unlike the present era (2021), cell phones don't capture every moment! There wasn't even a phone in the house I lived in up to age three! My neighbor Bill Wesling (see photo a bit later) got the call from the hospital that I was born, so he knew before my father knew.

ZERO TO SEVENTY-FIVE

1948, 1949

I distinctly remember being this old. This photo of me was a few years earlier than the walks I took, which I will mention later, with my older brother (nine years old then) and my older sister (eight then), but they were too young to supervise a rambunctious little toddler like me! I'll add details in a few. My older brother and sister told me stories along with our father (the same one who told me about his time on leave in Christmas time of 1945), and I'm getting ahead of my story yet again!

We three kids climbed the steep hill behind our Archer Avenue house (word choice of *house* is deliberate since none of the places we lived in felt like homes). We made it an adventure leaving on a brief escape. "There is a huge old monastery there," I remember being told. It was a church. It may have been a block or two away, but it was far from home at two or three with my tiny feet. I wish I had a visual memory of this adventure, but since there were no monsters there, I guess we were acting as good kids do!

I learned an early lesson around this third year, and I practice looking where I'm walking—a downward gaze, even today! In 1995, finally, this habit over the decades paid off big time! I walked across a parking lot in Kentucky and found a diamond pendant. I found out it was worth around $400. I have that gem, and it's now mine. It *always* pays to keep your nose to the grindstone and keep your eyes on the ground ahead of where you're walking! As a three-year-old toddler, I stepped on a $5 bill, and my cousin Peter Worthington was behind me (as I recall). He laughed at me and picked it up! Life lesson learned early, and I've not seen Peter since then. Did I not warn you how dysfunctional my family was?

I was having a fun early life until I was two. That is until I had to have plastic surgery when I was two! I was hit squarely in the mouth with a *steel pipe* that had an old rusty and bent nail sticking out of it on end thrown at me. It hit me in the mouth and split my lip wide open. Excellent plastic surgery, I was told, and that game is why I can never catch a ball or anything thrown at me to this day. My chances at playing any ball game were dashed at that point! While I was recovering from this, I was helping my neighbor, Bill Wesling, seen below, burn some *yellow jackets* out from around his wooden front porch steps. I was stepping on the yellow jackets that were getting away. The last step I remember was a rotten one that collapsed under my little foot.

Buzzzzzzzzzz. My mother told me I was stung over two hundred times!! I was covered head to toe with yellow jacket stings! I've learned your mind can remember many things, but not pain. I can remember playing here on the steps in front of my house. The wall was pretty high for a little tot like I was then, and it was where I got my lip busted open! My mother didn't drive, so she was the perfect nurse, and my only treatment was a dab of wet baking soda on each raised welt from hundreds of stings! I survived since I was not allergic. I would have yet another honeybee attack incident several years later when we review 1955.

Tom Byron visiting his birth place

Tom in 1952 with his favorite toy

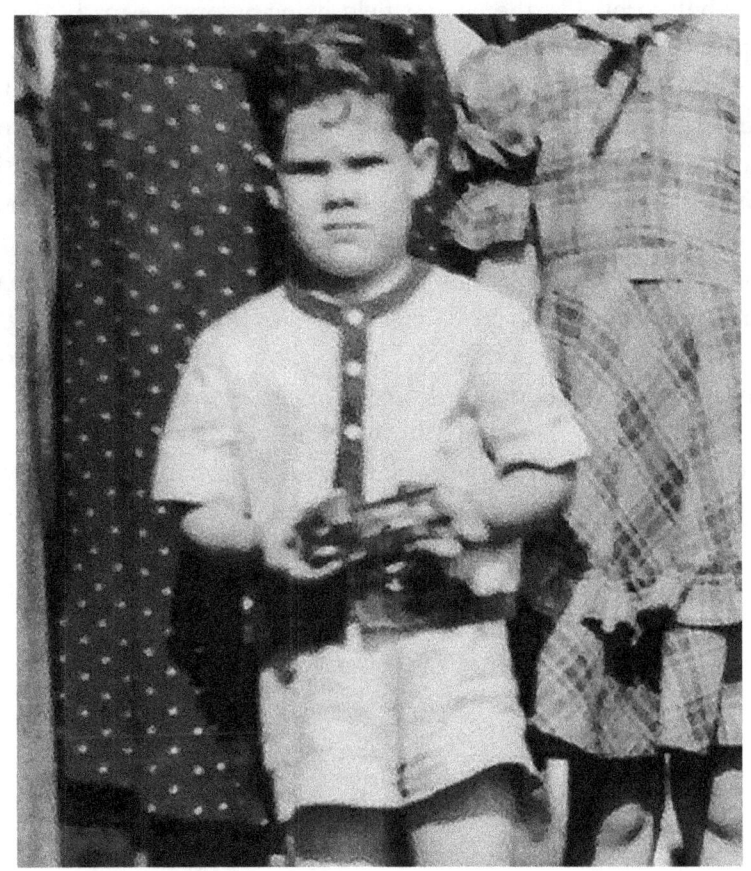

1950

This year, our family of four plus my parents moved to a very rural small town in southeastern Pennsylvania. Not a "town" but a merely a small dot on a map! This new place was not within walking distance of *any place* but cornfields, the nearest field being across the road from my duplex apartment. I remember being in our living room when my little sister Laura was brought home from the hospital. She would have been only a few days old. My youngest sister (number 6) was born in our next house, a vast and ancient three-story 1920s house. My father would leave his non-driving wife and four little children alone, none over twelve years old, for up to two weeks when he traveled on his sales job, *I do not know why he thought that was a good idea*! It taught me the charity of strangers and great neighbors! This time, he was working for Univis Lens Co. Recent research for my autobiography shows the company he worked for had some interesting legal issues.

The main business of Univis consists in selling lens blanks to wholesale dealers in the optical industry who grind such lens blanks by prescriptions for use in eyeglasses or who resell such lens blanks to others, including wholesalers, ophthalmologists, opticians, and optometrists, who then grind such blanks to the prescription. Univis itself also conducts at its factory a prescription department and has done so from the beginning of its business (*United States v. Univis Lens Co.*, 88 F. Supp. 809, 811–12 [SDNY 1950]).

Our father left Univis Lens Co. The year was forgotten, but the quoted research above indicates it was in 1950. He then went to work for Mr. Ed Freeman, whose position and his company's name had been lost to me and to time. He continued to sell optical goods in a wholesale business model until he retired.

What was it like to grow up in America during the 1950s? I will try to explain it year by year. Some years were memorable. Others, not so much!

It was an adventure. I spent 100 percent of my time outside unless it was raining. No one had a color TV, since they weren't made yet for home use. We didn't have a phone until I was seven or eight. Our first phone was a voice-operated ("Number please?" the operator asked) ten phones on a ten-party line set, we all shared that line. It was in the front hall of my Ambler house, and the only time I remember using that phone was on 09 June 1959. I answered the phone and was told, "Your grandfather has died." Our number was 1619J. There were ten on this party line, our four-digit number plus A through J. Ours was the tenth party with other homes that shared that same number, but that system depended on the ring signal (long or short, two or four rings, etc.) if the call was for you. Anyone could and sometimes did also answer or pick up their phone!

I picked wild berries and ate them at the vine (not Vine Street), but right off the plant and as I found them. Candy was not available. It was too expensive, even at 5¢ a bar! Cars didn't have seat belts, and they burned leaded, not *unleaded*, a gas which was 15¢ per gallon. Cars only got about 13 mpg, so we were (sort of) even on cost per mile driven. My future economics training was decades away, but I still find this an exciting way of thinking about those days. I hope you agree because I'm too old to change this habit now! I'm an old dog who can't be taught new tricks at my age!

I drank creek water. There was no such thing as bottled water. I flew in an open cockpit biplane at age six, without a seatbelt! A lifetime memory started me on a lifelong fascination with flying, with more details later. I must have entered the US Air Force in 1966 due to this. See item 7 at the end of this autobiography, page 321.

I had a box camera that used 620 roll film. I still have all my old cameras. We played marbles. We rarely went to the movies, but we sometimes went to the drive-in. You will read about a strange vignette later on page 37. Radios were the tube-type AM radio only, no FM, and radios were not portable! The only portable radio I had was a battery-less crystal set with earphones. It got one or two stations. My older sister Judy knew *the* Dick Clark personally. She was a regular on his TV show *Bandstand* (channel 6 WFIL-TV). We used 45 rpm records, of which I still have. There were no cassette tapes or eight-track tapes yet. Someday, I might get our 1948 jukebox working again! I read the original *Dick and Jane* books. I paid 10¢ at a flea market for my copy of this gem which now resides in my library!

I do not mean that everyone grew up or experienced this same lifestyle. Many people look for things and see life based on their experiences, as I did here. I didn't see what I didn't look for. Did I miss it? Maybe. Did I see problems and ignore them? Maybe. I have served on a jury and studied reports of eyewitness accounts. What people see sometimes is influenced by what they expect to see. Witnesses to the same event will always have different versions. Who is right and who is wrong depends on your experience. This was mine. And as a footnote, I had childhood friends in all three of the predominant groups in my small town—Italian; *Colored* a term not used in 2022; and White—where I grew up. From this Italian community, and the WASP community (not a word then but means White Anglo Saxon Protestant) and the colored, which was not pejorative then, but it is now (which goes to my point). We *all* got along!

1951

I have a few faint recollections of this time, but much of who I was has been destroyed in my being brought up in such a disharmonious house, not a home. I certainly have clear memories of a lot of my childhood, but they *all* involve my time spent outdoors. I have pitifully few family memories inside the house! I have related those few highlights that I can remember in the introduction. We might, or I *hope* we will, see what else my mind has hidden in its deeper recesses! As I relate these events, I find that other memories arise out of nowhere. Here is a perfect example. Was I too young to remember this event? Though I remember several events a year or two earlier, I did confirm it. Ricky, as I recall, during our time we lived in rural Skippack, had hit my little sister Laura on the head with a wooden croquet mallet. The inside of the hood of her little snowsuit was bloody, so it must have been more than a tap. This is a vivid memory of mine and not a story I was told. Quite sadly, I believe my parents ignored this. I will have Laura comment on this. She must have been around two years old when this incident or accident happened.

Laura's memory related to me today: "I do have a few scars on my head. I remember being hit and hit hard, but not why I was hit."

I think I overcame all of this, making me a stronger person. Or not. You decide. I gave up wrestling with this issue and other issues like that for too many years for it to matter now. Occasionally, I stop when I see a family from the fifties and ask myself, "Am I really over all this? Was this how my childhood was?" The answer to the first question must be emphatically "No!" To the second, a tentative "Yes." I thought one was supposed to let sleeping dogs lie. Is that why I love cats?

I "ran away" one afternoon with a neighborhood mom and her kids to go shopping. I say "ran away" because I left without telling my mom. Why? I was a four- or five-year-old! That was 1950 or 1951. I never told my mom where I was for several hours. She might not have realized I was absent without leave (AWOL). She did all the cooking and the laundry. She also used to grow her vegetables in our side yard.

She was always busy! Leaving home under unusual circumstances will come up in several years as a hitchhiking adventure in 1962. I would travel three hundred miles away and tell my mother I was a mile away at my long-time friend Johnny Pearce's. His father, Walter B. Pearce, was my scoutmaster, a true gentleman. Johnny's mother, Clara, a saintly woman, taught me how to fold and roll up a freshly washed and dried pair of socks. Why do I remember all of those minutiae? Why was she washing my socks? I did stay overnight at Johnny's quite often. She taught me how to twirl a piece of toast with my fingertips and butter it without going around the toast with the butter knife. Just twist the toast! My odd memory will be sprinkled throughout these ramblings of mine. I had to have been extremely lucky on this misadventure or secret road trip and many others. I never got yelled at about it. Looking back on that now, I wonder, "Why didn't I get asked if I was okay?"

My mom just asked, "Where were you?" Odd. Or maybe I'm great at not remembering all the bad stuff? I have erased so much of my childhood, and it is sometimes terribly fuzzy. Much of what I remember is my parents' arguments about stupid (s——t) stuff. Petty arguments my parents had over going out to see a movie or not going out to see a movie escalated into yelling! Random but upsetting to a young child. Fortunately, as a Libra, I sought and still seek balance, which helps. I think. I hope.

I knew during my early adulthood that my father was a closet alcoholic (at some point in my youth). Was that the reason for his mood swings? The reason I erased so much of my childhood? His alcoholic rationale was "You never see me stumbling around, do you?" His guilt spoke louder than his words! I do remember one particular late-night event. I never knew the time in my bedroom. I never had a watch or clock. All six of us children were lined up next to his room (a.k.a. his at-home office) and were grilled to find out, as our father demanded, "Who stole my pencil?" He spent every evening doing paperwork, which he bitterly complained about regularly due to his job as a salesman. He had a tiny walk-in closet-sized office where he hid/worked.

This was, and still is, a scary memory to recall. All of us were quiet. Either one of us was a liar, or he was drunk. I decided the answer was "I did it!" This stopped the madness that must have lasted thirty minutes.

I forget what my punishment was, but the yelling ceased! My little sisters still praise me to the present time for this act of courage. My mother must have heard all of this and retreated to wherever *her* safe space was!

My childhood is blank, except for some of these flashbacks. I will do my best to mention these events in sequence. But as much as I have to relate and as messed up as my childhood was, forgive me if I jump around at times.

I remember being awakened one night around nine and being told I was going to the local, and very popular, 309 Drive-In a few miles from my house. I remember I was in the back seat, but I didn't know the movie or even arriving at the drive-in. At my age, I mainly enjoyed cartoons. Saying that to you, dear reader, and myself, are we both wondering why I was taken to a drive-in movie show? Out of the blue! They used to show movies outside in a large empty field with a massive outdoor screen! You put a speaker hanging from a post next to your parking space on your car window and watch from the comfort of your car. An alternate plan was to go to the movie with a girlfriend and watch from your car "bedroom." Who wants to guess what or which happened?

As I sat in the back seat, not a good place for a small kid to watch a movie he didn't care about, he (my inner self) saw something else he *still* wonders about. Who was that woman in the front seat with my father? It indeed wasn't my older sister or my mother. Mmmm? I remember I was (half?) asleep in the back seat, and my father and "who?" were in the front seat. Just another weird memory from what's left of my childhood.

My father was not at home typically for two weeks. He was the proverbial *traveling salesman* of which old jokes were/are told. I'm sure by now you will believe me. They were jokes, but I saw them as reality. Maybe this explains where the child in me went. Perhaps the childhood me is hiding inside the real me. Perhaps *he* is dead. My brother took that option at age fourteen. We'll get to that later in 1964. I can't ask him, and I can't remember much about that, except one telling exchange. It was one of several of my life-altering events! They are fragments in my mind, like strangers walking around and talking to each other. I hear pieces of their conversation, but not much else!

1952

In the spring of this year, our family grew to seven members with my sister Laura's arrival. I actually *remember* her entering the front door, Mom proudly carrying her fifth little bundle of joy. Birth date specifics are omitted here for (those alive as I type this) security purposes. You can't be too careful!

Did I complete kindergarten at Creamery, Pennsylvania, school? Do you see the original report card somewhere? When I find it, you will get an email with a photo of it.

As my date stamps have shown thus far, I am slowly and diligently working through the most extended ongoing writing project of my life. The more I write, the more I need to edit and expand my history. I remember flying for the first time this year, at the age of six, in a red biplane with my father. It was an open-cockpit biplane, two-seater. The pilot—Stu Dowdy—sat in the back, and I sat on my father's lap upfront, of course. I was standing up, looking out, and leaning over the edge of the plane. What a view!

In late 2019, I came across the following post on Quora.com (my hangout for writing and where many of my recollections were written for the world to read). The reply I received about my first plane ride repeated above is strange! I will share it here. Hopefully, it will add to my first time on an airplane and corroborate my memory. If this were a rare coincidence, it would be mildly interesting, but odd coincidences are pretty standard for me. Notice in 1964–65, there is going to be another strange coincidence. See the last few pages of this autobiography for an enumerated list of my coincidences. The following item is (randomly itemized) number 28 at the end of my autobiography, page 325.

> Tom, we must be near neighbors. I'm in Skippack Township and maybe went up in the same plane—a 1929 WACO mail plane with teardrop wheel covers out of Perkiomen airport. Small world, eh? (Paul Metsch)

Also, see a list on pages 321 to 326 of other random events like this at the end of my scribblings, a.k.a. my life story, such as it is.

My father told me that all prisoners, like those below we are flying over in Graterford Prison visible from that biplane, "were only fed bread and water." I later realized that was a lie, but it was believable enough to keep me from crime.

Air travel has changed a lot since then, and it was years before terrorism controlled how we fly today, as I relate my life's events. Back then, you could go to any commercial airport, walk in, and go to the departure area and even get on the plane to see someone off. No screening. No ticket, except when it was you taking that flight. Everyone was dressed up, unlike today's travelers, like they were at church as we did then, not where I'm writing from. We always dressed well in public unless it was playtime. No security. No x-rays. The airlines let you smoke and even gave you small four-packs of cigarettes. Gave, as in free. Yes, I wish I had kept one of those as a souvenir. I still have a Hardee's restaurant aluminum ashtray, but my collecting is a habit from growing up poor. As a child, I remember playing store in our basement. Mom used to give us empty containers from the kitchen—cereal boxes, soap powder boxes, empty oatmeal cylinders. Remember those sizable round cardboard cereal packages that contained Quaker Oats™?

1953

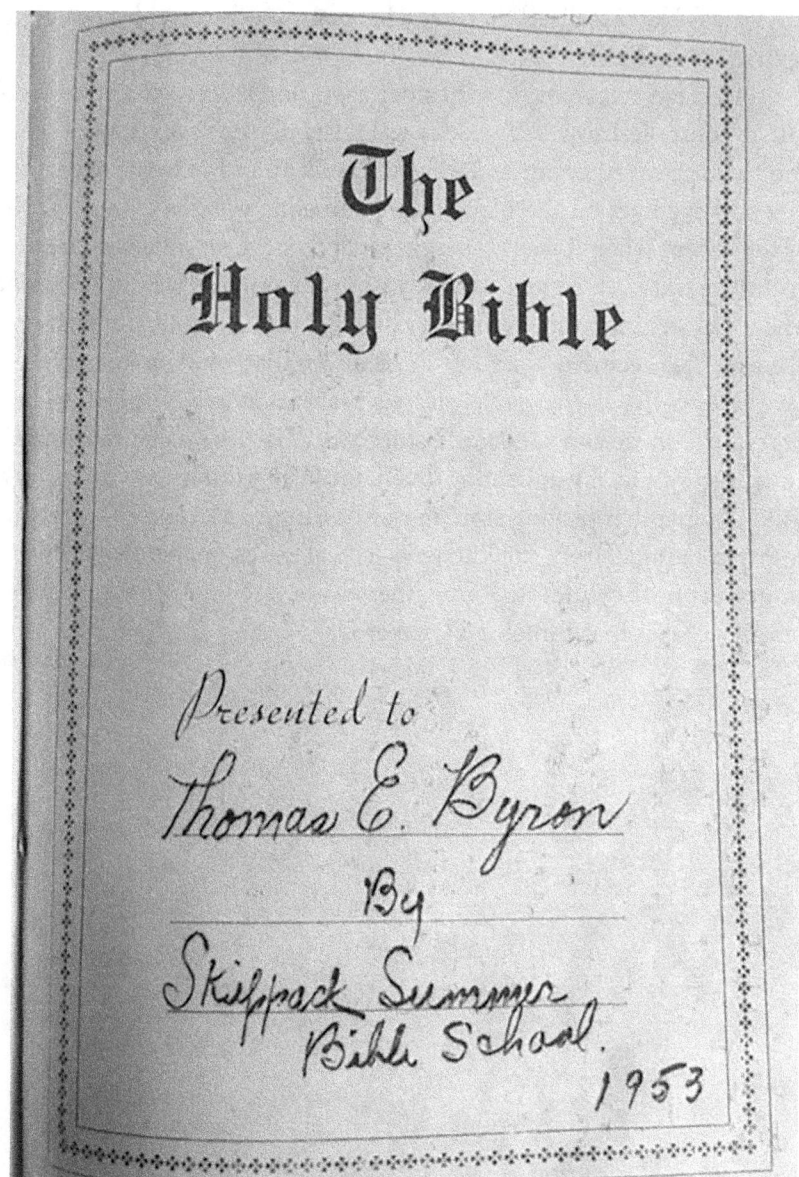

ZERO TO SEVENTY-FIVE

I went to summer bible school in 1953 in Skippack, Pennsylvania. I still have that same Bible that I was given then!

The drawing on the back cover is the only artwork that has survived my childhood. This was drawn on the back of a piece of my father's Univis sales paper, dated 8/12/52 by my father's hand, lower right corner.

I attended first and second grade and went to church in Creamery, Pennsylvania. As you have noticed, my memory is pretty good and not as bad as I thought when I began this tale! Exercising my memory will let you wonder (with me) why my memory is blank about that church and that school. Did something horrible happen?

There were only forty-eight states back then (no Hawaii or Alaska). This was about the same point in my young life when I realized that the Easter Bunny was a myth. I will explain it in a memorable Easter event next!

The Great Easter Heist

Here is how this "mystery" happened. This is a true story, though it was many decades after this event that I found out the *truth* about the event. Up until I was about seven years old or younger, every Easter morning, my brothers and sisters and I would come into the dining room and see six Easter baskets. They were little woven wicker (not plastic) baskets full of (fake) paper-green grass, not the plastic stuff that replaced it years later. There were chocolate eggs, a chocolate bunny, and those timeless candy jelly beans. After we overdosed on chocolate, we would be let into the living room. The egg hunt, the hunt for Easter eggs, was on! We kept the ones we found. It was a matter of how clever we were and where to look. The Easter Bunny hid those eggs pretty well. We didn't share our booty. It was every kid for himself. This family tradition would be forever remembered on a singular morning I will now relate.

After these Easter morning festivities, the entire troupe would dress in Sunday duds and go to Trinity Episcopal Church. We were regulars, and we always sat in the second row upfront or on the right side of the church. Paul and I were acolytes. Some of us sang in the choir, but the old man, Paul's moniker for *dear ole Dad*, lectured us the other six days! *You could count on that!*

SPOILER ALERT FOR THOSE YOUNGSTERS HERE WHO MIGHT BE BEING READ TO, OR MIGHT BE *READING*!

I have forgotten the year, but here's what happened. One morning, we all arrived in the dining room (average so far), and my Easter basket was *empty*! My two brothers' baskets were empty! My three sisters' baskets were empty! WHERE WAS THE CANDY?

No clue, no candy, and a very confused and sadder bunch of kids there ever was! Indeed, if the Easter Bunny was not going to deliver, I assumed he was a myth. So was Santa. He was a fraud as well. The whole thing, Tooth Fairy included, all fakes! About twenty years later, I confirmed my suspicions of the thief. It was my older brother, Paul. What did that mean? To me, it was made clear (to my young mind) that Santa, the Easter Bunny, and the Tooth Fairy were all fake, and my older brother was a thief! He snuck into the dining room that morning and killed the bunny and *ate the chocolate!* They had just been plundered by... who knew?

Years later, I heard from my older brother, Paul, who would say, "My friend Tim and I did steal that Easter candy." What a screwy family!

This year's October, the final number of family members reached eight, with the sixth child, Debra Jane, being born.

1954

On 26 April 1954, the Salk polio vaccine field trials, involving 1.8 million children, began. I remember how we got our pills to prevent polio! I distinctly remember being handed a small white paper cup. Visualize the old McDonald's catsup holders. There was a pill in that empty cup. You took medicine and put it in your mouth and put some water in that same now empty cup, and you swallowed your pill to prevent polio! A seminal year in every baby boomer's life.

Frank Fox and his daughter, Penny, ran the Ambler News Agency, and the joint was located two hundred feet east of the railroad tracks. I call it a "joint" due to its reputation and the illegal bookmaking (i.e., gambling) that was their primary business. The station master was named John C. (name omitted, but *not* forgotten), and I would deliver things from Mr. Fox to John C.

This was my first paying gig, and I might have made $2.00 a week for running errands and ringing up money for the sale of newspapers: the *Evening Bulletin*, the *Philadelphia Enquirer*, the *Racing Sheet*, *Sporting News*, and others I can't remember sixty-five years later as I write these words.

The cash register in Mr. Fox's store was an old machine, an NCR brand from 1902, if memory serves me. Google it and see what I mean. When the power went out one afternoon during a thunderstorm, I learned about that behemoth. You would insert a large crank into the built-in hole on the left side of this beast, and after you depressed the dollar amount of the sale, you turned the crank once. The sale bell/ringer went off, and the drawer opened! A few other memories come to mind. I remember the rainy summer afternoon I was outside near a power pole. Was I watching for the police for Frank or his daughter, Penny? I never thought about the thunder and lightning all around me. Then when I was about to go back inside because of the sudden downpour, a lightning bolt hit the pole and the transformer! *Kablam!* Gathering my senses, I quickly ran into the store, only to find it very dark inside! That was when you could manually use the cash register.

The transformer on the pole was hit by lightning had blown up, and luckily, I was not close enough to that pole to have gotten electrocuted! I think of that because a neighbor I lived near in Skippack, a few years earlier, fixed his TV antenna that blew down in a storm. Lightning hit his antenna. That was that for "the poor bloke," they say! I learned how to use the store's antique cash register—even then, it was old—to manually handle customers' sales, as I've just described.

On another occasion, Frank needed my help to replace a fluorescent light bulb in the ceiling fixture. I never did like being up on rickety wooden ladders. I still don't! Perhaps I only disliked ladders after this event. Frank was holding the ladder, and my feet were at least ten feet up off the floor. I was trying to take the old bulb out (not having anything for balance), climb down the ladder, and give Frank the old bulb and climb back up with the new bulb. Nope! I *sent* down the bulb! I mean, I dropped the sixty-inch bulb nearly on poor old Frank's head. *Pop!*

Disclaimer and sensitivity warning to an archaic reference to an African American follows. I'm writing about how it ——, not how I write this. In my summer career working for Frank, I decided to bet on a horse. There was this old "colored man" (I am using the language of that day) who was a regular customer. This was a specific language for that era, commonly spoken with zero complaints. If it were racist, then no one would have used that term. *Racist* was a rarely used word in the sixties—that *I* experienced. It wasn't until I was much older did I realize how well everyone got along up North and how ugly life was down South. Strange that a Democrat US Senator (Robert Byrd) was a high "muckety-muck" in the Klan and the United States Senate! That was disgusting then and isn't mentioned today. That man of color was the local bookie. Frank's daughter, Penny, and I split a $2.00 bet, and voilà, we split the $12.00 winnings. The reason I became suspicious of my regular visits to the station master was because of this bookie. I delivered a bank bag to the mob via John C., so I was a "bagman literally for the mafia!" I asked Frank, "What was in that bag that I just delivered? I was told it was, $1,500.00 in cash. Oh…my…*good*ness! (Said in Dorothy's voice from *The Wizard of Oz*.) That money was then a large percentage of a year's pay!

Since 1954, I remember my aunt's address: 40-25 College Point Blvd, Apt XX, Flushing, NY. Her telephone number was *IN*dependence 1-3421. I learned that number without an area code because I had to use an operator to place long-distance calls. We just dialed O for operator and said we were calling New York City. I recollect that all of us cousins, some of whom lived in New Jersey and my clan who lived near Philadelphia, were all told that our Aunt Grace's place was what we would later refer to as a safe space. I still remember this information though she passed away on 09 August 1995. She lived in that very same apartment for forty-one years!

My Earliest Christmas Memories

As a child of seven or maybe even eight, I remember the smell of the Christmas tree in our house. It was well over fifty-five years ago by now. The tinsel was shiny and so pretty all over the tree, and some was even on the floor. But what did we kids care about that mess? The view of the tree, from my height then, is still in my mind all these years later. It was hard to go to bed on Christmas Eve. Year after year, as I grew up, I think of those long cold nights waiting for Santa. I could not sleep well, but I did keep one eye open. And I never did spot Santa. I assumed it was difficult for him to climb three flights of stairs in the dark!

The first light of dawn crept so slowly upon my bed. It was always the longest night, regardless of any winter solstice. With the first hint of daylight, I noticed a Christmas stocking at the foot of my bed. Aah, the mysteries it contained! I reached down to get this surprise sock full of what? I never knew what to expect. I dumped it out on my bed like a cornucopia. It had an apple, a little box of raisins, some candy, and a few plastic toys. *Wow*! I stayed in bed for a little while, deciding which item to eat first, waiting to run down the three flights of stairs to the living room. My bedroom was on the third floor, and it had good points and bad points. Upstairs, nearly on the roof, I was away from all the yelling down on the first floor, but I got my exercise daily. In the summer, we had only a window fan for cooling. In the winter, warm air rises, so we are never cold!

My younger brother, Ricky, slept in the same bedroom as I did. It wasn't long before he would be awake and empty his stocking. We both decided it was time to head down to the living room where the Christmas tree was. Trying to be fast and silent is never easy, especially for two preteen kids. This might be where the term "a herd of elephants" came downstairs began! My brother and I were not alone in heading for the living room. We were *six kids*! What a racket we must have made running for that tree! But we were not to succeed since our mom stood guard at the entrance where the treasure land of gifts, under the tree, awaited us in the living room.

For a few years, there was a baby grand piano in the living room. The wrapped presents were piled separately on several different sofa chairs. What a sight! In later years, our father got rid of the piano and bought himself an electronic four-keyboard organ. He played "Tico Tico" way too many times!

"You must wait until everyone else is here!" We were admonished like that year after year. I had an older brother and sister who were not as anxious as my brother and I were. To our advantage (Ricky and I), we had two younger sisters to deal with. But *care* was needed, since by this time, ages six and eight, our two little sisters were two and four. You would surely be in profound something (trouble?) if you were mean to them! (We were a bunch, we were!)

You never cause problems with your baby sisters, or you *will be punished*. In this case, you would be held back (firmly but gently) as the rest of our crew dove into the pile of presents! Generally, we sort of all got along, most of the time. We were laughing—sort of, *really*?

Finally, after what seemed like noontime, but probably only 7:30 a.m., we all went into the living room and began tearing open our little surprises. Some gifts were on a chair or near a chair. Santa was a skilled wrapper! There was paper everywhere, but the mess we were making wasn't noticed by us anyway. We were so excited.

"Look what I got from *Santa*!" It was a happy morning, but it was over so fast, and we were each playing with our favorite toy in no time. The other toys would lie there abandoned…at least for now.

My favorite toy I ever got, or the only one I specifically remember, was a toy metal Erector Set like building a small house or something out of metal. Tiny screws and nuts everywhere. It was fun to make things at that age. What is/was an erector set? I glad you asked, because here's your answer!

https://www.etsy.com/listing/1283133473/vintage-1954-erector-set-no-6-12-w?gpla=1&gao=1&&utm_source=bing&utm_medium=cpc&utm_campaign=shopping_us_all&utm_custom1=_k_3e90ac332fce1cc9805acf28a9c842b6_k_&utm_content=bing_319339186_131061798

The rest of the day was usually spent sledding. It was winter up north where I grew up, and there was always snow to play in, or to throw as snowballs! It would be a good time for Mom to clean up our mess and enjoy some adult "eggnog", maybe.

1955

The following is my scary and unforgettable second and final (I hope) attack by honeybees. I was coming back from Shelley's Ice Cream Parlor (the home of hand-dipped frozen treats made there at that store. Ice cream was 7¢ a scoop) on Butler Avenue. I was in the company of Judy and Ricky, and we took the shortcut (a beeline, as it were) for home. As we came up the hill and approached the cemetery where the woods parted, the graveyard began, and I was stung once on my backside! Then again! And then several more at the same time. I started to run! *Fast!* It seemed as though the faster I ran, the more I got stung! Where did my ice cream cone end up? I dunno. Dropping everything, I kept running toward the cemetery, jumping the fence, and out of the woods! It was too painful to think about anything except, *Legs don't fail me now!* What a memorable way to remember that evening. No one else was harmed in my getting stung. I was the sole victim! The ice cream was lost, and the lesson about bees was almost over. Later in the early seventies, I was trying to kill a hornet or two and then knock down a hornets net under construction! With two young daughters out and about routinely I wasn't going to risk them getting stung. As I climbed my step ladder and attempted to use a can full of bee-poison (or some such stuff) here came the boss from inside his new home—still under construction! I watched in slow-motion vision as he flew up from the nest, made a u-turn, and dive bombed my hand. His stinger was aiming for my hand and he then landed, what felt like a thousand pound hammer, on my finger and rammed his stinger in to my hand! The pain was a lot worse than those yellow jacket several years earlier!!! (Note from the bees: We do not like your author!)

I remember going to this church for summer Bible school, Ambler Lutheran Church. I still have another one from Skippack in '53.

THOMAS E. BYRON

Thomas Byron Oct. 27, 1962 11th grade PHSHS ⑪	Thomas Byron Grade 8 A3 Jan. 19, 1960 ⑥	Thomas P. Byron Grade 4 November 2, 1955 ①
Thomas Byron ⑫ Junior (PHSHS) Jan. 29, 1963	Thomas Byron ⑦ Grade 9 H3 Oct 24, 1960	Thomas Byron ② GRADE 5 NOVEMBER 13, 1956
Thomas Byron ⑬ Mar 30, 1963 Junior WSHS MOVED MAR 25	Thomas Byron ⑧ Grade 9H3 Jan 10, 1961	THOMAS BYRON ③ Grade 6 JUNE 25, 1957
Thomas Byron ⑭ Sept 5, 1963 Senior WHS	Thomas Byron ⑨ Grade 10-3 Oct 18, 1961 MOVED OCT 26 1961 FRIDAY	Thomas Byron ④ Grade 6 Mar. 12, 1958
Thomas Byron ⑮ Jan 11, 1964 Senior WHS	Thomas Byron ⑩ Grade 10 March 11, 1962 (Penn Hills High Agh. 35)	Thomas Byron ⑤ Shady Shore Grade 7 A 2 February ...
Thomas E. Byron ⑯ June 2, 1964 Graduate of Wissahickon Senior High	Thomas E. Byron ⑰ Feb. 8, 1965 Antonellis School of Photo Phila. Pa	The Ministerial Assn. of Ambler Feb 26, 1959 (above entry)

Thomas E. Byron
Oct 16, 1965 ⑮
Famous Photographer's
Home Study Course

Thomas E. Byron ⑯
Jan. 7, 1966
FAMOUS PHOTOGRAPHER'S
HOME STUDY COURSE

Thomas E. Byron
191 Panther Street
K.I. Sawyer AFB
A2/c, U.S.A.F.
8 Aug 67

Met Heather Houston
2 July 66
   Chicago
Married Heather Houston
23 Jan 67
   Chicago

THOMAS E. BYRON

Going Up into the Church Bell Tower

Our entire family (all eight) attended Trinity Episcopal Church. That may have been because a few of us kiddies were in the choir as we got older. I tried to make a joyful noise (more than musical, but it was joyful) unto the Lord. Years later, in 1970, I would be called out during choir practice by music director Joel Youngblood at First Baptist Church in Erlanger, Kentucky. He said, "You're flat!"

I replied, "I quit!" I would not be complete in my narrative if I did not tell you about my memories, including a celebrity during our ten years we were members.

There was an "unused" door in the lobby/exit from the side of the church. I never saw anyone use that door. I'm sure I have wondered about this for a long time. *I wonder where that door goes?* You are getting ahead of me, grabbing the fifty-year-old brass doorknob, twisting, slowly pushing open. Think of an old horror movie with Bela Lugosi. Looking in and then upward, I saw an old set of wooden rungs on a ladder leading me, beckoning me, up to an unknown place, upward toward the light. Turning around, I made sure that no one was watching me as I closed the door. An adventure was unfolding before me. *What was up there,* My inner voice asked. I climbed up and was greeted by a new experience and a great view! There were several large and ominously quiet bells right in front of me! The hour was not twelve or six, so they just hung there in silence, blankly staring at me.

The Dick Clark Dance in the Church Recreation Hall

I was never a dancer, but to see Dick Clark, live and up close playing rock 'n' roll music, spinning "platters", was a tremendous treat! He was much shorter in person than on TV! I will mention another person, the Fonz, later on as our journey progresses. He, too, was much shorter in person than on TV. Camera trickery? My sister Judy was a regular on his afternoon dance TV show (*American Bandstand*) Monday through Friday on channel 6 WFIL TV. This was a fantastic privilege to see an actual celebrity in person (no, my sister wasn't there) in our church basement!

ZERO TO SEVENTY-FIVE

I was the beggar in the Good Samaritan story from the Bible in a play in this rec hall. I remember performing in a play to recreate an Old Testament biblical lesson, the Good Samaritan. My role was to act as the beggar who got beaten up and left by the road. No need to explain, but everyone would walk by me, the injured victim, and look at me with(out) pity! I had to lay on the road. It was actually the cold tiled floor. No lines to speak. No talent is necessary. I was too young to feel embarrassed.

The rector of Trinity Church was Father John Schultz. His name for me, as he wrote in my prayer book, was "God bless my little *Keg o' TNT!*" That original book has been lost for decades, but if you are family reading this sometime in the distant future and find this small black prayer book, look inside the front cover. I bought a similar copy in 1986 to replace my original. Also, I still have my sister Judy's prayer book from a few years earlier than mine.

Polio was fought as I grew up, but we hadn't yet heard about President FDR, crippled by this disease. Not until many years later would we understand. Decades later (October 2012), Sheila and I would visit Warm Springs, Georgia, where he vacationed and liaised (?) with his "friend" Lucy Mercer, and he would die there in '45. We also got those scar-producing shots to prevent smallpox (finally eradicated by 1980), which we wore proudly on our arms. Even to this day, our scar is proof of the vaccine. The girls could get them on their upper thighs to hide the scar if they ever chose to wear sleeveless dresses.

Our health, as boomers, was important. But curiously, our cars did not have seat belts then. It wasn't until 1968 that a federal law for seat belts was passed. Kids didn't wear helmets or kneepads either. I *did* drink creek water, though, and actual natural spring water along the Wissahickon Creek, where Ricky and I would sail on, with our handmade raft (think *Huck Finn*). I ate wild berries, crab apples, honeysuckle, etc., all summer, every summer. We didn't have gyms to exercise in. We never needed them because we never sat around watching TV or playing board games. I was "thin as a rail" (139 pounds, as I recall) until I married and settled down. Back then? Unless the weather was horrid (we never thought it wasn't perfect), we would always be found (but were never looked for) outside doing something. We built snow forts in the winter and jumped in vast piles of leaves in the fall. I even created my skateboard (before the term *skateboard* was in the culture). I made it from an old broken metal roller skate. I nailed it onto a board I found. Old nails. Old wood. No helmets were used. They weren't invented for home use then. I went sledding on a soon-to-be-antique Flexible Flyer. There was always snow every winter or swimming all summer. I'm surprised I never grew gills. Maybe that contributes to my skepticism toward evolution theories. That's a topic for another book much later.

I suppose it was around this age that I decided to make mischief. I earned a free ice cream cone for helping to put out a small brushfire at the local Howard Johnson's ice cream store. Odd that I was rewarded for this since I started the small brushfire. My career as an "arsonist" was over in two minutes. (Don't tell anyone, please!)

I have so far failed to mention the many summers our family spent at Dr. George Berner, ophthalmologist, and his lovely wife, Dorothy's, classic country estate/home with a swimming pool. I couldn't explain "the flipping of Dorothy" by my father, but I will try to, and that's not an exaggeration! Only three of us are alive now who were there when this happened. I, your narrator and guide, and my two sisters, Laura and Debbie. This pool was about a twenty-minute drive or thirteen miles through backcountry roads from our house. This country home, which none of us ever entered, was enormous. My father met Dr. Berner as an optical sales customer while employed as a proverbial, but literally in the sense of many a joke about "the traveling salesman". One could only suspect that in exchange for cleaning their pool every weekend, he dragged our brood to the pool for an afternoon of swimming and diving, shuffleboard, and sun. "The old man wasn't out a nickel!" He never wasted a nickel but never saved one either! He spoke about life insurance his entire life, but when he died, all that he bequeathed us kids was his last uncashed social security check that was split three ways from a scant sum of $390.00. Paul didn't want to have anything to do with, as he called him the old man! There are photos of us as a family of eight over many years, standing on the Berner's diving board! Classic!

Debbie (1956–20xx), Laura (1953–20xx), Ricky (1949–1964), Tommy (1946–20xx), Judy (1941–2004), Paul (1940–2016), mom Betty (1918–2003), father Joe (1914–2007).

My father had a habitual acting-the-clown streak in him. Does that surprise anyone who knew him or knew me? One memorable afternoon, around my twelfth year, he pulled the most epic blunder. *Ever!* He frequently swam up toward my mother from underwater stealthily. She stood there in about four feet of water and he swam under water in between her legs. He then quickly stood up flipping her backward over his shoulders and into the water and backwards and headfirst. Hahaha. Everyone was amused. My mother, at times, not so much! Dorothy was of a similar body shape (of course, as viewed underwater) as my mother. Though, and I would guess, a few years older. Dorothy was from a very decent, dignified society of the high peerage (someone you'd have seen in *Downton Abbey*). My father confused dear Dorothy one memorable afternoon as he swam up behind...yes... Dorothy! This was sixty-three years ago, and it's as fresh in my mind as if it were yesterday! Dorothy was mortified! Whatever was said between them, I do not recall, but I do remember her anger! She was livid, and she should have at least slapped him! Maybe she did, and I missed that while *I was* quietly laughing! But I can safely say that my mother was silently laughing too! She was laughing at how stupid the old man was!

1956

In fourth grade, I was out sick for a week from Ms. Searing's class. I had some nasty surgery, not because of the danger or severeness but the personal and delicate nature of the abscess on my rectum, which required surgery. I was eight at the time, so many things were a mystery. Some still are! I was in the Norristown Hospital for five days, as best I can remember. The beginning of my stay was memorable. As I was wheeled into the OR, I remembered being told to count down from 10, 9, 8, 7. Gas was going to be used via a rubber mask over your mouth and nose to "put you under." I think I remembered getting to 8. Then I was asking, "When is my surgery?" My mind was blank.

My recovery was the fun part. Since I was not allowed to walk (I had a sore butt, and walking didn't help me heal), I became accustomed to using a wheelchair to move around in my hospital ward. It was an open bed area/ward with curtains for walls. Lots of us kids around. It was quite public, but all young children. Naughty children. Creative children. Someone (me?) thought it would be nice to have playthings like those cardboard and plastic sketch toys. You could erase them by peeling the plastic cover away. *Riiiiiip!* It sounded like fabric ripping as you pulled it apart. When a nurse bent over, one would peel the plastic and "Let the page *riiiip!*" Amusing…until we were caught!

There weren't even any interstate highways until President Eisenhower decided, after his experience in WWII seeing the German Autobahn (built under Hitler's time as das führer, the leader), that we needed better and faster roads. I was a ten-year-old then, but currently, we have forty thousand miles of nonstop interstate highways. Fantastic. There were none when I was born! You can now drive nonstop across the US, except for changing drivers and getting gas. (Aside, I'll be amazed if I ever read about anyone driving and electric car cross-country!) This is why we now have motels and fast-food chains everywhere too. I have driven from the Atlantic Ocean west to Arizona (on separate trips) and only went *in* California after flying there to photograph my nephew's (sister *Laura's* son's) wedding. My first five minutes driving there were as long as it took before I almost got run off the road by a "blind" driver. It isn't nice to call them crazies. That had to be his problem unless they have "kamikaze drivers" that I don't know about. Perhaps I have some family influence to blame for my political interests, which were blossoming by now. My Uncle Clarence Francis[2], on my father's side, through his sister Grace, was in politics. He was a very successful "fruit peddler", referring to himself and his family stories. He retired as chairman of the board of General Foods, and he also served as President Eisenhower's economic advisor. I cast a vote for a democrat in 1972 for George McGovern, a mistake in retrospect. That was a Vietnam War protest vote, and as I recall, I was two years post-active duty then (1972) also! The Vietnam War was raging, and my peers were dying. I would become very active in politics in a few years. Life, I'm finding out, is precisely that—odd twists, turns, joys, and sorrows. "Incidents and accidents." It was unexplainable at the time, but valuable reference points in retrospect as we age. It also gives you insight as to my journey in life.

In 1956, or thereabouts, I remember a casual friend of mine whose last name was Haas, a young kid from the Haas family of the chemical firm Rohm & Haas. They harvested maple syrup into buckets and then poured that into large steel vats. They burned wood to heat the large (six feet-by-four feet and maybe three feet deep) metal vats full of sap, to remove the water content. They did this every fall at what I perceived as an estate somewhere in west Ambler. The place where he lived happened to be at the top of a long and steep hill where a grade school pal, Billy Pistilli, wrecked his bike. That hill was why I ended up meeting Young Master Haas. Billy and I rode down this long hill one afternoon after being at a fire we got to because we followed the local fire department to the fire. That being so, as going on our bikes to fires was a "hobby". How so, you ask? The volunteer fire department was less than one-fourth mile from my house on my bike (shorter if you use my ice cream-shortcut), and when I heard the siren go off, I immediately went to the firehouse. The fire trucks were already gone, but the location of the fire was written on the chalkboard right inside the volunteer

---

[2] https://en.wikipedia.org/wiki/Clarence_Francis?wprov=sfti1

station house. Other volunteer firefighters and I would show up. They were also off to the fire!

As Billy and I were leaving a fire one afternoon, we were riding down a long steep rural road. I was right along Billy's right side, about a foot from him. I watched him wreck! Nothing to do at *that* moment. He pulled the chain on his bike's handlebar to engage a small tire-driven siren. The siren slipped loose and became locked in the spokes, immediately stopping the cycle in less than a blink of an eye. I looked over at Billy. He was flying or "air-surfing" horizontally, still going the same speed as I was on my bike, before gravity slowed him down! He was *head*ing (literally) for the road! It would be just another blink of my eye, and he was simultaneously on the road and out cold! The fire truck was behind us and stopped to render aid. I don't remember more than that, except he had a scar for a souvenir on his cheek for as long as I knew him from "Tom and Billy's (not so) excellent adventure!"

Back to Young Master Haas. He lived in a nicely wooded old estate at West Mount Pleasant Avenue and Morris Road, not too far from Bobby Mueller's house. Yes. The same person as in the recent FBI fame and the Trump fiasco made up by the Democrats! Specifically, Hillary Clinton is now (as I edit in February 2022) known to have created this mess! We were Boy Scouts in Whitmarsh Troop 114 (see "1960"). Those vats of future maple syrup were collected in buckets hanging from nails hooked to taps to drain sap. They flowed down into the roots for the winter into the tree roots. The scene is embedded into my brain. Around this date, there was some discussion with my scout friend Johnny Pearce that he and I visit his grandmother in Baghdad, Iraq. I remember this was a serious plan. It never happened for many reasons, but it sure sounded exciting and fascinating! Johnny will be mentioned again in an entry dated 14 June 2020, in this autobiography. The oddity of tracking him down during the writing of my autobiography is a fitting conclusion. The years between our last two conversations would span from 1960 until 2020, or sixty years (my best guess)!

The year has been forgotten, but the church has not been. The Cathedral Church of Saint John the Divine, New York City. Here's a 2016 photograph of mine when Paul and Delores and Sheila and I visited in May 2016. I sang in my church's Trinity Episcopal choir there in '56 or '57.

ZERO TO SEVENTY-FIVE

1957

What do I remember from Ms. Tompkins's fifth-grade class this year? If I remember, I promised to add it to my last words at the end. But I only remember her name.

One scorching summer day, maybe in 1957, something occurred, but I'll relate it here. My little brother and cohort-in-mischief, Ricky, and I built a crude Huck Finn–style wooden raft, sans sail. We were then calmly traveling down a slow-moving, shallow, and very narrow local stream for our *"most excellent adventure"*. We were only five blocks from our house, but we probably thought we were in foreign territory! No one drowned, and we didn't make any discoveries, only to build something creek-worthy and fun. Most, if not all, of our playthings were homemade! Even as my brother and I were creating places to live in, in our small backyard, America worked with a former Nazi who came to America after he escaped from Germany. He brought a vast amount of knowledge of rocketry. Dr. Werner Von Braun emigrated to America and eventually became a part of NASA and the space race to get a man on the moon. History is always a bit odd. Aside: "I think that my personal history was/still is also odd." I learned that the Russians helped America defeat the Nazis. Ten years later (in the mid-1950's), a former Nazi was helping America win the US-Russia space race. I remember watching America enter the Atomic Age. It was a fascinating time to be alive! But I digress, and maybe Von Braun's reference will make sense in the following few paragraphs.

Sometimes my days were inspiring, like the afternoon Ricky and I decided to do some of our rocketry construction. You knew there would be a rocketry tie-in. Of course, you did...didn't you?

Materials: Empty CO_2 cartridge, an *empty* .22 caliber bullet shell, several books of matches, and a small tin container of Jet-X™ fuse.

Total expense: Mere pocket change. Greshe's toy store in town on Butler Avenue was a short walk. It was the place to buy the fuse for 25¢, and the rest was handy and accessible.

ZERO TO SEVENTY-FIVE

Construction: Remove the matches from a matchbook and fill the empty CO2 cartridge, and then seal it with an empty .22 caliber shell casing and a nail hole in the shell to thread it with a short piece of Jet-X.

Launch technique: Lay the rocket on something, maybe just the ground. Light the fuse, and 5, 4, 3, 2, 1, *poof* and *bang* launched! The trajectory was unpredictable at best! I calculated the speed at 118 mph using the speed=distance/time. Not every launch went as planned. Remember, we weren't NASA material. The fuse might not ignite the rocket fuel! We were poor, and not much was wasted. So one afternoon, we were doing more rocketry experiments, and we were in our backyard behind our three-story house. *Our secret missile launch site* was our private backyard. Too many Russian spies running about? This launch went poorly, but no one said, *"Abort"* at T-0. We knew the drill, the vocabulary, and the thrill of a rocket lifting off. A quick examination revealed that the fuse died as it passed into the .22 caliber shell casing, but there was still a tiny piece of fuse visible.

"Hold this," I told my assistant (Ricky). "I'll light it!" It took one nanosecond to ignite the fuse and another nanosecond to drop this bomb or rocket! I don't remember what he said as the rocket ignited and bounced off his chest and headed toward the house. *Woooosh!* We didn't have a flight plan in mind, just the launch. After some searching, we found a hot rocket out front in the street, still smoking but with no flame shooting out. It had traveled over the house and went about three hundred feet up, over, and out into the street! Quoting Ricky, "Owewiee! ——!" It wouldn't be polite to quote his actual words! Even at his young age, he was a master of foul language. He also had a cartridge-shaped welt on his chest!

1958

Since this school was very close, I walked only a few minutes to Forest Avenue Elementary School. In 2010, I made my first return visit to my sixth-grade classroom that I was ten years old the last time I was there! Below is that same room in a 2010 visit during a high school reunion:

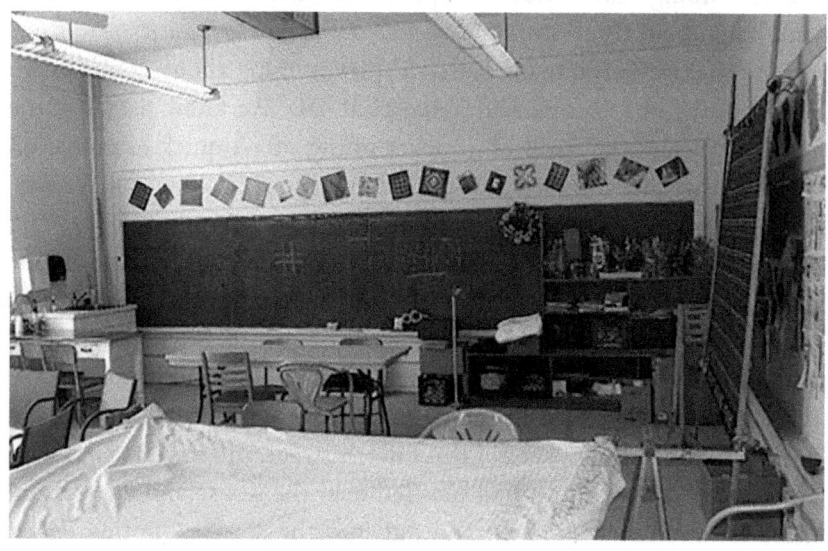

I remember *very* well an event in my sixth-grade class in the room (see below) with my teacher, Ms. Telanoff. We used the term *Miss* or *Missus* back then, and I don't recall their first names or if I ever knew those names. She was out of our class for a few minutes. Her mistake! This was the 1958–1959 school year, fifty years ago now. *Wow!* Billy N. and Eddie R. were roughhousing (horseplay). Last names are omitted as a courtesy, but I certainly *do remember* their names. Eddie got hold of Billy and flipped Eddie over his head and he fell to the floor. Laughter. No injuries.

No anger, just rough play. As if this were yesterday, I can remember our teacher walking back into the class and asking, "Who did this?"

Her hands were on her hips, as she looked at the bulletin board by the door to the classroom. She had seen the evidence. It was a sneaker print near the top of the bulletin board's paper-lined area. A sneaker print at least seven feet from the floor? *How'd* that *happen?* I remember this very well, but unfortunately, I've mentally eliminated the consequences, if any, of who was punished. My memory of that ends here. I can imagine that event as if it happened recently.

Seeing death in the raw at a young age and knowing that death is always only a moment away was well understood by me as a young adult. I was not yet a teen when I saw my first body. I'll get to that in a few more paragraphs, but it deeply affected me, and "I grew up in a minute!" Where I should have learned about death over a few years, that was *not* my experience! My neighbor died in a terrible car wreck when I was eleven. It rocked our small close-knit town. He was buried across the street from his home, a one-minute walk. It was next to where I ran out of the woods fleeing those —— *bees*! I knew the driver, the young and handsome Bobby Myers. He lived just about next door. This wreck traumatized our small town. Bobby came home from his senior prom around 1:30 a.m. and told his mom he was going to another party.

"Don't go, Bobby. It's too late!" That was their last conversation. He and three of his classmates were killed instantly when the brand-new '57 Chevy Bobby was driving after the car took out sixty feet of guardrails (best memory) as they slammed into a bridge abutment at 100+ mph. The impact woke up my classmate Joe Chinnici, who lived half a mile from the accident. They died upon hitting a concrete railroad bridge abutment!

From the photo, you can see how everyone reacted and sympathized with those killed. Ours was a small town of about three thousand. It was the first of two home town car wrecks I knew about, until I left for the military in 1966.

The following event in my life has been reviewed by my lifelong friend Doug Hill. Thanks for jumping in and helping out a classmate, Doug. This classmate of mine, Bob Jaffee, died in a horrible car wreck along with his mother and a baby brother who shared a casket. His father and sister survived. This happened toward the end of our summer break from school, and it wasn't long before we were back at school one Monday morning talking about this. It was a horrendous high-speed, head-on collision on the dangerous White Horse Pike (a two-lane road) returning from the Jersey Shore. It was a road that my father drove us on going to our annual two-week summer beach vacation. I knew that as I walked by those two caskets at the funeral home on Tennis Avenue, a few blocks from my house. While I'm on the death topic, I remember a second-grade classmate who got killed as he fell under the wheels of a local train at the Ambler train station, where John C. (remember, surnames omitted where incriminating) was the station master. That was scary when I realized how that happened, but it was not enough to keep me from becoming the local town crier as I went door-to-door telling my neighbors! I remember knocking on their front door and telling them what had happened. Strange? Yes! We agree.

I was almost twelve this summer (my birthday is in September), and I was with a church group this afternoon. The event was a bus ride to a creek somewhere in New Jersey or near Philadelphia. I don't know. As I've said and will continue to say, a large part of my childhood memories has been wiped clean! It isn't senility. It's been like this for many, many decades. The day was an outing to enjoy swimming at a state park. It has become one of the most vivid memories of my youth, like it was yesterday. At least parts of this day are etched like a carving in an Egyptian tomb. (That was a deliberate use of that metaphor.) I was thrust into adulthood quite suddenly, awkwardly, and permanently! It was a preparation for yet *another* event to happen a few years later. My youth ended this day, as you will see. I met death head-on, face-to-face, and not "funeralized" from my personal experience, not something I saw on TV or read about. Up close, and not yet a teenager, *in situ* is the Latin term. This event is barely censored (mentally) by all the time passed during these (fifty-five) years. But the details that matter have remained. We will revisit them now.

There were about fifteen to twenty of us kids and a few adults. Their presence and their names and faces have been shoved away into the back of my mind. The mind's handling of memories is like that. At least *mine* is! The muddy creek was wide, slow-moving, and at least six feet deep. This event is laser-focused on essential details, not the trivial details surrounding that day. Month? Day? Place? Gone. Gone. Gone. But *not* gone is what I will relate, from a kids'-eye view.

I am a highly visual person, no doubt because I'm a descendant of several generations of photographers. But I remember the landscape, view, grass, and trees as if I were there as I type. It was hot! There was a vast slow-moving idyllic creek. It was muddy but inviting on that hot summer day. Mr. Bill McClintock was our scout leader this afternoon. A rotund little man he was. I have a photo of him from a previous canoeing trip. Somewhere, another creek, and another date and time. Along the bank of *this* creek was a large overhanging tree with a big hemp rope dangling right over the water. We took turns pulling the string back to the shore and grabbing hold of it and swinging out over the creek and letting go. *Kersplash!* We fell into the water. I had never seen such a contraption. We laughed as one of us would try to show off and do a flip as we let go. Some were more athletic, some were lucky, but it was fun. It was a hot day, so the water felt great. We had no concerns about the muddy water or any hazards doing this. I think the water was plenty deep. Nothing to worry about.

As we gathered under this same tree, with the long rope hanging over the creek, maybe fifteen or more of us, I wondered who this young man was lying before my companions and me on the ground. I was also surrounded by panicked adults and kids talking to each other. I was walking around confused. Moments earlier, I watched a group of older kids playing out in the middle of the creek. Perhaps a hundred feet from us. They were yelling and roughhousing and splashing. We were jumping off this tree rope too. They were not with our group. Maybe four of these older kids gathered out in the middle of the creek, separately having fun away from us. I noticed as I waited my turn to grab the rope that their playing suddenly changed. Their voices came across the water in shouts! Staccato! Replies! Screams! Commands! *Urgency!*

As my attention focused on them, I noticed one, then another would disappear beneath the water for a few seconds. They were not playing anymore. Then another would surface and yell, followed by another who would dive below the water and suddenly pop back up. I could sense their panic and fear as I watched this. But what exactly was going on? Were they playing a game that I was too young to understand? An emergency? I didn't figure that out at this point.

Here I am, standing with a large and growing group of perhaps thirty kids and adults while also trying to see what was happening. An older kid was lying on the ground, maybe eighteen? There was an ambulance parked nearby on my left. He was splayed out on the ground, facedown, with his arms extended over his head. A grown-up knelt across him at his head. He *wasn't* breathing! They used the old-fashioned method of leaning on and pulling his shoulders up after pressing down on him. Afterward, I heard some of his friends talking to other adults. I found out more details. He had been pretending to drown but wasn't drowning. He would pop up out of the water and surprise the others!

Not the last time. Not now! He didn't come up, and they kept waiting, laughing. Their wondering soon became panic, and everyone nearby could feel the panic! He was in serious trouble. *They* must have certainly known something was wrong! *Very wrong!*

He was near my feet on the grass. His head was facing away and to my right. He wasn't moving. They kept trying to get him to breathe. After a long time (five minutes or thirty minutes?), they decided to turn him over. This is where my memory of this ends. I saw his face and his color, and I knew.

Was I being prepared for the shock of death three summers later? My younger brother would die suddenly by his hand, which was a pivotal moment in my childhood. I would say this changed everything!

Years later, I would read an article in the *Pennsylvania Packet* from 1785. An original, not a copy. Ben Franklin happened to have a piece published then, which is fascinating. He went into detail on "returning life's 'vapers' back into the poor victim." His treatment method was to place your mouth over the victim's and blow into the mouth. Exactly as you are thinking (mouth-to-mouth)! Yes, he was brilliant. My document was stolen when we lived in Alabama (circa 1988), along with my original wedding ring and G.O.K.'s what else!

Ricky's image Judy drew

THOMAS E. BYRON

17 February 1958

Was this a cosmic preparation, previewing the Death Angel's visit? A harbinger... precursor indeed! As I finished composing this and got a cup of coffee, I looked out the window here at my apartment. An ambulance next door backed up to that apartment, with the red lights flashing. Death Angel? (I am fast-forwarding to a present-day 2017 event.) The Death Angel has visited an elderly neighbor. He was taken away by ambulance. This is downright eerie and spooky. I am shaken. What did you see as a child that affected *your* life, dear reader?

1959

Sometime around this date, I recall a family reunion and the name Leeann (sp?) Secunda. How am I related, who, and where in New Jersey is this place? All are lost to history, and there's no one to ask anymore. Why did this happen once? And why am I the only one who remembers this? Oh, that's because I'm the oldest survivor in my family!

I once sold *Grit* (https://en.wikipedia.org/wiki/Grit_(newspaper)?wprov=sfti1) newspapers, my earliest job after working for Mr. Frank Fox and the Mafia. You had to find people who wanted to buy this quirky and obscure little-known paper, dwindling in popularity. You purchased the copies, and they were mailed to your house. I remember being excited when the package arrived monthly, as I recall. Now came the work—deliver them and collect the money. *Remember*, I pay my newspaper bill, they buy, and the difference is my meager profit! I don't think I lasted long in that business. I was now ready to deliver an authentic paper from a major city and a newspaper everyone knew—the *Philadelphia Evening Bulletin*.

Every afternoon, I would ride my bicycle (I'm visualizing this journey as I type) over to an old wooden garage/barn, uphill on my left, on a dirt road off Ridge Road, to collect my daily papers to deliver to around forty customers. These papers needed to be folded and placed in the basket I had installed on the handlebars at much expense. Each one was either thrown on the customer's/subscriber's porch, yard, or into the bushes, which then required me to stop and replace it properly on their porch. If it were raining, every piece of paper was walked up to the patio. One day, upon my arrival at the barn, everyone was hanging around, which was odd. Their newspapers were nowhere to be seen.

"Where is our stock?" I was confused (newspaper "stock"?), and I was later told the man who delivered the papers to us was named Mr. Stock! Not much of a part-time job since your paycheck was determined by your customers paying their bills. Mr. Stock always got his full pay, and the delivery boys got what was left since their pay remained after they paid Mr. Stock! I didn't stay at this job for too long either. Restaurant work was hard, but the payment was based on my hours, not whether the diner paid for their meal (like those newspaper customers).

1960

When I was in Boy Scout Troop 114 Whitemarsh, we went on an outing to fly in a C-119. It's a large cargo plane (known affectionately as the flying boxcar) used for troop or equipment deployment by parachute. The flight was fun and exciting, but it was the *end* of that flight that was *very* exciting! I was around fourteen years old and l had, not yet, been on a large plane. I had not flown since my first time in that red biplane I mentioned earlier in chapter "1952." This time the landing was terrifying! There were about a dozen of us seated inside this cargo plane when a voice came over the loudspeaker: "There's a problem with the landing gear…" I wondered if, perhaps, it was both gears! I probably remember (incorrectly) that there was a mention about using the parachutes we were wearing. Almost sixty years later, that might have been said. In any case, we landed safely! It was a fun trip, looking back on it. But I remembered being scared to death, I have a very vivid imagination!

On yet another scouting trip, we went to the Philadelphia Naval Base. We toured an aircraft carrier at the port, the USS *Kitty Hawk*, and then boarded a docked submarine; I forget the name. Preview: it wouldn't be until 2012 that I went to sea out in the vast Atlantic Ocean. We visited the *Titanic* wreck site (see <<page 261>>, *the* adventure of a lifetime, the Titanic Memorial Cruise 2012). The contrast couldn't have been starker. The deck of the *Kitty Hawk* was enormous (I remember nine hundred feet in length). While inside the submarine, I felt like I was inside a trash can! There was nearly no headroom in there, and you couldn't walk or even swing your arms, let alone a dead cat (a crude metaphor, but this is my story). Imagine living like that for months and months. No thanks! Maybe this was why I chose the Air Force to serve my country.

In the last two weeks in July, for many years, our entire family packed up five kids and parents and headed to the shore. A few years earlier, it was all six kids and our parents in one photo I have. We would be off to Jersey (pronounced "Joisey") shore. By now, Paul had left home upon graduating from Ambler High School, and he went sailing on many, if not all, of the world's oceans. I have a book about those adventures, *On Almost Any Wind*, which would add more details to his global experiences. My oldest brother was the first to leave home, and like a nest of robin eggs hatching, we all followed his example. Those hatchlings did just that as soon as they got their feathers to fly from their nest. His reasons for leaving and that story is "a long and tedious road" for another tale. Paul and our father did not mix like oil and water do not mix. Another time, I might cover that story. There were too many crazy stories that I've only heard about in bits and pieces. Was his father the same biological father as the rest of us five? My vote? A qualified no!

I remember loading into our family's 1958 light green Ford station wagon (no air-conditioning) and heading to the Jersey Shore. The third row of seats faced rearward to see the car behind us. Strange! He never owned his cars then. They were always company-provided cars. I remember the toasty-smelling tobacco smoke (Chesterfield Kings) every time he lit up. The smell of that smoke ensured most of us children became smokers. I have since quit (23 July 2012). In 2019, I had a chest CT scan and received a clean bill of health. Fifty years of cigarettes was enough! I did get bladder cancer from those cigarettes. January 25, 2017, was when I had my first surgery and my first catheter! *Yuck!* (It sure is smart to smoke, ain't it?) I'm still not clear, and it's been five years of treatment now as I'm typing.

What an adventure, walking two blocks every day down to the beach. What a troupe *that* was! It wasn't until decades later that I would like to learn more about the great white sharks would birth their young in Brigantine Bay. Right *in the bay* where we swam when not in the ocean! There was a very tall (twenty feet?) metal sliding board there. That slide was terrific. It was always wet from a watering pipe up to the top of the slide. Without that water, the fall would have burned your rear end, but you got a fast and wet ride down and *kersplat* into the bay! That was also before the movie *Jaws*, that excellent shark thriller! I didn't know to be scared; no one did. Not while we were there out in the ocean. Alone. Or maybe *not* alone…mmm?

One afternoon, from this time in my life, all these summers blend into one memory. It doesn't matter which of many years around this time I mention a vignette or two. I swam and waded out to a sandbar (half a mile out?) with little brother, Ricky. On our way back to shore, we had to stop swimming and wait for a shark (between us and the beach) to swim across in front of us. Too close, even though it was perhaps less than fifty yards away. We didn't even worry since it was pre-*Jaws*! Those days will never return. As I type, I can *see* that fin moving right to left slowly and parallel to the beach! We were too far offshore to recognize the faces of the beachgoers to give you a perspective of our distance offshore.

I have fond memories of Steel Pier, a place of arcades and *Ripley's Believe It or Not*, and the many miles walking the long and famous boardwalk. We were given a dollar or two (maybe less) for candy and were allowed to walk around. It was memorable once to see the real Mr. Peanut (you might have seen him in TV commercials) for Planters peanuts walking past me on that world-famous boardwalk. In the mid-2000s, there was an HBO TV series called *Boardwalk*. It was set in the twenties or thirties, very similar to my memories of Atlantic City!

Every fall, before school started, we would go, one by one, to the local shoe store, Reagan's Shoe Store, and get new shoes. They had an ancient Fluoroscope™ where you could stand there and look into a small greenish-looking screen and see an eerie moving x-ray image of your feet to make sure your toes weren't being smushed in your new shoes. Clever. We also made a trip to *Sears Roebuck & Company* for the only new clothes for that entire school year. I would also wear my brother's old clothes as I grew into them, even after he'd long since left home! I had an older brother and not just an older sister. There is no telling how I might have dressed.

Just one more incident my older brother, Paul, told me about. It was a 1960-era event. He drove from Pittsburgh to Ambler on the PA TNPK (Pennsylvania Turn Pike). It is about three hundred miles and a very boring drive. Some people have their way of dealing with this boredom, but Paul's idea cost him dearly and provided me, the younger brother, a valuable lesson. He was exiting the turnpike at Ft. Washington (the exit for Ambler) and handed the attendant his trip ticket "IBM" punch card and the $4.00 fare. He was given his receipt and a ticket for speeding. It isn't rocket science to calculate speed based on time/distance. (Do you remember that calculation I showed you about my rocketry story earlier?) He arrived sooner for that road trip than he should have and was fined for speeding. He laughed when he told me this, and it's been etched in my brain since then. To further my brother's adventures with his 911 Porsche, he let his insurance lapse when he just happened to wreck his Porsche. That was the final blow to the Paul-Porsche "Union" and their adventures!

1961

The world was indeed a crazy place. It still is! My childhood is always remembered because of the odd yearly events that used to trigger my memory. Take 1961 as an example of my craziness. My grandfather was three in 1881. I was fifteen in 1961. Both were upside-down years. Flip 1881 or 1961 upside down (literally). They read the same. I thought about that *then*! If he had lived two more years (he died in '59), he would have seen two upside-down years! The next upside-down year is 6009, if you're interested.

I was told a few fibs by my parents (and some significant lies) as a child: "Step on a crack, break your mother's back." Or the devil's back? There was a Sandman, a Tooth Fairy, a Santa Claus, and an Easter Bunny. Oddly, two of those myths were religious-centric, but that's another story I will get to when I was an acolyte at the local Episcopalian church. Getting to church for an early morning mass on a weekday, on a school day, on foot. It was a thirty-minute walk to and thirty minutes from, then I walked to school before classes started. All of us kids were a bundle of energy, and now I view it as a shame to waste that potential energy on kids today. But I digress.

I *had* to clean my dinner plate. All of us did! Was it referred to then as supper? I think so. When the eight of us sat down to eat (I *know* it wasn't to "dine"), six kids grabbed at a bowl of food being passed around the table and were always fussing! If you didn't eat it, someone else might. Plus, wasting food was a taboo in those days! I grew up eating my meals without drinking my milk during the meal. Our mother got tired of cleaning up the inevitable spilled milk, and I still don't drink and eat at the same time.

Sometime around this date, Ricky built a working crossbow. Was it a school project he was allowed to make? I will never know. But I *do* remember he caused quite the kerfuffle!

Fall 1961

The Bay of Pigs Invasion, Cuba

This occurred while I was in high school when America's CIA tried to oust Fidel Castro.

https://en.wikipedia.org/wiki/Bay_of_Pigs_Invasion

Fidel was alive in Cuba in 2016, but his brother Raoul was now in charge. The Cuban public still drives old cars from the fifties. Great economics there that we seem to be experiencing a preview of in 2022! Also, we are looking at the possibility of a US-Russia engagement over Biden's (Hunter and Joseph Robinette) connections in Ukraine. We came so close to war during the early sixties. The Russians had our military ready for battle. It would be ironic that five years later, I would join the United States Air Force and be assigned to a squadron of F-101s. Those Voodoos, as they were called, were used as reconnaissance aircraft (the RF version) to photograph those Russian weapons all over Cuba. There are details in a later chapter ("1968") of my chance to fly in one of these Voodoos after making a nuisance of myself for at least a year. Some events are never forgotten! This was one of those I'll discuss in a few chapters.

As I do my final reviews here, the long-forecasted invasion of Ukraine by Putin's Russian army has begun! Biden referred to them as Uranians (you read that correctly), as in people from the planet Uranus in his State of the Union address a few days ago!

There was a massive wall separating East and West Berlin from 1961 until 1989, and my cohorts and I consistently grew up under communist threats. We practiced duck and cover in schools! We also read a Bible verse in class to start every school day. That is true! The Berlin wall came down, and I have a piece of it. I also have a bit of coal from the *Titanic*. I hope they are both authentic! I was never comfortable standing up in front of a class or any group ever after these Bible readings. It wasn't reading the Bible. It was the fumbling of my words or being in front of thirty classmates thinking I was doing a lousy job!

1962

When my generation was fifteen, in 1961, we had already seen real Russian threats. We were actively testing nuclear weapons aboveground because of actual USSR threats. Soviet missiles were found by aerial surveillance ninety miles from these United States! That was a terrifying reality! Aside from 2022, the Russians again appear to be threatening to deploy nuclear weapons in Ukraine! (That sentence was written well before it *did* occur in March of 2022.)

1. The USSR was supporting the failed socialist Cuban economy and trying to install offensive weapons in Cuba. (https://en.wikipedia.org/wiki/Cuba%E2%80%93Soviet_Union_relations?wprov=sfti1).
2. President Kennedy stood face-to-face with Nikita Krushchev. https://www.history.com/news/kennedy-krushchev-vienna-summit-meeting-1961
3. I am jumping forward sixty years. Please grant your author, or at least allow him, to make a comparison. In the sixties, we had a Communist threat. It is/was evident to everyone. Today, in 2021, we have a Socialist/Marxist threat. And as I make final edits here, I must add the Taliban and al-Qaeda terrorist threats post the fall of Afghanistan! Quite exciting news tidbit that the CNN and the MSNBC of the left will keep downplaying. Why is this not front-page news? Does this item make sense in today's current events and where we are headed? If you have any reason, you'll tell two people. Yesterday was too late, and tomorrow's getting sketchier! Patrisse Cullors is a trained Marxist and a cofounder of Black Lives Matter. (https://en.wikipedia.org/wiki/Patrisse_Cullors?wprov=sfti1)!

Do we have to destroy this country to balance race relations in this land that we call America? I sure hope not! In 2021, when Biden was elected—or in my wording, "emasculated," which I prefer—it was okay to promote or hire his cabinet, et al., based solely on immutable characteristics. Race or gender were their preferred choices for the filter he used to staff his cabinet. To which I say, a plain *"wow"*! His recent appointment to the Supreme Court (SCOTUS) bench has one qualification he touts: "She'll be the first Black female justice!"

In my sophomore year of high school, I was on the rifle team. It was my only high school extracurricular activity (excluding chasing girls), which was an ironic team to be on as time would play out in my early years. Our entire entourage (read "family") moved three hundred miles west to Penn Hills, Pennsylvania, in my sophomore year. So did my best friend, Steve Clark. I didn't realize Steve had moved to Penn Hills until I saw him in the hallway at Penn Hills High School! His mom didn't like me; she thought I was a hooligan! We were lifelong and long-distance friends until his sudden death in October 2012. **R.I.P. Steve**

Steve Clark and another classmate, Terry Kelly, and I got locked up on mischief night, the night before Halloween, *only* for accidentally setting fire to a street, as I will now relate! We were out in our neighborhood acting like hooligans. We weren't hooligans, just kids acting a little stupidly. We had a can of kerosene and a torch ("t.p." on a stick) we lit as we walked around. As a car came up the hill and the sun had set, it was very dark. I was re-soaking the torch that had gone out. We had to have a torch since it was too dark to roam the streets. Great kid's logic, right? I dropped the can of kerosene as I relit the torch. I decided to scare the driver of that car, and I also couldn't see the details of that car with the headlights shining in my eyes. Had I noticed it was a cop car as it approached, I would have kept the torch in my hand and ran. I dropped the torch, and we ran very fast as the cop car drove over the torch. We scattered! Not fast enough! After a brief chase on foot, we were nabbed and placed in the cop car. Then after a short walk through the jail, the screw (a.k.a. jailer) locked us—*clank!*—up! We three spent the next couple of nervous hours making up a similar story to tell our parents. Around 9:30 p.m., we were released. We were only told, "Behave! Go home!" *(A collective and silent gasp went up from us to heaven.)*

On Monday at school, we met up in the hallway or at lunch and asked, "What did your mom say, Terry? What happened at home,

Steve?" It took only a few seconds to learn we each had the same reaction at home—*nothing!* The cops never called our parents, and their plan worked. We were scared ——less, and no one got into any more trouble...ever...that I know of.

Without checking my old tax returns (which you're not surprised that I have), my first taxpaying job with a W-2 was around this year at Frank Lee's and Eddie Swirk's restaurant. It was a first-class restaurant—*not a joint!* President Eisenhower once dined here, and since this location is/was about one hour by horseback from Philadelphia and was built in the mid-1700s, I think the rumors that George Washington slept here were probably accurate. I became friends with Doug Hill from my high school. (Thanks for your permission to include your name here in my autobiography.) Since Steve had a car, and I didn't, we carpooled. This restaurant catered to a wealthy clientele. How could I explain this better than by pointing out how they collected their income in the days before credit cards? Yes, they relied on cash in the form of $5, $10, $20, and probably $50 bills. I vividly remember being in the bar area eating while they were preparing to turn the "Closed" sign over to "Open". They sorted out the cash register drawer and then unwrapped new ones, fives, tens, etc. The crudeness of giving change with old, rumpled currency was forbidden. That's how they treated their customers!

What would my time at this restaurant be without mentioning Willie? He worked in the kitchen as a dishwasher and was a "wee bit daft," as the Irish would say. Looking back now, all these decades later, I know now what I was too young to understand then at age sixteen. He was disabled mentally, but there was one other thing about him I should point out. He had a lifetime job, and he lived upstairs above the kitchen. He was also the sole inheritor of his parents' restaurant! The very same one I was working at!

Doug Hill's comments:

> "Had the same thing at Blue Bell Inn with one of the employees. The Lamprecht (sp?) German owners of the BB Inn kept him on, and he did a great job, except he would go off the deep end once in a while. I recall his chasing someone with a

butcher knife one time! The BB Inn kept our family going, with my brother Don and I working as busboys and my mother as a waitress. We made enough to pay for our car and clothes and dating etc., and still had some to help out with the family expenses too. My dad's factory job at Leeds and Northrup in North Wales, PA, wasn't enough for a family of seven!"

We moved to Pittsburgh and then moved back to Ambler. We were only living in Pittsburgh for eighteen months, and it was a *busy* eighteen months! My father was transferred from the eastern side of Pennsylvania to the western part of Pennsylvania. This was a three-hundred-mile move, and not everyone was pleased. My classmates commented on my moving away then moving back in my high school yearbook more than once. It lasted eighteen months, and we were right back in the same house we moved out of! Fortunately, there were no going-away parties, or I would have felt very bad about moving right back!

Late summer on 04 August 1962, I was in a car with Marsha Silver, an adult mom, and friends. This was due to a sudden summer rainstorm that caused us to get out of the *pool*! Now! Several of us, with a parent who drove us to the Crestwood Hills Swim Club, were in her car. I was in the back seat, and her mom turned on the AM radio for some music. It wasn't very long until a news bulletin came over the radio. It was on that rainy afternoon in August that the reporter announced, "Marilyn Monroe has been found dead." Many years later, fifteen to be exact, on another August afternoon, I would hear about another celebrity's death. See "Elvis" P. 152 August 1977.

I hitchhiked six hundred miles round trip on the weekend to go back to Pittsburgh, Pennsylvania. Why did I do this? Because I wanted to visit a girlfriend. I did this in three days and told my mom I was at a neighbor's kid's house. Probably my friend Johnny Pearce. Several of my rides were in large semi-trucks (a.k.a. eighteen-wheelers), and I was fascinated by the tandem gear shift requiring some fancy shifting. *No wonder*, I thought, *they hate to slow down for 4-wheelers and downshift.* Many years later, I confessed to my mom about this adventure, and we both had a good laugh. It was a pretty dumb stunt! While visiting a girlfriend, I slept in my old backyard, in a giant playhouse. It was not comfortable but away from any rain that might fall, and there was no chance I'd get into trouble since our house was still for sale and empty. And securely locked up. I checked!

I've hitchhiked back home to Ambler. There is/was no hanky-panky to mention. It never happened!

November 1963

As I was at the beginning of my senior high school year, President Kennedy made a campaign trip to Dallas, Texas. Only after forty years did Sheila and I visit Dealey Plaza, where the most famous TV news of all time was broadcast to the world. It was like we were in a movie or a documentary, and it seemed like walking around in a dream. It was a surreal visit. Indescribable. Sad. Moving. I remember when this happened, and I was in a senior day's last class. The course was generally dismissed at 2:35 p.m. EST, but I remember this afternoon, silently and numbly, slowly walking down the hall to the bus. It was around 1:30 p.m.

Dead silence! November 22, 1963, was my future wife's seventeenth birthday. She and I would not meet until many decades later. This was a Friday, and Thanksgiving was the next week, so we probably would have had next week off. I do not remember. We were all relaxing and wasting time in the shop class I was in. I was not an academic student. I tried to have fun. I was a kid. We would all be turning seventeen that year. I never looked at the clock, but I heard the radio in the teacher's (Mr. Faulkner) office where a small group had gathered. We were all about to become adults at that exact moment. Here's how we saw the news, on B&W TV: JFK is dead. Cronkite informs a shocked nation! It was one of those rare and momentous events of life you can remember and date yourself by and with.

Where exactly were you when something historic happened? It was one of those times. Life was fractured, and we were collectively a nation of zombies. It was mortifying, and it took a lot of time to wear off! Life is marked when time stops, and we can gather our thoughts, blocking everything else out. You know then you will remember something forever. Getting married in the famous 1967 Chicago blizzard was also a moment I would not forget. The 1969 moon landing was also one of those dates. The 1986 Challenger explosion was yet another one of those dates. The 1987 murder I witnessed was one as well. 9-11 is the most recent date that's etched in millions of people's brains. Life *is* a series of incidents and accidents, *isn't* it, dear reader?

1964

Post-Ricky Period Begins a Month after Graduation!

On 06 June, I graduated from Wissahickon High School, twenty years and four days after the D-Day invasion on 02 June 1944. Fifty-two years after the *Titanic* sank, I worked at my first job two days after graduating from high school, and in different Wanamaker's building in nearby New York City was one of the places where the famous *Titanic* SOS signals were heard that dreadful early morning in 1912. There was also a telegram sent.

A telegram from *Titanic* proves owners lied about hearing nothing from it. Yes, here is one. I have not held this telegram in my hand, but a telegram from *Titanic* proves owners lied about hearing nothing from it. This copy says telegraphs still exist from that night (https://davidsarnoff.tcnj.edu/2013/08/30/radio-to-the-rescue-david-sarnoff-and-the-titanic-disaster/).

I might point out that the founder of NBC, Mr. David Sarnoff, listened to his radio at his telegraph machine on the upper floor of John Wanamaker's Department Store in New York City and received many more messages from the *Titanic* that night.

On 08 June 1964, I started work on the first Monday after graduation from high school! My first job as a high school grad was selling film-cameras and taking in the film to be developed and printed in-house for the camera buffs at Wanamaker's Department Store. I *still* have my 35 mm Pentax I bought while working in that department! My boss was Henry Black (or was it Blacker?). Interesting fellow, not to put too fine of a point on it. One of the customers I waited on many times will come upon another page in a while. When we get to that event, I will ask you to remember these pages for reference. A memorable event if ever there was one, just as impressive as realizing that Mr. John Wanamaker Jr. was one of my customers. I would wait on him to get his snapshots developed. A few other celebrities like Norman Fell, Mr.

Roper from TV, and others I can't remember for now, also frequented the store.

While working in this sizable ten-story department store every day, I got to eat lunch in the company cafeteria. The lunch area was on the tenth floor, so I took the elevator instead of the stairs. In those days, they were still using people, a.k.a. elevator operators, to open and close the doors. They didn't have electronic eyes that sensed you going through the door. Interesting how technology works now. As the months went by, I got to know this polite gentleman in a company-branded uniform. Everyone in the store took elevators to the various floors where different departments were.

I learned one of that regular elevator operators' names (now forgotten). We might chat briefly about this or, as we often did, travel floor to floor, just the two of us. At some point, the subject of opera came up, and Philadelphia had a world-class opera company. He and I enjoyed the opera, and I was eventually invited by Mr. X, as I shall call him, to go with him as his guest to see an opera. I've long since forgotten the opera I saw, but I've also never forgotten this one-time event. After that opera, sitting in a box seat as two private guests, I was invited to his apartment as the opera performance concluded. My senses told me, at the age of seventeen, that something was odd. Then I merely declined, but in retrospect, did I know he was a gay man? I'm as sure now, based on more experiences that I didn't have then, that I was correct. He might have been a friend of Henry, my boss. Mmmm... We continued to meet in the elevator, and no future offers to go to the opera were made. As I've gotten older and older, my decision from back then to ride in that elevator car is reaffirmed today.

Another unique thing about this store was that every day, we would turn our cash receipts and paperwork in at the company bank. On payday, which was every Friday, we'd be paid in cash. *Wait*, there's more. Our paycheck (money, not a check) would always include a $2 bill as part of our weekly pay. I was told that the store monitored these $2 bills to see when and if they would turn up inside other departments' cash receipts. The store could assume accurately that the $2 bill came from an employee spending their pay in the store where they worked. Clever, if I do say so!

THOMAS E. BYRON

I was working in this photoshop department, and it took almost a week to see if the photo you took was out of focus or my friend's head wasn't shown in the image. Oh well, I did come from six generations of photographers—Byron and Company in New York, James Byron Clayton & Joseph Byron Clayton, photographers in Nottingham. Color film, in 1964, was new and fun since TV was still BW with only three channels to watch: ABC, CBS, and NBC. Sunday at 7:00 p.m., *Walt Disney's Wonderful World of Color* (1961–1969) was a treat. Our family gathered around to watch. If you had an expensive color TV, you were lucky. It was probably an RCA model that weighed about fifty pounds. It happened to be a warm summer evening while watching TV. There was never any air-conditioning in our house or most homes. That's a deliberate change in wording—I never felt as if I lived in anything other than a house! It was a sweaty evening, but the color was great to watch. I don't remember it being hot. I was used to it. There wasn't even air-conditioning in our family car.

The following memory is why I don't like city life. This event convinced my young mind that much of what happens in big cities do not foster camaraderie. You end up with hundreds of small friend groups and not a wide circle of friends. Then there are thousands of non-interconnected people who do not care about anyone outside of *their* clique. To wit: On one occasion during my regular job related commute in Center City, Philly, I saw a man drop (literally) dead right in front of me (across two lanes of traffic) at a bus stop. I did witness too many adult things at a young age! He was standing, with his back to me, on a concrete curb/divider with posts every twenty feet or so and a chain. The chain discouraged pedestrians from jaywalking. He merely sat, slowly, on that chain, and then he slumped over backward, toward my direction, and continued to lean back. And finally, he slammed his head on the cement. An ugly sight I saw. No one appeared to help him, and there *were* ten people within a few feet of him, and I had a train to catch. They were adults, and I was a teenage kid. What I did seemed logical then. Should I try to fight across two lanes of traffic to get to him with the people next to him? I did not. I still don't have a good feeling about all of that! City life was not for me, and perhaps it was events like that which made me a suburbanite for the rest of my life.

A friend of mine, Bill Dunlap, invited me to attend a Hollywood movie premiere after party. It was 18 June 1964. I remember the event, but as I still am today, I'm uncomfortable being around many wealthy people at a party. The movie was *The World of Henry Orient*, starring Peter Sellers and Merrie Spaeth, a friend of Bill's. I've since been to another premiere movie of my wife's granddaughter, Belle Adams, *This World Alone*.

11 July 1964

I came home from camping up in the mountains of eastern Pennsylvania on Sunday. It was a *hot* July afternoon. Another escape, you say? Probably. When I came home that day, on that life-changing July afternoon, I carried my pack into the house. It became apparent why our narrow street was crowded with parked cars. My older brother, Paul, greeted me when I came inside. He said, "I thought you were dead!" Call me "Mr. Obvious", but I was not quite dead yet, and I'm still not! I soon realized that our little brother had committed suicide the night before. Death became very real for the first time. My seventy-nine-year-old grandfather had died a few years earlier. I'm not quite that old, but I'm very close as I type this. Deaths of strangers were not as traumatic as someone you loved and were around daily! The rest is also blank, erased, as I have previously mentioned. I can't explain why Paul or Ricky were back in Ambler since my memory of this has always been fuzzy! Blocked out? Those critical memory gaps are not random. They are what I will label as trauma blocks, or me trying to save my sanity!

Paul left home when I was in the ninth grade (1960–61). He never lived where I lived again. He and his friend Tim went to the state of Washington, as far west as you can go. He had just graduated from high school, and I was in the ninth grade, I think, or at least six years behind him chronologically. He spent the last years of his life, as did our sister Judy, in a desert climate. Paul chose New Mexico, and Judy chose Arizona!

My child-self died on one of those hot summer days over fifty years ago now. I am here, trying to write all this down as that child's unauthorized substitute and replacement: "The show must go on, right?"

Ricky had said to me one day, "I dreamed of a color I never saw before." As I write this in 2021, I still don't know what he meant or how intelligent he was. I just *know* that he was!

Back to where we were. I went on a weekend camping adventure, and I assumed Ricky would come home from running away by the time I got back Sunday. It would be rare times that I would go out into the wild and sleep in a tent, a.k.a. a canvas house! He did come home. I knew he would. Then he probably wrote his suicide note after he learned he was trapped!

The old man was coming home! I know that's what he thought. My older sister, Judy, at one point, read it and told me about it. The details of that note are now lost to history. I remember frequent references to the current time as he wrote and his remaining minutes alive ticked by. His time remaining on earth was growing shorter by the minute. Could I have talked him out of this? Would he have killed me to stop me from stopping him? I will never know.

The events of that camping trip are also lost to eternity, as is much of my childhood, as I have said before. I was lost in a fog of yelling and bickering. That was the background noise—the soundtrack of my early life.

Our younger sister Laura was told, "Go up [stairs] and tell Ricky there was ice cream served downstairs." No one particularly enjoyed trudging up and down those dang stairs! I learned from mom never to go up or down those stairs empty-handed! I still follow that rule all these decades later in our second-floor apartment. *Thanks, mom*! When she entered his room, her world was turned upside down! She was around ten years old. Such *horror*! I cannot imagine.

While I was camping, my little brother came home and asked (about his father), "Is he home?"

He was told, "He isn't home. I don't think he'll be back until next week."

The following is my sister Laura White's account, used with her permission. (*Warning:* she uses adult language, and it is *graphic.*)

> I was twelve when that happened. Ricky had turned fifteen on February 6, and I turned twelve

March thirty-first. I never heard that shot. All I can tell you is Ricky used to play games. He'd hide up in those rooms from me. I went in and called his name. No answer. But I did hear something. Something I'll never ever forget. This swooshing, gurgling, muffled sound coming from across the room. I had already checked the other bedroom/storage of old stuff. Then I checked the bathroom. No Ricky. Then I zero in on the sound. The bed. Bedspread off of the bed, mostly all of it. I was not in the mood to be playing hide and seek. I wanted to go to my room. I didn't want dessert or be anywhere near dear old shithead sperm donor. That was my father. I go around that bed, and as I'm pulling the bedspread up, telling Ricky, "I'm tired of playing this game. Mom says it's time for dessert, and she wants you to come down for it."

I pull up that bedspread, and the first thing I notice is the strong smell of gunpowder. Like the overpowering smell while watching fireworks up close. Years later, I realize that the smell of fireworks is a big bad trigger to me. It all comes back. I see him lying on his back, his head turned and the gunshot wound (already the blood has dried). I scream. Take the ten to fifteen stairs down to the second floor screaming. "Ricky, Ricky, something's wrong with Ricky!"

The first one up the stairs is the jackass. Hollering and shaking, screaming in my face. What are you screaming about? At this point, all I remember is just crying and pointing up. Then Mom comes up the stairs. He won't let her up there. I guess he called the police and the doctor. The utter chaos that was in front of our house. Lights flashing, sirens blaring. My head is spinning. Doctor comes up to see Mom. To comfort her. I'm standing there crying. Then suddenly, I start laughing—hysterical laughter. Doctor was going to give Mom a shot to calm her down. I know that was the plan. But after I went into this (my first nervous breakdown), I'm dragged into my room and given a shot. I don't remember much of that summer after that. What strikes me as strange, is it was in my room, under his room. I was that close and never heard a sound. That bothers me to this day.

More unedited from my sister Laura, in her own words (*adult language*):

The sounds of that night haunt me. The body after death is not quiet. Stuff still is functioning. Process I don't get. That sound and the smell are my triggers. Fifty-three years later, I'm still a fucking mess.

One other cruel thing that that man did to me. I was told that I had to go to school and let them know Ricky wasn't going to be attending school. I told Dad that the whole town (three thousand) knows he's dead. Why should I have to tell them? They already knew. He insisted I be the one to go to the office and tell them. That was cruel beyond words.

I never saw the suicide note, never saw the weapon. I was told I couldn't go to the funeral. It would be to upsetting. WHAT'S MORE UPSETTING THAN FINDING HIM DEAD?

Then every time I was in the car with them, he would turn around and ask me every time. Why did Ricky do this to him (sic)? Why did he kill himself? For years on end. Even in the house. It was an obsession to nag at me. Why, why, why? One day, I remember this. I told him, "He killed himself to get the fuck away from you." I told him I'd thought about doing the same thing but hadn't. "The only reason was as I didn't want to hurt Mom. But if it was just you left, is kill myself to get the fuck away from you too. But I love my mom too much and hate you, you fucking asshole. You killed him. Now leave me the fuck alone." That outburst was the end of those questions.

Okay, so I ask and get my own phone and phone number in my room. Not sure what age. I don't remember much about how I got out. It did help me connect with a few friends. I was so lost most days, I missed so much of my classes. I needed to call some friends and get some help. No problem. I spent time in there to escape from him. Too late to go out and play. My room was my sanctuary. So here I am almost finished getting caught up over the phone. *He* struts in and says, "GET THE HELL OFF THAT DAMN PHONE!" I tell him I'm almost finished getting caught up. I'll be off in a little while. He didn't like that I didn't immediately hang up the phone. Oh well. The next second, he comes over and rips the phone, wires and all, out of the wall and throws it across my bedroom. Then storms out yelling I was supposed to be in bed.

You know me. I'm a smart-ass. I push back when I'm pushed. So I'm not stupid. I know how to put those wires back together. I fix, called my friend before, and apologize for Dad pulling the phone out of the wall. Now let's get back to what we were working on. A few minutes later, after explaining to my friend, we got back to work. The door flies open, Dad screaming, "I TOLD YOU GET OFF THE PHONE AND GO TO BED!" And repeats what he did the first time. He rips it out and tosses it across the room. He does this probably five or six times.

By now, I've had enough. I try to be quiet on the phone. The sneaky bastard was outside or in his room with his ear to the wall, listening in on my call. Boom, door flies open—same thing. The phone was ripped out of the wall and thrown across the room. I'd had enough. So I reached for the phone (what did they weigh, like 10 lbs.). And before he got the chance to slam the door shut, I had my arm back, ready in full swing. Perfect landing. Hit him (heard a crack, his head, I was hoping). That phone bounced off the back of his head and fell inside my room. My last words to him were "Come back and try that again. I'll pick the fucking phone up and beat you with it." He never did that again. (No edits made by Tom, as he copied this verbatim.)

Not much love in this house that never was a home. Paul left for Washington state, Judy left for Vermont, I left for the military, and Laura and Debbie left for Vermont. *Ricky took his life!* Sounds like an old country music song, doesn't it? Today in 2022, Laura's in California and Deb's in Vermont, and I'm in Georgia! What a dysfunctional, emotionally crippled family I'm from! Family? By the way, my mom and my father moved to Florida!

Returning to *my* account of this weekend, I had been camping with my then girlfriend Ruth's dad, Mr. Dowlin, and a few other guys. I remember very little (read that as zip) about that camping weekend, other than it happened. We were arriving home on what must have been a hot Sunday afternoon and noticing there were several extra cars parked along the narrow street in front of my house. ("What's going on here?" I said to myself!) I got my camping gear together and got out of the car. As I walked up those seven or eight front steps, the day would become oblivious to me. As I met Paul at the front door, my world would become a nightmare! All the scary stuff was real, though!

Saturday, the night before, less than twenty-four hours earlier, around 8:30 p.m., my brother took his life. Upstairs in his bedroom.

Alone. He was living in an absolute hell and took the only choice he felt he had. Exit permanently, without consulting *anyone* for a second opinion!

I doubt several aspects of what I've been told. Please allow me to explain. How do you shoot yourself in the head with a rifle? I don't know! Please follow me here. I'll get to my alternate theory soon. You have also just read earlier that Paul was conceived out of wedlock. The wedding date was a lie. You've seen the proof earlier in my saga, a.k.a. *this* is an autobiography. I suspected Paul's *bitter* scores of years of hatred was because he, Paul, learned or assumed or was told by Mom (the most likely answer) that they weren't married in 1939 like we kids were told. Certainly by his father, but not by his mom.

Paul, no doubt, felt he was an unwelcome child. Did Paul and his father have words before the suicide? Did Ricky threaten to tell the cops or the police to be polite?

His front-of-the-house bedroom was across the hall, and Ricky and I shared the other back-of-the-house bedroom. Paul, being the older, had his room that had a third-floor deck and a fantastic view. When our father returned early, angering Ricky to a state of rage, did he, Ricky, want to kill *his* father? There could have been a struggle over the rifle, and he, our father, "who art a monster," committed filicide? I'll never know. I have watched TV dramas where a rifle was ruled out as the weapon in a suicide. That's a significant reach involved in aiming, holding the rifle outstretched, then pulling the trigger. Murder, on the other hand, to save yourself, is a much easier choice.

Alternate Theory

My brothers Paul and Ricky discussed their lives in the bedroom. Paul told Ricky he was conceived out of wedlock. Ricky must have thrown this in his father's face when he came upstairs. His work/office/cubbyhole was close to the upstairs, and if Paul and Ricky were talking loud enough, the old man could have come upstairs and confronted Ricky. Paul would have just gone downstairs, and it was just Ricky and his father alone, arguing! To end the yelling, Ricky was shot by his father after he read the suicide note. Many people talk about suicide but never carry it out. When Ricky was found dead, the rifle was there. I still don't believe he could have held the rifle *and* reached the trigger. There were never any fingerprints taken that I knew about. I've never heard one word from anyone about any terms between our family and any police! The lie my father told until he was ninety-three was that his marriage was fine! (It was a scam.) Life was good from my father's perspective. But know this: Paul hated his father with a purple passion! A deep crimson, loud purple! He said that to me *many* times! This was many, many long years after "the suicide." Did Paul know the truth? I never asked.

The rest of that day, the next, and the next must have been traumatic. I have a mental blank (gap) about that period. I very *much* erased my memory! The events, and who did or said what, have been blocked out of my mind. What I *do* remember is being in our Trinity Episcopal Church a day or two later.

The Funeral

His casket was like a monster made of wood and metal! My mind was not connecting what I saw with what I was thinking. The priest (Father Shultz) said, "Blah blah blah… We know what Ricky did was wrong, blah, blah, blah." I remember those words as if he told me to write them as I type them here today, fifty-six years later!

He was cremated, and his cremains were interred with his paternal grandfather, Percy Byron (1878–1959), unmarked in that graveyard in Moravian Cemetery, New York. And then there were seven of us as a family (06 February 1949—11 July 1964).

As to any funeral, I remember his ashes were interred at Moravian Cemetery (Staten Island), New York City, but I was not present for that. He's finally at peace.

Question for you readers: I think this event was what turned the old man, a.k.a. Dad to some, into an alcoholic. He was never the same, and I believe it was the actions that sent/moved him "into the Vodka bottle" until his death!

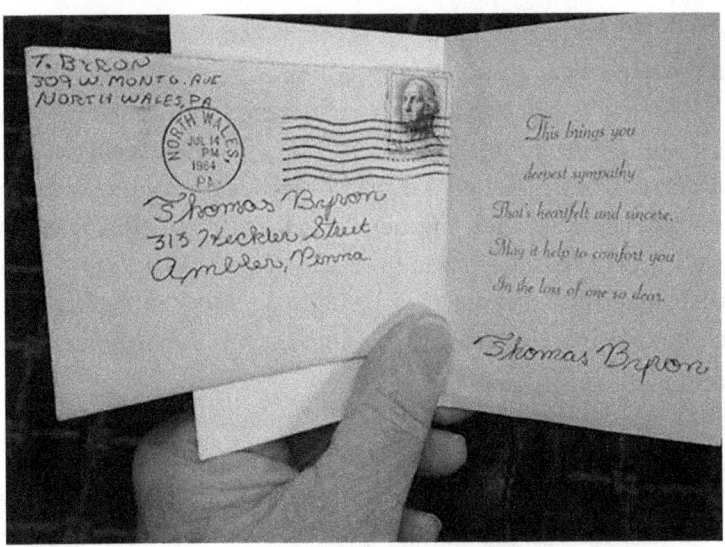

Late Summer '64

I have been privileged, on two separate occasions, to be face-to-face with some amazingly glorious pieces of history. Twice I have seen some breathtaking views of godly and empowered artists' creations! Once was in 1986 in Birmingham, Alabama, and once in New York City in 1964.

In 1964, I had to wait in line for a very long time, and it was a hot summer afternoon in Flushing, New York. The occasion was the 1964 World's Fair. My brother's funeral was already behind us, and someone (I assume) suggested we'd visit the fair. Nothing more than that. It was one of those out-of-body events. I was there, but my heart, mind, and soul were *not*! These few words may cause *you* in the future to visit his grave, though his name was never engraved on the Byron gravestone. There's a fantastic view of NYC and the Verrazano-Narrows Bridge from there in the winter when the leaves have fallen.

The 1964 World's Fair was literally across the street from my cousin's government housing apartment. I would visit the 1982 World's Fair when I lived in Knoxville, Tennessee. We'll get there in a few chapters. When I moved from Tennessee to Louisiana, there was another World's Fair that year (1984). The Murtaugh's lived in Flushing, New York, from the late forties until Patty moved to Minnesota. That would be from the late forties until 2000 something.

I do digress, but that's how my strange mind operates! As we Byrons stood in line at the NYC World Fair, the sounds of weeping and hushed gasps could be heard over the sounds of children murmuring and babies crying in their mother's arms. Amazing! No cameras were allowed. I imagine that I was in the same space, as in the same distance, as Michelangelo must have stood when he looked at his creation 465 years before me. Michelangelo's Pieta. (https://en.wikipedia.org/wiki/Piet%C3%A0_

That blows my mind! Years later, I would stand a few feet from King Tut's golden sarcophagus in Birmingham, Alabama! Absolutely two incredible events I will relate back to for impact. (https://en.wikipedia.org/wiki/Tutankhamun?wprov=sfti1) It was in 1986 that I spent a lunch hour in line or a few unique moments at the art museum near my office in downtown Birmingham. The exhibit was close to my office and only a short walk from HQ at 601 N. Nineteenth Street. The King Tut exhibit was not something to put off. No one I knew ever said, "I'll be in Cairo next year on vacation and see it then." *No way!* This three-thousand-plus-year-old sarcophagus of King Tutankhamen, "the Boy King," was gold-covered and a mint condition piece of antiquity! *It! Was! Breathtaking!* A treasure among treasures, it was the primogeniture relic among the ancient world's many treasures!

Fall 1964

One lazy summer evening in Philly (the nickname for Philadelphia), I walked several blocks from PhotoCine Shop at 129 S. Eighteenth Street to Twenty-First and Delancey Streets to visit my sister Judy's apartment for some gin and tonic! Her specific invite mentioned this drink! Spur-of-the-moment events were so typical then, and I realize now, twenty years into the next millennium, exactly how lucky I was to have had all that leisure time! I had a lifetime of hard work ahead of me, and any dream I set my mind to was all mine! I didn't do many crazy things when I was young, but I'd be remiss if I excluded *this* dinner event here in my final version of *Zero To Seventy-Five…*, the shorter version to which I recklessly gave limited distribution. C'est la vie! Live and learn!

Judy worked at Penn Mutual Life Insurance as their in-house graphic artist. I worked in Philly. I was a camera salesman at an expensive shop in a wealthy neighborhood a block from Rittenhouse Square. Princess Grace of Monaco also lived there around this time. My sister Judy and I occasionally met for lunch since the PhotoCine Shop was only a few block's walk. Everywhere back then was a short walk. I never took the first cab ride! Where we met, I can't remember.

She and her Roman husband, *not Italian!*, his R-word not mine, invited our parents and me to dinner at a Lebanese restaurant on Sampson Street named Eddie Taeoon's (phonetic spelling) Middle East Restaurant. The restaurant was old (I was young), and the interior wood was dark paneling, with a live band up on a balcony at the far end of this cozy place, made for intimate dining experiences. The dining area was long and narrow, with tables along the walls with a center aisle for waiters and servers. Imagine a movie set and an older B&W film, and you have the visual for this memorable tale! There was room along here for a belly dancer as well, and with music and alcohol! It was festive.

As we were eating our appetizer of Hummus Tahini, a young lady came down the aisle, her colorful silken dress flowing and finger tambourines jingling in her hands. My eyes followed her as she approached closer and closer, slowly. And as she reached the end of the aisle, she turned around. She was now coming toward our table and facing my father and me. My sister, her husband, and my mother had their backs to her as she approached our table. To my delight, she stopped right in front of me. Smiling, she said, "*Hi* there." Then I realized what had just happened as she continued down the aisle. My father looked at me with a *very* puzzled look! You don't know, but this father of mine *was* the epitome of the traveling salesman. He looked at me in awe and showed pure unadulterated jealousy. Shocking! I knew this young lady as a customer from Wanamaker's Camera Shop. She took pictures of her daughter who was a pre-teen learning how to dance! My father was clueless! And nary a peep out of me. Not then. *Not ever!*

In the fall of this year, I enrolled at Antonelli's School of Photography in Philadelphia, Pennsylvania. I don't know much about what I might have learned there in the year I attended. I was too young to stay focused on night school and work forty hours per week. I remember a classmate, Anthony Zannoni, was my running buddy on our photo class assignments around town. I still have a few B&W prints in a file (one of him as well), but I did learn how to shoot with a 4"x5" press camera. I never graduated, but that would serve as a future life lesson. *Never quit!* When I exited the military and decided to earn my college degree, in total, I never stopped attending classes until I had graduated! It's worth noting, and I will dwell on that point momentarily. It was a seventeen-year saga that never seemed to end. But I showed myself that I could complete a task no matter how arduous the plan was. (Add this autobiography to that shortlist.) Raising a family, being the sole breadwinner, attending a rigorous schedule *would! Not! Stop! Me!*

1964–1965

New Year's Eve

A New York City trip with two friends, Bill Dunlop and Rick DeVoe from high school, would be memorable! At least a few parts would be incredible, not that being in Times Square on New Year's Eve in person wasn't unique. "But wait, wait, there's more," as the ad goes! After a short ninety-mile train ride from Thirtieth Street Station in central Philly to Grand Central Station in midtown NYC, we would join in a party with a quarter million other partygoers. We were each a stranger to anyone in the Big Apple, just the three of us. Aaaah, youth! Why not? Police on horseback monitored the crowd. We watched. As a small-town suburban kid, I knew nothing about horses. It was intimidating to stand next to a horse that towered over you, and you had to look up at them while simultaneously needing to look down and watch what you could step in if you didn't ~~smell~~ and see where you were walking!

Everyone had a grand time, and I even had a bonus to cap my night. I will record and relate one of my multiple coincidences as we proceed. My cousin Bart lives in the Borough of Queens, Flushing, New York, and several millions of other people! My brother Paul was born there, and President Trump was born there, as were my cousins Bart and his sister Patty. It was crowded for a kid from a town of three thousand people where everyone knew your name (like the *Cheers* TV show). I was standing in Times Square and was backing away from a moving flow of people celebrating when I backed into someone. Not seeing who they were, I said, "Excuse *me!*" Then I turned around, "*What* are you doing here, Bart!"

I knew why he was in Times Square, I thought, but how and why was he right behind me? We then turned around, and we were both amazed. Neither of us knew the other would be here. Try telling someone, "Hey, meet me in Times Square on New Year's Eve!" That isn't happening...but it did. This is the second coincidence (see 1952 on pages 38, 39). More random events like this, or even more incredible, will happen. I'll get to them later, I hope! Remind me if I forget.

1965

New Year's Day, or the morning after, I got some much needed sleep on a public wooden bench in Grand Central Station. Or was it Penn Station? I forget. It was only a few hours from 2:00 a.m. until the train back to Philadelphia would be ready to board at 6:00 a.m. The Brits refer to this as rough sleeping. The Yanks today call it homelessness. I call it crazy! I would do this one more time in Chicago in 1966.

I spent a week in a Philadelphia YMCA while my parents were on vacation this year. *"What?"* That is exactly what I said to myself at that moment in time when I was asked to leave while the family went on vacation! *"What?" You read that correctly.* I felt I had been abandoned, but at least I had a job, so no vacation for me.

I remember the creepy feeling I had in this crazy place. Remember, as a child, you heard the saying, "One of these things is not like the other." Everything was not like any bleeping thing I had ever seen before! Sheltering me at this very adult place, "Young men's *what?*" (*Hah!*) "*Christian* Association?" What a bone-jarring experience I had *that* week. I can't say for sure if this didn't cause me to think about joining the USAF seriously! I can't recall any specifics (memory scrubbed). Still, the atmosphere struck me like a gut punch in the stomach. My parents thought this would keep me out of ~~my~~ their, not *our*, house and any mischief. Well, they were wrong then! I got into zero trouble while being surrounded by a twenty-four-seven crisis! No tellin' how my brain and psyche were abused!

Joined the US Air Force, 1966

The Vietnam War was a huge mess. I had registered for the draft back in 1964. It was the law!

Life began to require something from me—to think and make choices, to take life-altering risks, and to take on primary responsibilities. I was *not* told what to do, and I had *no* mentor. I had no *input* from my parents. For the first time in my life, there would be significant choices that would have serious long-term consequences. Join the military and run into a random bullet? Just like I randomly ran into my cousin in NYC. I would exit civilian life at age nineteen, and as life would have it, I grew up quickly in uniform. I was away from home, in a place where I was a lot more in charge of my life, my choices, and my everyday decisions. Every day! Well, sort of in direction, in order of who and what I wanted to become. No one with my lowly rank was in charge of much. I would have one responsibility by August of this year.

Would military rules be for me? Would I rebel? I had to find out. When spring arrived, I had tried to understand what I could about Southeast Asia, the VietCong, etc. I failed (it was too complex and constantly changing), but I tried. I knew what my best option was. My cohorts were being sent there by the military, and they were returning home, some not alive!" Life was demanding my closer attention now, perhaps some minor consequences for which I would have some input. I was nineteen and knew I would get drafted soon. I would end up in Vietnam, so my choice to volunteer was the best option with the most choices I would have control over. I had few choices for sure, just better chances of staying out of the jungles of Southeast Asia. I would become a flyboy that April and never live at home again.

Instant adulthood! After you finished the induction process, you got the "turn your head and cough" exam. You were naked. You had to bend over en masse and be rectally examined while the entire line of your fellow young recruits were doing precisely the same. Embarrassing? Yes! Required to make you feel less human! Indeed, you were now merely a piece of government property with a serial number—AF15757xxx. Like a wrench or a building or a sack of spuds! I was simply a GI, a government-*is*sue piece of property. It was all a series of lessons for life!

After my first long flight from Philadelphia to Baltimore to someplace in Texas on Ozark Airlines (a.k.a. the "Tin Goose Line" on a propeller-driven aircraft DC-3), I ended up on a blue Air Force military bus heading for Amarillo AFB, Texas. Most of our brief trip from the airport to base was on the original Rte. 66, the same route of fame, movies, and music. The road along there is now a boring Interstate 40.

I am wearing my tags as I type, but my hair is way down my back (ten inches, guessing, and a primarily white beard).

Besides the decision to sail on the Titanic Memorial Cruise, which I will get to when I discuss it in much detail in 2012, there was the possibility of injury or death with both choices. Sailing across the ocean post-9/11 was a little scary. I would also consider it a dangerous adventure that occurred during my time as a hydraulic mechanic in the US Air Force in 1968. I've jumped ahead again. We'll get to that at length in 1968.

I will now relate, for the first time to anyone ever, a troubling and severe event that happened during my brief time in training at Chanute Air Force Base, Illinois. No one else—except myself and one other person—knows about what will follow here. I'm prepared after fifty-four years to relate an event that shocked me to my core, that explains my behavior to this very day, that I do not wish to discuss and something I do not want to carry (alone) with me to my grave.

I was on an adventure exploring Illinois one weekend (dates are lost in my memory), but I do remember being in Springfield, Illinois, and seeing Lincoln's tomb. I did not have a car since owning a car during training was not permitted. I didn't have the money for a car anyway. It was easy to hitchhike in uniform always... but I digress. The one other person was Bob Cherry, but allow me to say that I might be misremembering that name, and when this matter comes to my mind, so does that name.

I was hitchhiking, and I got a ride. I did not think about it at age nineteen as being a wrong decision. Hitchhiking was very common in the fifties and sixties. I had already hitchhiked 300 miles across the

Commonwealth of Pennsylvania. The rest of this story gets fuzzier in my mind. You'll see why. He was a little too nice, and I was ignorant of the world's ways. Returning to my memories, he invited me into his house. Where was I going? Did I ever get there? How did I get back to base? No one knows those answers. I remember my mind going haywire, or my mind is blank in areas where I hide bad things.

I suspect I was drugged when he gave me a glass of beer. The next and last thing I remember was being raped and sodomized! This might or should answer your questions about my feelings toward the homosexual population—period, full stop! That's off my chest.

One of my many new life adventures was in '66 while courting my first wife. I was nineteen. Economics would again force me to sleep on yet another empty park bench under the stars in Grant Park, in the heart of the city of Chicago. That was bold, but that was also a long, long time ago. Remember, I did this in New York City three years earlier! This time, I was visiting my future wife at her home, north of down town.

Upon leaving basic training in Amarillo, Texas, America's dust bowl, I flew to Chanute, Illinois, via Ozark Airlines. Their air service was the DC-3, the same aircraft the military used in WWII, the C-47 troop carrier. It was originally designed as a glider. This was like walking into a time warp upon getting on board. The flight was smooth, and we flew low enough to count the farm animals below as we flew over them!

Early Summer, 1966

02 *July, Chicago, Illinois*

I went to Chicago for the weekend with a fellow airman. My base was the exact location where the famous Tuskegee Airmen were trained during WWII when it was Chanute "Field". We rode there on the Illinois Central Railroad, "The City of New Orleans" (hear the song below). Not expensive if you go in uniform. I met this young Midwestern man in Tech School at Rantoul AFB in Chanute, Illinois, Ira J. Burd (I still have my thick notebook from my Air Force days to reference his name). He wanted to ride on a subway. *Groan*…in the big city. I was from Philadelphia, Pennsylvania. He was from a small farm town in mid-America. I was tired of the subways and the hassle. They were too crowded, not safe, noisy, and dirty! I am a nice guy, so I decided I would humor him.

We started the weekend by taking Amtrak north to Chicago. The train was still called the City of New Orleans (https://youtu.be/TvMS_ykiLiQ), as in the song made famous by Woody Guthrie. We were having a good time on this weekend adventure which would be life-changing, but the entrance down into the city's bowels was still ahead. Did I mention I don't like subways? I don't like subways at all! If I write another book, I can go into many strange things I've experienced in that underground world.

Here we were on the subway platform. In uniform. Two dudes, GIs, or chick magnets" for the ladies. I suppose women always like a man in uniform." We were just waiting for a friend our train, and we noticed two young ladies waiting on the platform for a train like we were. (https://youtu.be/MKLVmBOOqVU)

"Do you mind if we ride with you on the train? It is kinda late, and we will keep ya safe," I said. Or something like that. They were Dawn Herl (spelling is my best memory after fifty-three years) and my soon-to-be wife, Heather Houston.

We talked for maybe ten minutes as the train stopped every few blocks, station after station. We had no particular place to go, so we decided we were exiting when they exited. We were brave, and we were soldiers! A dangerous mix, but it was a lovely eighty-five-degree summer evening. We were allowed to walk them home. We would yak for a while and see these young ladies home safely.

One weekend later, that same July, I visited her again, and while exiting the el train (short for elevated train) at the wrong stop, I ended up in the Southside! That neighborhood, even then, had a terrible rep! A mile or so away from there and two days earlier, Richard Speck had visited a nursing student's dormitory. Multiple deaths. Sad. That convinced me that parts of Chicago were not for tourists. Still aren't!

On 28 August 1966, I arrived on base at KI Sawyer.

Along with my fellow five or six fellow hydraulic repairmen, we maintained and repaired the hydraulic systems of twenty war machines, also known as the McDonnell-Douglas "Voodoo" F-101B aircraft. The squadron had a duty that wasn't discussed, but we all understood why this base was so far north. We were freezing and living like Eskimos because this base was part of our Air Force defense on the DEW line. **D**efense **E**arly **W**arning system stops Russian bombers from flying across the Arctic. Think of the movie *Dr. Strangelove or: How I Learned to Stop Worrying and Love the Bomb*.

Barracks, number 815, became my temporary new home until I got base housing in 1967. Everything in the military had a number, even me—AF15757xxx! They now use your Social Security number as your ID number.

There must have been a bus that took me to my work, also known affectionately as my duty station. I didn't own a car until sometime after our wedding when I coughed up $500 for a beat-up 1960 Chevrolet Bel-Air, two-door, black, and not a beauty but rather a black and rusted beast. The flooring beneath my feet when I drove was rusted out. A rubber floor mat covered this quite nicely. Thank you! I learned a lot about auto mechanics at the Base Auto Shop, where I attempted to keep this "hooptie" running! On the topic of older cars, my boss was SSGT Richard Romano at my part-time job where I was employed as a *paid* KP worker at the Officer's Club (Col. Carmen DiBiaso was the OIC). My boss owned a 1950 Chevy, which he told me he had gotten when he traded a $10 mattress for and got legal title to that car. They do last forever. Chevies, not mattresses! Aside: Sergeant Romano was and still is the only person I ever knew who was in a real and very deadly serious earthquake. Anchorage, Alaska, 9.2 magnitude in '64.

My Chevy was an automatic. Too easy to use. Place in P-R-N or drive D and you were good to go…most of the time! The transmission did all the shifting. Fine. I hear you asking from across the decades, Why are you telling me this? Here's why. Fast-forward a few months in my story, and one afternoon, I was told, "Take this part out to the flight line and, pointing at an air force vehicle, use that truck." This was said while pointing to an old late fifties to early sixties blue unknown type of government truck.

A minute later, I returned and said, "I've never driven a *stick* shift!"

I was told, "Just put it in gear, any gear, by pressing the clutch in and hitting the gas."

Some loud grinding sounds were heard and were ——horrible! I was told, "Not to worry. It's a government truck." Oh my, I had learned to drive a stick shift, sort of. I did get from point A to point B. I didn't get in trouble or get injured. Eventually, I mastered this rite of passage. It was an excellent example of a GI's mindset toward our government's everyday property. Did we care in general (no pun intended)? Not much!

I used to commute between Chicago and KI Sawyer AFB. Without any interstate highways, it was a slog, a long and monotonous drive. No internet maps. No cell phones. Four hundred miles one way on two-lane roads!

There were 400 miles of two-lane roads, and I drove late into the night. As a youth, as I was then, or even now in my dotage, I didn't require a lot of sleep! An eight-hour drive was acceptable. But after six hours, things took a *sudden* change! A red light was staring me in the face, and I stopped suddenly, just short of sliding. As I think back, it must have been summertime because there wasn't any snow. In the UP, there are only three seasons, though: "this winter, last winter, and next winter." Luckily, I stopped and immediately realized I had a significant problem. No, my foot hadn't gone through that rusted floorboard. The police weren't behind me with lights flashing! I was lost as a goose. I must have dozed off, eyes wide open (shut?), and automatically stopped at a red light. Where was I? No idea. How'd I get here? No clue! I nonchalantly cleared the intersection and found my way back onto the main road for two more hours of monotonous driving. I saw things on the last leg of my trip I had not ever seen before. My eyes were as wide open as an owl's! I had nearly died from fatigue, and luckily, I saw the red light before I went to see my maker!

Speaking of death, at some point in my tour of duty, there was a forest fire off base. I helped...as in obeyed a command and was put to work on the fire line. We were rounded up as volunteers (translation?). We were breathing, and we were GIs! Government-*issued* property. We were involuntarily "volunteered" and summarily loaded into the back of one of those sizable canvas-covered troop trucks. In a few minutes, we were off base and on an old logging road. Where we were, besides in the woods, no one cared or asked.

"Grab your shovel and get your asses off this truck!"

I recall smelling the smoke and digging the best trench I could muster! There was not much fire to be seen, but the piney smell commingled with smoke was, in a word, nasty! The best part was it didn't last that long since we were the best trenchers ever seen in these parts! *Ever!* I know the locals still talk about that day when "those flyboys saved our bacon!"

During my vastly different duties as a GI, I was given an opportunity. There are no opportunities in the military. They are called *orders*! I remember being told to be the bus driver during some crazy plan that some crazier higher-ranked person thought was *not* a crazy idea! The project lasted all night, as best as I can remember, fifty-five years later, writing this. Even then, I didn't know why we were doing this. Just obey my orders and drive the "darn" (it was probably a f——ing) bus! Everything went just peachy until...

(*Gulp!*) Until I found myself seated behind the wheel of a twenty-nine-passenger school bus! A government school bus, probably salvaged from a school nearby. My Pennsylvania driver's license wasn't a CDL license, but who worried about that? Interesting that now, if you want a CDL license, testing (expensive) and training (more expensive) are required to apply for and pay a lot. Hint: Uncle Sam is a *hypocrite*!

It was late. I was tired from working all day. Finally, the exercise was over. Everything in the military is called an "exercise"! Parking the bus required backing up. Okay... I hadn't done this before. I just drove in forward gears all night. I had to back up and say, "Here goes nothing!" A few seconds later, I heard a quite loud and bus-shaking *kerBANG!*

What the —bleep—! The back bumper hit something that my mirrors hid from me. Thinking of the use of a spotter...not happening.

My immediate instinct was to move forward and then go back there and see what happened. *Error!* What you don't know *can* hurt you or the bus in this sorry tale. The bumper had run up and over an (ill-placed) fireplug. Moving forward only moved the bus' fender backward! It was now pointing at a ninety-degree angle back and away from the bus. I was then told to drive the bus to the base welding shop. Another GI was told by his superior to fix the bumper and turn in a bill for his time and materials (a welding rod was the only material).

The bill came to $4.13. I paid for it! End of story, but distinctly remembered and placed here in my autobiography forever.

1967, Winter

The *worst* blizzard in the history of Chicago! True. Concerning my first marriage, I think Mother Nature was trying to warn me. Not much to say. There were no wedding photos, no reception, no guests. It was just her parents, her sister, us, and the preacher. At my second wedding was our BellSouth friend Foster McClain, Sheila's friend Kathy Kuegel, and a judge. That was our wedding. Strange that years later, I would be a wedding photographer who covered five hundred weddings with more photographic images than I can count! I only covered one court house wedding. He looked like DB Cooper. Message me on Facebook, I have photos and more details…

It had been six months since I met Miss Heather, and we got married in January 1967. The wedding was on the same day as the worst blizzard in that city's history. I married one of those "subway-young ladies." History repeated itself. Life was never to be the same! Oddly, and as an aside, my parents also met on public transportation, the Staten Island Ferry, in New York City many decades earlier. Still valid in 2020—that 1967 snow was the worst blizzard to hit Chicago (https://en.wikipedia.org/wiki/1967_Chicago_blizzard?wprov=sfti1). "The **Chicago blizzard of 1967** struck northeast Illinois and northwest Indiana on January 26–27, 1967, with a record-setting 23 inches (58 cm) snow fall in Chicago and its suburbs before the storm abated the next morning. As of 2022, it remains the greatest snowfall in one storm in Chicago history."

The day before we were married, three NASA astronauts died in a fire on the launchpad. On our last wedding anniversary, before we were divorced, the Challenger blew up! The cruel irony was that to get to the wedding, I rode (I still didn't have a car then) three hundred miles south to get to Chicago from the Upper Peninsula of Michigan, which is a barren, snow-covered wonderland from October until May. Then I put the tire chains on for the winter. I only got stuck in the snow once in four winters, and it was due to my stupidity. But first, that other snow story!

I drove a fellow airman, Bill, twenty-five miles into town one afternoon (all the years have erased his last name). It was too far to walk, and there never was any traffic! It snows nearly every day in Michigan's Upper Peninsula (I think you know that by now). There was plenty of snow on the road for our twenty-five-mile, one-way journey. It rarely goes above thirty-two degrees. Once, I survived below-zero weather for thirty days! I remember feeling comfy working outside in the sun on a fifteen-degree day as I completed a task requiring my sense of touch.

Before we put the car in D and proceeded along this two-lane rural (read that as isolated) highway, between a base and Marquette, there was one crossroad with a gas station. There was a steep hill going into town the last mile. Otherwise, it was just me, my passenger, and many pine trees. No scenery, just trees. In the trunk, I kept a shovel, a flare, a blanket, and some anti-skid traction plates to put under the drive wheels to help get out of a snowbank you may find yourself in, with no one but you to get your sorry butt out of a jam.

We were a mile or so down the road. The skies were clear, and it was 10°–15°F. Straight road. I came up behind a slowpoke and passed them. As I was still driving, a faster car approached me in front, leaving me one choice—move immediately to the right and pass him on my side of the road. The pass was successful, but I was not parallel to the road when I competed the pass. Turning the wheel sharply to the left would have been disastrous! I would probably slide, lose control, and end up GOK (God only knows) where! We were now traveling safely away from the oncoming car, but we were also heading almost straight toward the woods at a forty-five-degree angle.

We knew that hitting a pine tree would destroy the car and kill us. But we were alive, and I was lucky we ended up in a massive snowdrift, hitting zero trees! No problem, except that in driving off-road about ten feet from the paved road, I noticed the engine had died. Bill and I got out of the car and began our inspection. Nothing we could see of the car was damaged, but then again, we couldn't see the car's hood under all that snow!

We got the shovel from my well-prepared trunk and started digging. No traffic to worry about, and the car's back end was off the road! No one was going to stop and help us. We just kept digging since priority number one was to get the engine running to keep us warm! After maybe fifteen minutes, we found the hood, cleared off the snow, and opened the hood. Phew, but no time to relax yet.

Where was the engine? Nothing but snow. *Keep! Shoveling!*

We were locating the engine. Getting the engine running meant heat! Emergency passed. Then we dug and dug at the rear end of the car to clear the drive wheels and dig a path to maneuver back onto the road. An adventure like no other in winter, stuck in snow cold as ——…until the next snow apocalypse.

In a separate incident (as I said, there were incidents and accidents along my way), I argued with my State Farm insurance agent about an accident resulting from an on-base ticket at KI Sawyer with my State Farm Mutual Insurance agent. I argued with them for about a year, and finally, I got my deductible returned! I spent that check to fix a fender on my good old '60 Chevy. I also got a written apology (now enshrined in my memorabilia file) a year later!

1968, Julie's Birth

Julie's birth! A fantastic event/miracle to see your firstborn child! Unique describes a sunrise or sunset. This is *totally* beyond that! Details? The waiting room, the photo of her birth, etc, *nothing* like it! I do remember being in the waiting room, but I was a lowly airman, and my waiting room companion was a lieutenant. We paced, and I smoked. The event was terrific! I was very proud but too poor to buy a bunch of cigars to give out. Hell, maybe I did buy cigars and I forgot. I didn't take many photos, and the few I might have made are now Julie's mother's property. She took the hundreds of 35 mm slides I made (captured the images). Here's a newspaper photo of Julie's nurse, which I noticed sometime later. I don't remember reading this paper very much. I was primarily working on planes or in the Officer's Club, where the brass played and I worked in the kitchen after my work as they relaxed!

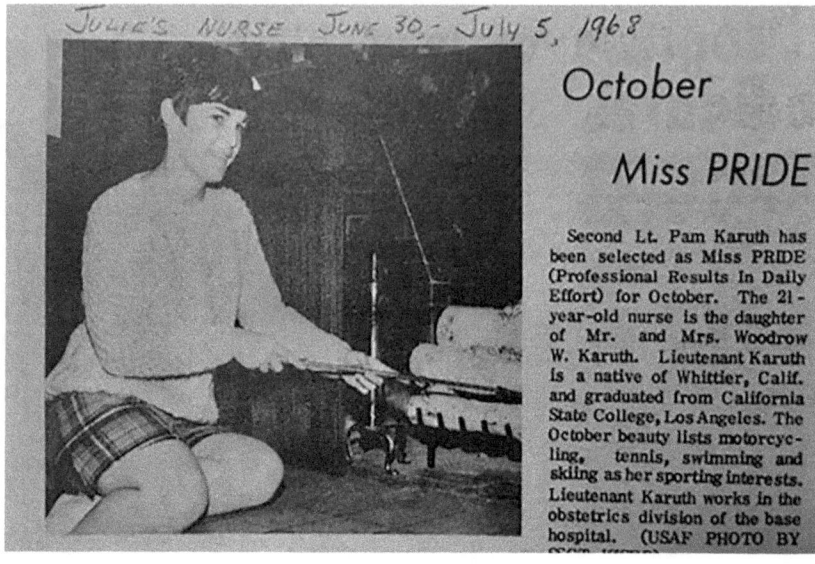

While we lived in the UP of Michigan, we only once traveled east along the beautiful Lake Superior shoreline and saw Pictured Rocks National Park. Then farther east and into Sault Ste. Marie, Ontario, Canada. We did a little shopping, then 169 miles back home. This had to be during July when we had a few summer days. One afternoon, on a different outing, we took our dog "Lucky" to Marquette for a beach blanket picnic on the beautiful shore of Lake Superior. When we left, about twenty minutes later, it was getting very windy. I distinctly remember the time/temperature sign on the bank had fallen nineteen degrees! That same bank can be seen in the movie *Anatomy of a Murder* (1959). No picnic that day! We never tried to have a beach picnic again.

I was a hydraulic mechanic on the F-101A Voodoo. Having pestered many test pilots for a "free ride," I was suddenly offered the chance one August afternoon in 1968. Here's what a Voodoo looks like: (https://en.wikipedia.org/wiki/McDonnell_F-101_Voodoo?wprov=sfti1).

Major VanHorn (my best recollection of his name. There was a pilot named Major VanHorn, that much is true. Was it him? Dunno) asked me, "You wanna go for that ride?"

As quickly as I knew how, "*Yessir!*"

ZERO TO SEVENTY-FIVE

The pilot then took me a short distance over to the flight ops building, and we found a flight suit that I could wear, a parachute to strap to my chest, and a helmet for my head. Background to this flight: it was not approved to fly in these fighter jets unless you passed the course called "altitude chamber school". The school was at Wright-Patterson AFB in Ohio (where the alleged aliens are rumored to be stored). I never did this since it was not part of my work routine. I was a ground crew member, not a flying member. Break the rules if an officer was involved. Okay, I guess. But, oh well, it was a fine afternoon to suit up and go up into the wild blue yonder in a government-maintained aircraft! At least I had installed a few critical parts.

After getting some quick instructions on when and how to eject (a good plan for just a fun ride), the engines started, and we went out onto the runway. It would be pertinent to mention two minor details at this point. (1) I had just finished a minor hydraulic repair to a flight control system, the flap up-lock actuator. (2) One of the two Pratt & Whitney J57 engines had just been replaced by the engine crew. The purpose of the test flight was to make sure the new engine worked adequately. Mmmm?

I love to fly. My first flight was in an open cockpit biplane at age six or seven (1952) if you are skipping around. I assumed, that as we got airborne, I would experience a nice view of my air base, flying like it was a routine flight. Wrong!

The pilot and I sat at the end of the runway (he in front, me behind him). And before takeoff, he ran the engines up to takeoff power. He then idled a few moments and got radio clearance to take off. As he released the brakes and accelerated, we began our takeoff roll! At this point (eighty kilometers per hour?), he flipped the two switches on the throttles and lit the afterburners. *Boom!Boom!* (180 kpm)! I had heard these engines roar to life many times before. At the same time, I was standing around on the flight line. It's a different thing than working around these engines and having your butt only ten feet (a guess) from those twin roaring monsters!

There was no view to see since I had, guessing, about 3 Gs (G being gravity) pressing me back into my seat. I weighed three times my average weight as the engines were pressing me back into my seat. We took off and climbed straight up! That "boom, boom" was something

I just heard moments ago as I felt those afterburners and us riding up into the stratosphere *like I was a Roman candle*! We were at twenty-five thousand feet in no time, or thirty thousand feet. We leveled off around thirty-five thousand feet, and it was surreal. The glass canopy allowed an unimpeded 180-degree side-to-side view. As we rolled over, the view of the ground was even more spectacular! It was a fantastic feeling being inverted in flight and looking *upward* at Lake Superior with the sunlight rippling off that dark blue water!

The real reason for the flight was the next phase. It was to test the new engine. Simply put, this involved turning that engine off in the air. *That is what you just read.* (mmm... What were those ejection rules?) Nice! As he shuts the new engine off, we immediately slowed down, dramatically, then using the forward movement from the remaining engine, he "air-started" the new engine. In a car, this would be equivalent to popping the clutch if your starter or battery were dead. *Whoa!* More G-forces again. Having completed this part of his job, he decided to do a little showing off for me and put the jet through some loops, rolls, twists, and turns. Interesting, to say the least! Very expensive roller coaster. The Immelmann maneuver was an experience!

Aerobatic maneuver

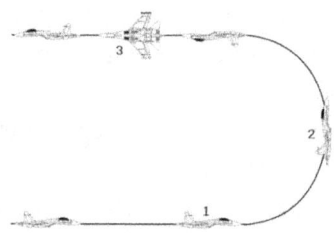

Schematic view of an Immelmann turn:
1. Level flight
2. Half loop
3. 180° roll to bring aircraft back level

The aerobatic Immelmann turn derives its name from the dogfighting tactic, but is a different maneuver than the original, now known as a "wingover" or "hammerhead".

The landing was not what I was expecting, nor was it your typical commercial jet landing where it takes several miles to descend twenty-five thousand feet. We did this in three or four miles, not fifty to seventy-five miles, approaching our landing strip like a brick! I was glad to be on the ground finally. As we taxied, I made a hand gesture, opening and closing my hand and fingers for the pilot to open the canopy. I was sick, and I needed to…you get the idea. But it was more fun than you can imagine! The ride of a lifetime, fifty-three years ago, as if it were yesterday! Dangerous? Yes! Scary? Yes! Fun? Heck yeah! Engine and hydraulic repairs all checked out fine. Now it was time to be sick to my stomach and hope my ears stop bleeding and my hearing was still okay. *What an experience!*

Sometime about now, on the other side of the planet, with the Vietnam War raging on and on, there was one afternoon at Sawyer, I remember. Vividly. Not the date, just the pain! I stood in a long line (in hangar 800) to get the business end of an air gun medical shot. *Blam!* The plague shot! Wow! That was the most painful shot, as I write this. I never contracted the plague, nor did I end up in the Southeast Asian jungles of Vietnam. During this time, I was considered for a language school then deployed to Vietnam. I would have enjoyed learning a second language, but not over there!

1969, Lisa's Birth

I remember very little about the only ice hockey game I ever attended. There's not much to do in the Upper Peninsula if you are not into hunting moose or skiing!

Sometime this year, I remember the event but not the date. Julie had a severe encounter with a pole lamp in our living room. Her balance and steps weren't as sure as they would soon become. While Heather and I were in our living room, she lost her balance and grabbed for something to steady herself. As she fell, she knocked down a pole lamp. I saw her little arm was lacerated from the shattered glass fixtures, and I calmly wrapped her arm while seeing to it that she elevated it to stop the bleeding. It may have been during the winter. Otherwise, thinking back on this event, she never saw a doctor, and I believe this was wintertime, and the weather must have been the reason.

If you count mischief night in Penn Hills in 1962, which we've already discussed, I was now locked up for the second time. This time, in a military jail! 21 April, 1969. What does that mean?

1. They shave your head.
2. They give you a new mug shot. (*I still have that jewel!*)
3. They put you in the brig.

4. You walk around the base picking up trash and being publicly humiliated.
5. You are busted (demoted) down a rank. (They take away the last stripe you just worked very hard for.) And they reduce your meager pay!

After five days away from your job, you get out of jail. The jail wasn't much worse than boot camp anyway. Then five months later, on 15 September 1969, and out of the blue (that's an unintentional flying reference), your First Sergeant comes to your defense. He finds out that you were wrongly charged and that you were off base for the weekend with permission from your superior (SSGT John B. Kaiser). You did not go AWOL. You took a "known to the boss" weekend off. One big lie from my staff sergeant has been made right. Then you find out that your First Sergeant (CMSGT Clayton Teem) has sent your boss (SSGT) to Vietnam as punishment for you getting put in jail. *Ouch!* Of all my military (non-family) experiences, this AWOL story is my second most vivid memory. My flight in a Voodoo has to be at the top of my *non-family* memories!

Now, fast-forward fifteen years in 1985 to "the rest of the story," as Paul Harvey used to say. (He was a famous radio personality.) I will post a photo of the newspaper article if I find it! I noticed SSGT Kaiser's son (a junior) was stationed in New York State, where his father used to be stationed before I met him. He regularly flew C-130s as his job. There was a plane crash, and he was killed. I spent some time finding his telephone number. I made a brief call to my old boss; no doubt, he was dumbfounded at my calling.

Julie's first step has a recorded date: 05 June at 7:30 p.m. See the photo of the business card I still have (see next page). We went on military leave (vacation) to present Lisa to her family.

THOMAS E. BYRON

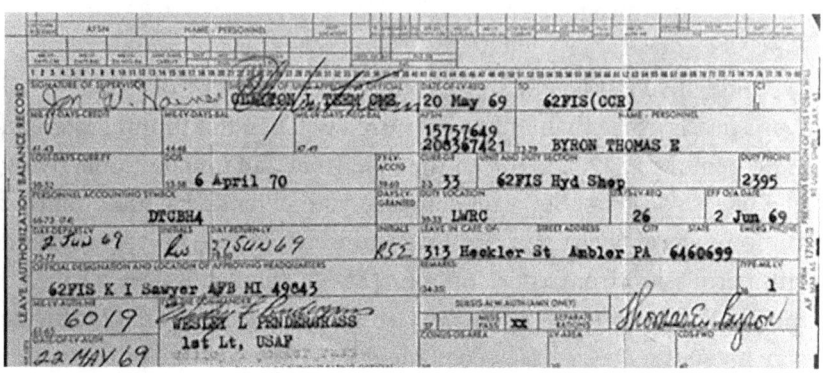

GREEN LANTERN MOTEL
14944 Pearl Road
Strongsville, Ohio 44136

16 Miles Southwest of Cleveland on U. S. Route No. 42
1½ Miles from I-71 and Ohio 82

ALL ROOMS HAVE AIR CONDITIONING AND TV
⅛ Mile to Restaurant and Shopping Center

5 JUNE 1969   7:30 PM - JULIE
STARTED WALKING !

Telephone (Area Code 216) 238-6997

More notes on the first events by Julie and Lisa.

6/7   LISA ROCKING CHAIR IN PINK · JULIE & GIRAFEE
6/11 LISA ICECREAM
6/12+13 LISA STANDS ALONE 20 SECS.
6/14 LISA - WHOLE PEAS
6/17 Julie 24 lbs.
6/21 JULIE ICECREAM
6/25 LISA 20 lbs
6/28 JULIE 24 lbs
7/1   NEW V.C. BAG
7/5   T+H BAPTIZED 7:30 PM
7/11 LISA TOOTH #3 UPPER FRONT HER LEFT
7/17 Cleaned basement
7/23 LISA TOOTH #4 UPPER FRONT HER RIGHT

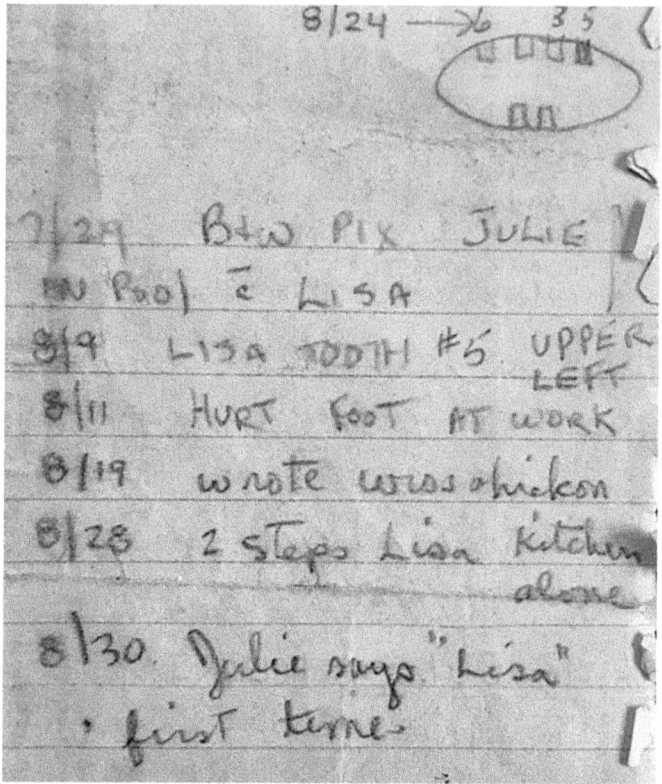

What a great year it was! *Lisa* was born on 08 September 1969. Julie had a little sister to play with or fight with or get into mischief with. They were a team. I'll tell you that!

In August, there was a rock festival called Woodstock. You might have heard of a significant party that summer. We had a young daughter, Julie. Her mother was pregnant with Lisa, and thus, we did not attend. Even earlier than Woodstock, America landed a man on the moon! We watched that live (viewing was delayed due to the great distance from the moon) on a B&W tube television with rabbit ears and saw the images of that fantastic event! Two significant events—Lisa and the men landing on the moon. What a year!

Later this year, we traveled four hundred miles south to Chicago to visit family and check in with the employment office in Illinois Bell. I successfully applied with Illinois Bell for a future job at Cincinnati Bell. Always the planner, Heather's father, Richard, was an intelligent guy. His advice was to apply at a Bell Telephone Company office in Chicago for a future job in Cincinnati when I exited the military.

Return to Civilian Life, 1970

02 February. I am now out of the military and working for the oldest telephone company in America. Cincinnati Bell Telephone & Telegraph Company was founded in 1873 as a telegraph company before Mr. Graham's phone invention. I would learn that gem during the year "we turned" one hundred as a company (https://en.wikipedia.org/wiki/Cincinnati_Bell?wprov=sfti1).

It would be a cold and snowy trip early that winter morning as the four of us headed south to Chicago in our bright yellow '66 Ford Galaxy. We spent the last night in the same trailers the pilots slept in when they were on alert duty! We were a few hundred yards from the very busy runway! The place was free, as I recall. We were young. We were brave. We were determined. *We were free!* Now I had a civilian job as a telephone installer at the North Bend garage in Cincinnati, Ohio waiting on me! I was always the planner.

But before I could begin my long and sometimes rocky career with good ole Ma Bell, I was required to drive a company car, and that required I take (and pass) a driving test. Cincinnati, if you've not been there, isn't referred to as *the city of seven hills* like Rome, as in Italy, for *nothing!* It is very hilly. Very! The test was easy—drive around and properly obey the instructor's orders and make turns and stops. All the usual stuff one would expect. Fine. Then my last test was to park the vehicle and hand the keys to the test-giver. Parallel park, please. Here on the hill. About a fifteen-degree slope, maybe twenty degrees. Steep enough. With a stick shift. *Groan!* I remember the fear. The zinc taste in one's mouth when fear is present! That moment right before I nearly died. I passed. Otherwise, I might not have a job, and I was the sole (income) provider. I had three young ladies to feed!

I remember my time being in the military from 1966 to 1970. Everyone who had worked for more than one enlistment (four years) told me, "You can't make it on the outside [being a civilian]!" They were persistent and convinced of this. I wondered why. Here's my reasoning. They worked for a large group, the military, the government, who spent their time and the taxpayer's money in a closed system. No one competes with the government, but venders compete to do business with Mr. deep pockets, the government makes nothing but *red tape*! No one ever, or rarely, discussed the costs of anything—your time, the supplies used or the time spent consuming those supplies. The pay wasn't that great, but the benefits were good. Free health care was good, but the doctors were not competing for patients since it was a closed group. It was an assembly line lifestyle.

I wondered, what if I competed with a skill that I could learn and then take it into a larger and more competitive society for more pay and more benefits? Even more security.

I had decided it was time to finish serving my country, so I became a civvy, as in civilian. I then decided I would go to college at night and continue to support myself and my family. I went into a significant competitive group—America and two hundred million people, not one million in the military. Numbers are relative. They do not need to be exact.

An education would transfer to a lot of different careers and companies. There weren't many companies that needed military people to repair fighter jets. Note: the civilian mechanic's job required a license and a test. USAF training wasn't good enough? Companies did not have to trust the military's way of doing things? I decided to study electronics, and I earned an associate's degree in applied science with honors. This skill was a lot more marketable. Then I decided to get a bachelor's degree in economics. Even more marketable. I spent twenty-two years as an engineer in the Bell System.

I had decided to be responsible for myself, not reliant on a massive government bureaucracy. That was why my fellow brothers in uniform told me, "You should put in your twenty years and then at age forty, retire," to which I added, silently to myself, "With no marketable skills, and then you find yourself looking for a second job to support your family and yourself?" You'd be looking for a job because your retirement income would be 50 percent of what you were making when you were enlisted. You would, no doubt, need a part-time job to supplement your military pay with your career at a profit-driven company. Private businesses are interested in efficiency and profit in a competitive job market. In the military, you are sitting around too much. Not for my tastes. Those were not the traits I saw in the military. I served in the Air Force as a hydraulic mechanic for three years, nine months, and twenty-seven days. I was let out of jail (euphemistically speaking) early, and it was time for me to regain my civilian life again. I was a free man again, and as a married man, having two small children, it was more severe than going into conscription in the USAF in April 1966! I had fun in the service and only spent five days in jail. In February, I had a job at Cincinnati Bell Telephone, a phone company "marriage" that lasted twenty-two years.

My *first* of three jobs was working as a telephone installer. As a new hire, I got the worst part of that job. Only one was given to the new hires. I had to go to those houses where people had moved out, not paid their bills, and left their phones behind. In filth. With the roaches. The dirt. The spiders. Just in one word: *horrible!*

I wouldn't say I liked that job, so I applied for another and was hired at the General Electric Evendale branch. I made much better pay and was working on the assembling of the TF-39 and CF-50 turbine rear sections. Huge engines! Much, much better pay. Noisy place, larger floor area than a football field! Union piece work decided by the UAW on how long and consequently how many units you needed to complete during your four-hour shift, meal break, then four-hours and it was quitting time!. The Union (UAW 647) sets your rules, *not* your supervisor! When you reached your requirement (you completed what should take you four hours longer) for an eight-hour shift, in four hours, you and your pals met in the cafeteria downstairs. The bosses left at 5:00 p.m., and my shift began at 3:30 p.m. Timecard punch in, punch out. Too easy. Too much free time on night shift, but work ended at 11:30 p.m. (eight hours).

As the US government's SST project got canceled by President Johnson, GE decided to lay off the lowest seniority workers, myself being (least) prominent among the lowest seniority worker!

I took a manager's position at McDonald's. Big pay increase! That job lasted ninety days, and a few weeks of that was Manager's Training Class No. 1 (certificate in a file somewhere), but my boss used nepotism by firing me and giving *his* son my job!

My *second* job at the phone factory then began! I was now a drafting clerk. I rose rapidly in the union rankings from a level-8 clerk to a level-6 and then a level-4. The next promotion was assistant engineer, which never happened. Thank you, Mr. Union Boss. I got laid off. "Oh, *snap!*"

Before I got laid off, things were fun. I did work in a department where the manager, Mr. Russ Schaefer, celebrated a special anniversary. I only witnessed this one time during my entire working career. It was his fiftieth anniversary! Not a typo. He was hired as a co-op at the age of fifteen. My father-in-law, who then lived in Chicago, had encouraged me to work for the phone company since this was a stable job with great benefits and friendly people. I recall visiting an Illinois Bell office in Chicago and our plans to move to Cincinnati. This preliminary work allowed me nearly instantaneous hiring when I arrived in Cincinnati.

My first direct boss/supervisor was Helen Castelli from Crittenden, Kentucky. I would later learn on 28 May 1977, that she and her husband, Norbert, had died in the very terrible Beverly Hills (Kentucky) Supper Club fire that killed 165 people. John Davidson was performing to a packed audience. RIP, ma'am!

After a brief time, one year, I quit the phone company for the first two times, each time getting a better job than I just quit. I recommend *not* doing that! The installer job I had was filthy. A *nasty* job! My job was to go to empty houses where people had left their phones and didn't pay their bills! Roaches! Spiders! Creepy things!

Never give up! I then went to General Electric as an aircraft engine assembler for double the pay I earned at the phone company. It was a temporary job, but one year later, I was out of that job, too, because of a government-caused layoff. This layoff was President Johnson's decision to reduce people making jet engines driven by the SST (a supersonic jet) production cancellation, but it was an exciting job anyway! The work was also supercritical and essential. I still see those engines on commercial airplanes and military jets that fly over our apartment near the local Martin-Marietta Co. and Dobbins Air (Force) Reserve Base. I worked at GE in the Turbine Rear Section in building 700, a massive building more significant than the giant Walmart. I assembled the TF-39 and CF-50 turbine rear sections, the monstrous six-feet diameter intake. They are visible when you look at the rear of these engines as the are installed on their variety of different aircraft. This seemed like a good move, but within a year, due to the vicissitudes of the UAW union I belonged to and the politics of government, I was summarily laid off! Zero income... and this was the end of my associations with unions. While working my second shift job at "Generous" Electric, I received my first and only speeding ticket. After work, I was driving home with my carpool buddy, and I forgot there was a speed trap. He and I even talked about it the night before. As I passed the spot and the blue lights came on, I knew I was traveling 64 in a 55 zone. My fine was a nasty $35.00, and at a $150.00 per week check, this was hard on our budget. That was forty-nine years ago (as I type this), and not another ticket for speeding since. I tried the Spiro Agnew defense "Nolo contendere", and the judge wasn't having any of *that*! My faux legal career lasted a nanosecond. "Pay the fine! Get out of here!" was his reply!

ZERO TO SEVENTY-FIVE

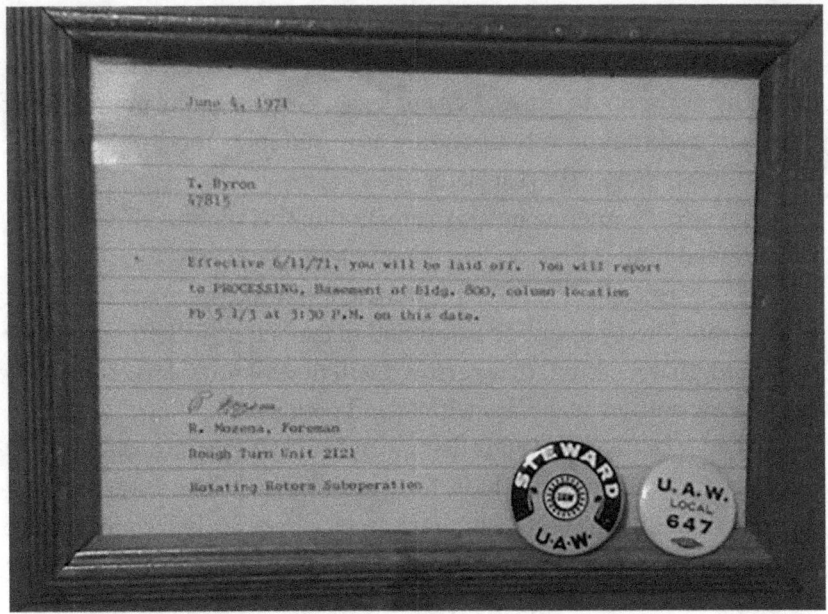

I began working for Ma Bell, a.k.a. Cincinnati Bell, for the *second* time in 1971 as a drafting clerk. This work was exciting and fun, or as much fun as a job could be. I was promoted several times, and my tiny paychecks grew. Eventually, as I was incrementally promoted, I took one step toward becoming an assistant engineer. I was ignominiously bumped by the union contract under the local CWA to a mail clerk. Not able to live on this pay, I began looking through a telephony magazine, and I ran across called *Telephone Engineering*. In the back of this magazine were jobs offered by contract companies. I remember going down to the lobby at work and using a pay phone to call Burnup and Sims and talking to a Mr. Roy Seibert about a job. *Success!* Now we had to sell our house and move to Tennessee.

Before we leave Cincinnati Bell, a few events should be mentioned. During my tenure as a clerk (that makes my clerkship sound important), I will relate a one-off experience. One of my jobs as a low-level clerk was running errands. About two blocks from the telephone headquarters office where I worked was the power company headquarters. Con-*veen*-iant isn't it (remember *Saturday Night Live*'s Dana Garvey's voice?). Jim Poteet was my contact at CG&E, and we regularly chatted about stuff, long since faded memories. *But* there was one occasion I've never forgotten. I will say, upfront, this is an exact and not a fuzzy memory. Why my brain does this, I *do not know*! Getting to the point, one of us mentioned the room temperature as unsuitable. Too hot, too cold? That's lost all these fifty years later.

Jim said, "Someone needs to ameliorate this situation!"

I asked him, "What do you mean… a-*meal*-e-or-ate?"

He corrected my sloppy pronunciation and explained what that word meant: "to even out or adjust and make better." Why I remember that word, that location, that person, I will never know. That is the *only* word in my entire vocabulary with "word pedigree!"

I had recently signed our first mortgage, $104 per month on a $70 per week income with two kids, for a brand-new home. I was the first owner of a small house! The military service benefits kicked in. We got a government FHA235 loan. Subsidized. A year later, I would apply for more GI benefits and begin an epic adventure attending colleges. In this order of enrollment: (1) OMI–Cincinnati, Ohio Mechanics Institute; (2) OCAS–Cincinnati, Ohio College of Applied Science; (3) UC–McMicken Ave. "on the hill" Cincinnati; (4) UT–Knoxville, Tennessee; (5) McNeese State–Lake Charles, Louisiana; (6) UAB–Birmingham, Alabama. I graduated (exhausting!) after attending six different universities! I could say that I stuck to my plan! And it's a life's lesson well learned!

At some point in time, while I was attempting to begin my plans for what work I'd enjoy, I went to Xavier University, within walking distance from the University of Cincinnati. I used my excellent GI benefits, and I undertook a career psychological examination. Dr. Cosgrove was my advisor and analyst. He tested me for what I was best suited for. Why I remember his name, I can't explain. We met once, and I was asked lots of questions, and our acquaintance was that brief.

Results that remember? The priesthood was a possibility, and an undertaker was also a potential match. With this information in mind, and perhaps in my unorganized stash of notes and paperwork I had with me, I went to the Cincinnati (city) Library. I decided to look into the business of undertaking. Bear with me. I went to the reference desk and made a life-changing request: "Do you have any books on undertakers?" I was handed a thick, rather heavy book with lots of photos. I returned the book to the reference desk within a few minutes. "Thanks, but… I'm seeing more than I was prepared to see."

Engineering sounded better than embalming! Mission accomplished. It was engineering for me. I made the correct career decision. Thank you, Dr. Cosgrove! And I never told the shrink/doc that he was 180° off the mark!

1971

I started my college career. The GI Bill helped, and I still have my accounting pocket notebook to track my payments! This is not the easiest way to get an education after starting a family, but why not at least try? Uncle Sam said this was my GI benefit for being in the USAF. I had a family, a mortgage, a fledgling career, and night school. Oh, and a total of three kids (after 1974)! Without them, it would all have been *meaningless*!

I've probably had the same problem as 99 percent of every other commuter stuck in traffic. Our urban commuting areas are generally years and years behind engineering changes to adjust for choke points. Bottlenecks occur and have all types of bad results. Have you ever been stopped/stuck in traffic? No accidents are visible. No bad weather. Just at a standstill. We've all seen it.

That's my problem, as it is yours. So what's the point in *me* telling *you* this? Someone[3] out there knows this story I'm going to relate to. It's a fantastic event that solved my commuting problem, at least for two days. I'll *never* forget. We both lived in Kentucky in the early seventies. Anyhow, where was I?

---

[3] Message me if you read this.

ZERO TO SEVENTY-FIVE

Was it the time I was commuting, and I had another driver pass a beer to me on a hot afternoon as we were both going around 55 mph side by side? I saw him drinking a beer. He was the passenger. I motioned to him with my empty hand to my mouth, mimicking the act of drinking. He held a beer out, and as I held my hand out while I was looking straight ahead, a cold beer was passed to me! Wow! But that's not my only story like that. Another time I had a pack of cigarettes handed to me. I took a cigarette and passed it back. Then a little down the road, I had a lighter from the same car. That happened. But that's not my only story either. It is the same road as the above events in the following vignette of my life's story.

Here's the significant part. These are all *not* made up. They are incredibly accurate. I have no photos or eyewitnesses, but they happened! I was traveling this very same road (a few miles closer to my home) one afternoon after getting off work at rush hour. That part happened every day. It was during rush hour that my factory shift ended. I was in Cincinnati, Ohio. I-75 South was heading for the Brent-Spence Bridge across the Ohio River and into Kentucky. It was a funnel and a major merge point, six lanes blending into two to cross the bridge. Travel five feet, stop. Travel two feet, stop. I was crawling and stopping. It was a nightmare to frazzle even the calmest of nerves.

I was looking at other drivers and studying their moods, listening to the different music coming from car radios. I was bored and mad at the same time. Windows were down to save overheating my engine. Grrrrrrr. I looked over to my left at this young lady, and she smiled as she looked at me. We were both getting ready to cross the River Styx (maps show it as Ohio, but that's a misprint). She stopped. She was going three miles an hour. I was going 3 mph. *Then.* She motioned me ahead of her, and I nodded and smiled and waved a "Hi!" at her. Smiles were exchanged, and we slowly proceeded across the bridge from hell and went home.

The *very* next day, at the *exact* location, I was crawling along with this *same* patch of concrete that never moved faster than a dead slug! Traffic sucks. It was hot as hades. I looked to my left in a smog-choked gaze at the driver next to me to see if their patience was about to break, and they'd mash down on the gas pedal and bulldoze their way through this mass of steel and angry, tormented souls. Nope.

The very *same* driver! The exact section of roadway! Same result! She saw me, and with a huge smile, she excitedly realized we must have been in a time warp, and she could slow down and let me merge in ahead of her. That was over forty years ago, fresh as if it happened yesterday. I retired and do not miss those days of "whines and rows" of traffic nightmares. That was my story. An actual event. Karma? Time warp? BDL?[4] I do not know. I know that commuting is a curse placed upon the daily schlep who sit in traffic-purgatory…every…day…until death do we part.

---

[4] Blind, dumb luck. h/t Jeff Salyer

1974, Mark's Birth

Mark was born. The trio was complete. Everyone was pleased! Cigars are supposed to be given out. The family name continues. Dr. Brunamen came out of the delivery room and said, "Congratulations! You have a healthy little boy!" Any son would need to grow healthy and robust with two older sisters. I don't know how long it took you to exert dominance and control. You did! And you three were the ultimate and proverbial barrel of monkeys!

Now everyone should know that during my entire time being married to the mother of three young children, I was responsible for the three children and their mother's well-being. I was always the sole provider. I worked a forty-hour week and went to night school from 1970 until 1987. It was as grueling as it sounds, but necessary to improve my family, my employer, and myself.

Around this period, the details are etched in my brain. The date is not. The fact that random ideas come to me should not surprise you, dear reader! I have always had a creative mind. I was thinking and tinkering but never getting over the hump. Ideas are great; implementing them is an entirely different animal, as it were. Sometime in 1981 my upside-catsup idea would be stolen. Here's what happened. I had this brainstorm once, stemming from poverty and being a miser. Why not make catsup bottles with a more oversized flat top? I found an invention submission place, pre-internet. I drew up some very detailed plans. Remember, I was a draftsman with the phone company back in the seventies. I mailed in my idea, and after a month or so, I found out that the next step was to pay them a $5,000 fee! This fee deflated my goal of becoming wealthy. This amount was entirely obscene, and I gave up. I think I told them that, but no matter.

Some five years later, I saw my concept in use! I was angry that they (it's always *"them"* isn't it?) had stolen my idea. I was stupid enough to blab about it without thinking about the next step. Theft. I am a permanent resident of the skeptic-camp of strange people! I will never take that path again.

Only one of you will remember this event. I had a crazy notion that catsup and shampoo bottles should be made to sit upside down! How strange, but how *convenient*! This is a true story. Being a draftsman and making neat drawings, I submitted a plan to a now-forgotten place: "invention submission." Many years later, my plans stolen, I saw my invention in a grocery store! I still cringe all these decades later, what could have been!

By the time you, Mark, were around one year old, you were exploring your surroundings more and more each day. As I told the doctor, "The last thing I remember was he said, *'Eye!'*" Little Mark was comfortably sitting on my lap. His sharply trimmed fingernails were a weapon no one realized. Least of all me, your humble correspondent. You pointed at my eye with your index finger, right *at* my eyeball. *Owie! Wham!* That tiny weaponized finger cut my cornea! Until you've had a piece of iron sliver (which I did while working at L&N Railroad for two or three weeks and then I got laid *off*!) or a fingernail in your eye, you *do not* know pain! Earlier this same year, there was a massive tornado north of Cincinnati! April 3, 1974 (look up Xenia, Ohio,) was a terrible day. I attended night school at OMI (Ohio Mechanics Institute), and I experienced my first and only air raid siren. It was scary, but the tornado that caused the alarm was not a long way away from Cincinnati.

A couple of my classmates and I went into the building and took the elevator to the top floor to get a better view. We forgot that the *lower* floors were where you should go during a tornado! I remember seeing hanging clouds swirling and looking quite ominous! I worked for

Cincinnati Bell and went out the morning after with my boss, Frank D. Davidson (from Hazard, Kentucky), to explore the telco damages. There were several significantly large, as in nine *hundred* cable pairs, which is 1,800 wires, plus each wire is insulated—cables severely damaged, and there was one giant trunk cable that would knock out service to nine hundred people. (I have a short piece of a nine-hundred-pair cable on my library shelf.) I will never forget an elderly couple sitting, dazed, on their front steps. They were looking out toward us but obviously in shock! There was no house behind them. They lost everything. Maybe even their front lawn was blown away! It was that severe. I heard about a pair of scissors blown through a telco cable! That took some mighty wind to do that!

In 1974, I bought a 1966 Dodge Cornet column shift for $400 (cash)! With three kids and one car, I finally solved that problem. This old beauty was a necessary purchase and cost-effective addition. It was in excellent condition, though it was a very loud *yellow*! And I had learned to drive stick shift cars through trial and necessity.

I don't remember where I was when the following history occurred, except that I worked at Cincinnati Bell as an engineering clerk. I do remember seeing the news that evening. I had followed the political career of Mr. Nixon, now an embroiled president. Watergate took its toll on politicians, and I can still see him saluting as he got on the presidential helo. I'm paraphrasing from memory, not googling it. "I shall resign at noon today…"

Sheila and I finally went to Emory University in Atlanta and heard Woodward and Bernstein speak about Watergate. In person! Exciting experience about thirty-five years after the event!

My Three Children

In this chapter, I will remember some of my joys and sorrows surrounding Julie, Lisa, and Mark's adventures, accomplishments, and challenges usual to every family—I think. *Julie Ann* played some school volleyball and basketball, as I recall, and I still have these memories, Julie.

Lisa Dawn would become her big sister Julie's loving little sister. Mark nicknamed Julie "Hister-Goolie". If these two weren't playfully squabbling, one was asleep or not at home. Young girls are like that, and I suppose it's training for motherhood.

Lisa also played school basketball and volleyball at Moss Bluff Middle School and Cedar Bluff Middle School in West Knoxville. As soon as high school was finished, she married her sweetheart, Tim.

Mark Edward was *"the"* (pronounced with a long *e*, rhymes with *me*) adventuresome child. He once brought home an empty RPG launcher in 1983. You read that correctly! No grenade present, just a green tube with a handle. Mom nearly had that proverbial cow. I tried explaining that the thing wasn't dangerous, but she'd not hear another word. I think Bubba LaBleau (spelling?) had some involvement. He and Mark were friends in Lake Charles, Louisiana. We had moved from Knoxville and a Cincinnati suburb. After Lake Charles, we moved to Pelham, Alabama. We moved around because I followed what my company told me to do. It was not voluntary.

Mark and I hiked through Shiloh Park in Tennessee, and on another adventure, we hiked up Cheaha Mountain State Park in Talladega, Alabama. We camped overnight in tents at Mammoth Cave in Kentucky. He was always an explorer and attended an advanced class called SPARKS in Moss Bluff, Louisiana.

Mark went on to become a VW enthusiast. Other incidents and accidents were his first helicopter ride, post-skateboard mishap, his T-ball experience, and our entire clan's trip to Disneyland in Florida in 1977, if memory serves. Along that line, I was the family photographer. My children's mother has all the photos, and I have a precious few of them.

1975

Thinking of Bertha and Ammon Carr, Heather's maternal grandparents, allows me to recall memories from a Chicago watch factory. Mr. Carr was an inveterate tinkerer, bar none! They lived near the Westclock factory and, separately, a Whitman's (chocolate) candy plant. There were always secondhand candies and repaired alarm clocks to be handed out as treats. I preferred the former items!

In his own words, he was "an alley picker," and his retirement was spent building and refurbishing things that he kept in his cozy basement workshop. He had drawers full of clock parts, small motors, cords, blocks and wood, glue, tools, etc. He also had a few bicycle castoffs from kids wrecking them or parents not wanting them anymore. Nothing he picked was wasted. It was made like new and given away. Sometimes he created different things in his busy little private factory. I remember once he made a box about eighteen inches square, the sides of which were louvered wood strips with a small electric motor inside this box. Ammon had constructed a small engine which used a small fan, which he then attached to the motor shaft. He had a quiet and small, as well as efficient, air cooler for his shop. The air did not blow on him or his work area. The air moved up and then from lower to higher, where the cooler air naturally settled. Free. And genius!

Then came his workshop's demise. The clock company caught wind of his hobby and crushed all their unneeded clocks! *Time's up!*

I remember hearing that he was taking various pills, like I am now in 2022, when he died. When I learned about that, I thought it frightful to need so many pills. Now at seventy-five plus, I take about five every day. Bertha found him in his room before dinner, having passed away peacefully, taking a nap (I think). I also remember her going to the bank and closing the joint checking account the next day before anyone knew he'd passed away. A bit sneaky, but legal…

Early 1976

Based on my phone call (I mentioned earlier), I worked as a contract telephone engineer in Sweetwater, Tennessee, for Burnup & Sims. My coworker was an older (sixty-plus-years-old, and I was a mere child of thirty) contract employee who went nuts, and I started smoking again. (I apologize for forgetting his name!) He went outside to smoke, but before he came back into the office, something in his mind went *snap*! Another employee and I helped him out of traffic and moved him toward the office building we worked in. He was mumbling and making no sense. "Who am I? What am I doing here in this town?"

We packed him into a car and drove him half a mile to the local hospital. I heard through the grapevine he had had a complete mental collapse and was off work for six to nine months. Poor bloke! But the telephone engineering/design work was tedious and mind-twisting. Telephone engineering was not rocket science, but it was bland, sort of like three-dimensional chess using numbers, not game pieces. It was all in your head!

This was the year when Mark broke his leg just as he was beginning to walk. The grass was wet and tall. Lisa slipped while carrying him, as I remember, back into our rental house, on Cessna Road, for dinner. He was, and still is, a free spirit! And Lisa is a sweet and caring girl! She'll always be a girl, not an older person, even though she's a grandma by the date she's reading this! *Wow* is my thought now that having children who are grandparents' makes one feel almost old... but *proud*! She will never forgive herself for helping her mom round up her little brother and then watch him hobble around with a leg cast up to his knee!

I left the contract engineering world, and my career began afresh this year. I finally had the job title of Engineer. JD (Jefferson Davis) Creel was the big boss. My friend Bill Schrader was a telco employee (my entire phone company career ended up as a twenty-two year adventure) and must have told his boss, JD, about me, and I became a salaried management employee! "The third time was a charm!" We moved to Tennessee a year later and would stay in the south, even as I type this. I began to listen to country music and joined a Baptist church. I was entering my thirties. We had our second chance to sign a mortgage.

This telephone work would have me sent to Louisiana, Alabama, and Kentucky. My kids liked/hated this, but they now have friends from several states. My lovely wife, Sheila, has three grown children and three grandchildren and a great-granddaughter living in Maryland with a Navy father! I have a son in Ohio and two grandsons, a daughter in Kentucky, a granddaughter and great-grandson in Alabama, and a grandson who moved to California. Life is full of additions, changes, and corrections as we get older. I had a twenty-two-year-long career with Ma Bell, a.k.a. the Bell System. I'm now seven years into my retirement, as I type. My story goes back long before this event and a few years before I received this bronze trinket marking the official breakup and end to the Bell System! (See <<p. 168>>.)

Remember, I began my telco career in 1970, immediately after leaving the USAF. By 1976, I was a non-degreed outside plant engineer in management. I was still going to night school. I designed cable distribution networks to handle the growth of subscribers (customers) in the rural parts of the American South. We signed our second mortgage, a mortgage without government assistance! A proud feeling.

THOMAS E. BYRON

May 1976

I worked in Sweetwater, Tennessee, where the PSC (Public Service Commission) ordered the phone company to discontinue all eight-party telephone services. With this shared service, one telephone cable pair had eight customers on that line. Only one telephone could be used at a time. Allowing everyone to have a single cable pair for their telephone meant we needed to provide eight more cable pairs to allow one cable pair for each customer. A private line! That meant that more cables needed to be engineered and put into service. This, in the past, was what was referred to as a party line. It was two, four, eight, and I had a ten-party line phone (1619J) when I was a lad of seven.

How was this work done to provide everyone with a single-party telephone? Tediously and rapidly. Tens of millions of dollars were invested as well! Here's a brief explanation of my tech engineering job:

1. Use a very detailed county map.
2. Overlay the service area boundary from the tariff books on this map. Each exchange (area code-338-XXXX exchange telephone number).
3. Overlay our telephone cables from the engineering maps of our lines and the cable wiring information. As an entry-level clerk at Cincinnati Bell (1970) I was a drafting clerk and updated these plats/large drawings.
4. Using this map, get in a car and drive every road to the end. Count every dwelling—trailer, house, apartment—and then add them up by route.
5. You can see i.e. fifty-seven customers along a route, so you need a large table for everyone's cable pair. *"No sharing cable pairs like party line service."*
6. Cables come in incremental sizes: 25 pairs, 50, 100...and more significant for core routes 100, 200, 400, 600, and 900.
7. Then it starts to get complicated:
    a) Cables have transmission factors in six-thousand-feet lengths which must have inductance added to a resistive cable. It gets messy, and that will suffice for here. They

are called load coils and refine which cable pair can be used.
- b) Cables then have to be installed aerially on poles, new or added to power company poles, and required private property owners' permission (more permits and person-to-person negotiations).
8. Then while we were doing all this, the main switching office (Central Office) was being rebuilt to handle the additional cables and newer type switching required by the Public Service Commission. The older offices were outdated by decades and couldn't provide all the latest service offerings.
9. After a few years, my work was completed, and then I went from Sweetwater to Sneedville and finally to Newport, Tennessee. This was a *memorable* part of my career to work on upgrading telephone service to Eastern Tennessee! It happened a few times in different areas, it was not just a one-off event.

August 1976

It was a summer afternoon in East Tennessee. Hot. I was twenty-nine. My job involved a long commute covering many miles of open interstate highway. Boring. Tiring.

I needed better transportation and required a decent car to get me to and from work six days a week. I bought, and *rebuilt the engine,* in the vehicle I purchased from my neighbor, Jim Haynes. Much cheaper than a new car or a used car lot purchase. And as I mentioned, I worked forty miles from home and had little free time. In Tennessee, there are two rules for drivers that apply: (1) new drivers have ninety days to get a Tennessee driver's license, and (2) a car has to have Tennessee tags within sixty days. Failure to comply with either of these can get a fine and a ticket by the police.

I try to obey the laws, and I am obsessively attentive to details to avoid getting in trouble. I had my Tennessee Driver's Brochure actually and literally on the front seat of the car for reference and as a reminder to pay the fees and be a legal Tennessee driver. Great! I was also twenty-nine. *Arrogant* or *assertive* is a better word.

Anyway, here I was, driving home from work on an empty interstate, and since I spent so much time on the road, perhaps I got a little cranky. If there were *any* way to shorten my driving time, legally, I was in favor of that. It was a summer afternoon. It was not dark for a few more hours.

Noticing a Tennessee State Trooper passing me and seeing no lights and siren, I realized my 60 mph (limit) found me slowly but noticeably falling behind him more and more as we drove along I-75 NB.

What did I do?

I decided he was a cop. An example. He surely must be obeying the law (as he sees it). *Fine*. So I decided to pick it up a little and stay the appropriate distance. I did. For several miles, I was cruising along at 75–80+ mph, not sure because I was keeping up in traffic, of which there was none, or this wouldn't have happened how it did.

Since the traffic consisted of him and me, there was no one anywhere around in either direction. After a while, he slowed down, so naturally, I slowed down. I was now in front of him, at a legal speed, and he turned on his blue lights and flashed his headlights at me. *What?* We both pulled over correctly and politely. I handed him my valid Ohio driver's license.

"How fast were you going," he asked tersely. "Where did you get this car?" he snapped at me again. He must have been about twenty-six, and he might have even been thinking about his first service anniversary with the THP, coming up in six to nine months (I am wondering). He asked me, "Do you *know* your Ohio driver's license is not good?"

Okay, I was wondering what was up here. I explained to him that Jim Haynes was my neighbor from Cessna Road (where Mark broke his leg), and I had recently bought the car (a pale blue Chevy Vega station wagon). They were his tags on the vehicle and in the database the officer just looked up.

Now I realize that since Tennessee had front/back tags, while I was cruising behind him, he had run my tags and knew who the car was registered to.

"You have thirty days to transfer those *tags*!"

I was stunned. I knew he was wrong, but he was the law. I politely told him the handbook said otherwise. I pointed toward the manual on the front seat. No reply.

"You have sixty days to get a Tennessee driver's license! Do you know how fast you were going?" he asked again.

"No, sir, I do not know," I said calmly. It was followed by "I was just following you." (Hell, I knew I was *way* over the limit.)

No reply from the trooper.

I added, "And I have ninety days to get a Tennessee license. The booklet says—"

He cut me off. "I don't need to see that *manual! Here!*" He handed me my license. "*Have a safe afternoon!*"

No ticket.

Did I convince a cop that I was not speeding and he was the guilty one? That's *ridiculous*! But it is also a true story!

Winter '76/'77

I remember Earl B. (the last name omitted to protect his reputation, but it's a color) jumping out of his truck and pointing his .38 revolver at me! I was terrified. I was also a little drunk. Let's look at that in the sequence of events as they happened. Earl was *way* more intoxicated than I was! I was *nearly* sober.

Earl and I decided to go to a pool hall and have a few beers. Earl had met two young ladies at our hotel lobby, and they asked him if we wanted to go shoot pool and drink a few beers. Why not?

It was a *cold* winter night. It was late. We had to be at work at 7:00 a.m. Why not go out and have a beer? We were in our youth, forty years ago, when all of this happened.

We said, "Why not let one of you ladies drive? We don't live around here." We rode in the back seat of this bug, and in about fifteen minutes, we were literally in the middle of nowhere! There was a bar along this country road. An illegal bar since Cocke County Tennessee is dry. (Alcohol is not legally sold.) Woods all around. No streetlights. In the middle of nowhere!

As I recall entering the bar, a young man was seated on a bar stool and playing an air-drum near the front door. The music was loud behind him as he sat alone, playing his air drum with the music he was enjoying. It was indeed interesting, mmm?

What a place! Jam-packed. The smell of cheap perfume, smoke (cigarettes and weed?), and the aroma of spilled beer filled my nose. I got accustomed to the light, and with beers in hand, Earl and I shot pool for a while.

How many "whiles," I do not know, not all these years later, and not *then* for sure. But we had a good time and a few beers to drink.

"We need to get up at six a.m. and go to work," I told the young lady. Her name is lost to history.

She said, "I need to finish this game of pool I'm in, and then we can go."

I told Earl, who didn't care. The ladies didn't care. I just smoked another cigarette and ordered another beer.

Somewhere around 2:00 a.m. or 3:00 a.m., we pestered our ladies, with whom we spent very little time, or none, to be more precise. "We need to go." She handed me her car keys.

Now it was game on. My first and only VW experience began. "I'll bring your car right back after we drive back to the hotel, get Earl's truck, and come back here with your VW. Okay?"

It was an uneventful but slow trip back to our hotel. It was still snowing, and there were a few inches of snow on the roads. A dark and lonely two-lane windy country road. They wouldn't be plowed, but the sun would clear them in two days.

I was chosen as the designated driver by my *much* more drunken friend Earl. He didn't know I had never driven a front-wheel VW bug. Why scare him? He was drunk enough for both of us! It was dark. It was snowing. *Oh, what a night!* That's an old rock 'n' roll song by the Dells, I think. (https://youtu.be/Z1ozQT8yQXA).

Only a few miles to go.

We arrived safely(?) at the hotel. I had figured out how to drive this small gadget that I had previously seen only when I passed one on the road.

It was now sometime around 3:00 am. It was still snowing. Still dark. I was still a *bit* drunk. It was a short trip back to the bar, and I wonder if I can find it again. I could still see it today if I wanted to because my engineering taught me to be a visual person. But Earl got in his truck, and I got into our borrowed bug, and we headed out into the dark, cold, and wintery night.

About halfway there, Earl, being the drunk-mother-trucker he was, began swerving a bit more than the last mile or so than before. I was sobering up. Before I realized what was going on, Earl stopped dead in the middle of nowhere! In the middle of the —— road! I was right behind him. Not for long, though. I ran directly "slap-ass" into the rear of his truck with her VW. It was a slow-motion event (2–3 mph). It hardly jolted me as I gently hit him.

The next instant, as I got out of her car and he got out of *his* truck, I realized how drunk he *really* was! He turned around as he stepped out of his car into the dark and saw a driver standing there. Wait for it... Earl pulled out his .38 and (aimed?) pointed it at me and yelled something, probably obscene! He didn't realize that I was following *him*!

No shot was fired. We delivered the VW back to its rightful owner. A slight minor dent on the front bumper was her reminder that she had been asked several times to take us back to our hotel. She never even noticed it the next time she drove to her job. She was a pool shooting schoolteacher who owned a VW Beetle, and she let me drive it the first and still the only time I had ever driven a VW Beetle.

February 1977

I drove to my introductory engineer training class from Knoxville, Tennessee, to Birmingham, Alabama. It was wintery, and *it was* cold! There was just enough snow to make the trip several hours longer than usual and very tense!

When I got out of the car, I could hardly stand up! *My back!* I had severe lower back pain. I went to a chiropractor in Birmingham and got limited relief. When the class was over, after two weeks, I wasn't much better than when I arrived. More chiropractic work in Knoxville and some electric shock treatments did not work.

My friend at our church was an orthopedic surgeon, Dr. Gilbert W. Pratt. He could do my surgery. Wow, finally some relief, but that also came with some problems.

Heather and I had realized that since our free insurance didn't become effective for ninety days after I hired in, I was (we were all 5 of us young and uninsured)…but I was fortunate. Dr. Pratt would allow me to pay cash over a one-year repayment schedule. After my surgery, when I finished my last sixty-day follow-up visit, the good doctor gave me my bill and said, "Give this to the receptionist on your way out. Good luck, and remember the exercises I told you about."

I gave the bill to the young lady as directed, and as she looked at the details, she was shocked! "Where'd you get this bill?"

I replied, "Dr. Pratt said this was my bill! Why?" It seemed that he charged me his fee only, not the insurance rate! Years later, I heard Rush Limbaugh talking about this kind of payment when he had a heart attack. After his treatment and after being released from the hospital, he handed them his MasterCard. "Put my bill on this card. Thank you." It was a lot less than if he'd paid for insurance policy premiums and then paid his deductible. When I heard that, I recalled my experience in Knoxville.

A week or so later, I bought a ten-speed bike at JC Penney's and rode the one-mile trip home, per my doctor's orders. I suppose my wife, Heather, drove the car home. Dutifully, I would go on a one-mile evening bike ride. Every evening that I didn't have night school. I was feeling great. It's now been forty-two years, and my back *still* feels excellent. All he did was remove a blown-out disk, no fusion. A small scar and some nerve damage, with minor numbing, including the skin on the outside of my right leg. It's still like that as I write…but I do not notice unless I think/write about it. [I fell on my face in a 2021 stress test on a treadmill. See 2021 about this.]

The exercise would strengthen my back muscles and help me heal. The last bike ride of my life occurred a few months into my routine practice to enhance my aching back!

I always went out from our house situated on a short cul-de-sac, and made a left turn, down the hill, and eventually left and uphill for a while, then two lefts and home. Fifteen minutes, I think. That pretty much comprised a small part of our nice suburban Crestwood Hills subdivision.

Not this evening. I turned left and started down the hill. (see P. 176)

Some unknown time had just elapsed. I was unconscious from impact, getting an ambulance ride, getting into the hospital, etc.!

I woke up in a strange room, on a small and narrow bed. I had no idea what, where, and why. Huh? When I opened my eyes, my friend from church, Alan Parker, attorney-at-law, was at my bedside, waiting for me to wake up.

"What happened?" was all I wanted to know. "Where's my wife?"

Alan said, "I'll handle this if you'd like." He did, and when the case was over, I had won! My neck still makes crunchy sounds when I turn my head.

Alan told me a dog was sitting on his owner's front steps, blocked by shrubbery from my view, as I went 25 mph down the hill. The dog broke free (was let go) from his master and ran out into the road and hit (attacked) my bike. Disaster. He attacked the front wheel of my bike as if it were his enemy. Centrifugal force stepped in and kept me moving, but not the bicycle. It stopped upon being attacked! The bike and I parted company, and just like Icarus[5], I came crashing down, with my

---

[5] Icarus, Greek mythology

arms useless and limp by my side, as I soared upward toward the setting evening sun. The landing was not artfully done. No hands, dead man landing... on my face. My arms were useless and akimbo, and it was the closest I've ever examined asphalt pavement!

A few weeks later, I received a check from my attorney.

I had a grand time with the local salesman at Reeder Chevrolet. We haggled over the price of our new car for several days. With three kids, we definitely needed a larger car! After many phone calls, a deal was struck! *Gadzooks*, I surely hate car salespeople!

After we settled on the price for the brand-new car, I was asked, "How would you like to finance this?"

My last words were "Will you take a check for the total here?" as I pointed to the figure on a piece of paper between us.

Was he mad? Nope... he was *furious!!* No financing kickback check from GMAC (the financing arm of GM). It was an excellent brand-new '78 Caprice station wagon for the five of us! I love lawyers and a fresh car smell. I loathe used car salesmen. They remind me of the movie *Jaws*. They circulate on the lot, looking for victims and unsuspecting meals... I mean people!

Later this year (or my best guess, anyway), my sister Judy mailed me a Cheap Trick cassette tape from Cris and Stephanie. The year 1978 is my best estimate. I still have that tape! The music was making her crazy, and I know this because I remember her being a jazz fan. John Coltrane and Thelonious Monk come to mind.

Look! A Gorilla!"
The Story

It was later this summer: "*Look*! A gorilla!"

With my three-year-old son, Mark, in tow on my left hand, we're walking across a parking lot. It was a *hot* summer day. I had been told by "She Who Must Be Obeyed" to quote Rumpole's name for his wife, Hilda, go to the store and pick up some "Vim". "Vim" was the pseudonym for some "useless" household product, so far as I know. He was in tow on my left hand as we made our way across a forever-long parking lot of car after car. We were on a mission to purchase some critical supplies! The car in my story here was an old beater truck. Nondescript. Just as we were right opposite that truck, the driver must have been sitting there for a long enough time, probably waiting on *his* wife to do *her* shopping for "widgets and thingamabobs". He was blankly staring at the windshield from inside his hot truck. My young Mark saw a "gorilla" in his mind, and being surprised to see such an actual beast in person, right there a foot from him, he was proud to tell me such! "Look, a *gorilla!*"

It wasn't a gorilla sitting in a truck, having escaped from a local circus. It was the blackest man he, or I, had ever seen! Mortification immediately set in. My feet went as fast as his little feet could go to keep up with me! We went across the parking lot, hoping to blend into the confusion of cars, people, and shopping carts. Immediately! Aaaah, lovely darling children and their ability to speak aloud precisely what's inside their little brains. Aaaaah, my youth and knowledge to walk superfast and not have a heart attack.

Kids are both a joy and unique little creations! I imagine this fellow in the truck laughed if he heard this kid. He did, or he was a deaf-mute. No time for mental debate. Get in the store. *Get in the store*! Do not look back. Do not act scared. And yes, I've reminded that young son of mine, Mark, as the years passed. He's now well past forty years of age.

Elvis died on 16 August 1977. A tragedy had just occurred in Memphis. Ten years later, the love of my life is a (the?) *number one Elvis fan*! I was at a local bar in Newport, Tennessee, Gene and Polly's Supper Club, after work with a few coworkers. I was in the parking lot of that local bar after work, standing around smoking and chatting. Someone had a (car?) radio on, and I heard the answer to what would become a common question: "Where were you when Elvis died?"

The other question was already famous: "Where were you when JFK died?" I was in last period shop class back in 1963, as I've already mentioned.

I may be writing about this next event in the wrong year, but it was around this year that I was assigned Spring City, Tennessee, as part of my engineering territory. I never worked as a telco engineer in an urban area. Watts Bar Nuclear Plant was under construction on the Tennessee River. I spent some time in and around this area. Being assigned to work on telephone service to a power plant was blasé *but* very exciting since it was nuclear. Part of my design area for telephone cables resulted in my entry into the reactor core area of the plant. Aside: one could reasonably assume a phone line in an emergency nuclear power plant would be "mission critical!" It was. As I measured and made construction/design notes and plans, I made mental notes. All these decades later, I can still visualize that room. The uranium-filled control rods would be lowered into the water-filled tubes. The reactor core, dry when I was there, would soon create heat that would produce steam to spin the turbine generators. In an emergency, and an overheated reactor, the method to combat this was simple. In a separate building immediately adjacent to the core was a continuously replenished room full of ice. There was a large (twenty-foot-diameter?) door that would automatically open, dumping tons of ice. That lowered the reactor core temperature and prevented a Chernobyl, Russia meltdown! I would be a telco engineer, not a nuclear engineer. Sorry if I misstated anything.

1978

This was during my engineering days, working with multiple counties. The following piece of history I experienced is interesting trivia and worth reading. The Melungeons (https://en.wikipedia.org/wiki/Melungeon?wprov=sfti1). These people were unusual because of their long-rumored ancestors. They mainly lived along Snake Hollow Road in Hancock County near Sneedville, Tennessee. I never confirmed it for myself, but I did make several engineering visits to that location. I can say many unusual people lived there, and they were very hesitant to talk with outsiders, and I was *very* much *the* outsider!

Summer, 1978

While we lived in West Knoxville, a friend asked if I wanted to go on a hot-air balloon ride. It would only cost me $100 for propane. As tight as our budget was, I had to decline. That explained the noise I heard one Saturday morning, a loud *whooshing* sound as my friend floated by our house in his balloon. He was about two hundred feet or less over me!

November 18, 1978. I vividly remember, all these decades later, staying up very late and watching the TV news about Jonestown, Guyana. It was sad, graphic, and tragic! I think I stayed up alone way past my 10:00 p.m. bedtime until 2:00 a.m. The news was shockingly brutal and unimaginable—even unfathomable! Then again, I have been a news junkie for a long time, even till this day!

Prelude to the Afternoon of a Fool?
(Alternate Claude Debussy Reference)

Location: Birmingham, Alabama
Place: Mustang Lounge (bar and pool room)
Date: 1978–1981 era

The Story

The joint was empty when we walked in, around late-thirty a.m. Let me back up twelve hours to what the instructor told the class I was in: "There is a nasty, rough, mean bar/pool hall. Don't go to the Mustang Lounge."

There were probably twenty-five to thirty young engineers in my classroom, and we were given the evening's instructions. We were told about some restaurants. This one was good, this one was within walking distance. We were all from out of town for this two-week class, which was helpful. Also, we were all in our late twenties to early thirties. His one last piece of advice about where not to go was necessary!

The question I heard from a nearby seat-mate was "Did you hear where that Mustang place was?" Someone remembered to ask about where not (haha!) to go. We were all youthful and obedient.

The Fateful Decision

It was a little hard to find the joint, but after driving my Mustang II, I got the four of us to where we were supposed to avoid. This was me back in that time. This was my car.

THOMAS E. BYRON

The Situation

Here we are, parked in a lot of my soon-to-be memorable Mustang Lounge. It was not busy, the parking lot was nearly empty, and there was the first mistake. We entered without considering if our instructions were correct. I first need to describe the (joint) facilities. There were three pool tables, two in the main entrance area and one in an L-shaped room off to our right. The atmosphere was stale cigarette smoke and old spilled beer. *Classy.* Someone asked about getting a beer. We weren't minors, but immediately, several significant, nondescript, troublemakers came around from the L-shaped area. They were very *mad!*

"What are *y'all* doin' here?" That was the beginning of the end of our visit to this establishment. Remember the scene in the *Blues Brothers* movie at Bob's Country Bunker? Beer bottles were being thrown at the band, and in this story, we were on the receiving end of this anger. *Splat! Smash! Clank!* The annoying sound of glass breaking. That's what we experienced. Briefly.

As if we had rehearsed our plan, we exited where we had just entered. Faster! A dead run, and we all dove into the car. *Start!* The engine was roaring to life as I was getting seated, and we were heading off the lot! I didn't make any long-term plan other than *exit*. Having done that, I planned on heading left, needing to cross any oncoming traffic. Check. Clear. Snap the wheel hard left to head back to our hotel.

Second Mistake

Being unfamiliar with this particular road, I didn't realize there was an eight-inch-high concrete lane barrier to separate traffic. *Bang! Whoomp!* I hit the barrier as I turned left and slid up and over the concrete. Before crossing the road completely, I had a brief airborne experience. *Thud!* Back on two wheels, bounce, then on all fours! Not looking in the rearview mirror. Not now! The drunks in the bar hadn't followed us, and I knew this because the initial sounds of beer bottles hitting the back of the car very hard had stopped.

Conclusion

Overall a decent evening. There was a little excitement, and I took the Mustang Lounge off my list of places to visit. My apologies to Claude Debussy. The title of this story is about a fool, not a faun. Some calming down exit music is needed to calm down a foolish driver! Names were omitted or forgotten to protect them and me.

Thus far, my first and only helicopter ride happened in Tennessee around this year. It was an afternoon I won't forget. What a way to spend a lunch hour! My engineering jobs took me to all places that needed a telephone line. It was interesting to end up at a small hangar in the country, as most of my area was very rural! After talking with this young telephone customer, and me thinking it was time to say goodbye and grab lunch at the who-knows-where restaurant, he said, "Ya wanna go for a short ride? I have to check out my repair work, and you're welcome to join me!"

"What?" I said to myself. I answered assuredly, "*Sure!*"

In a few minutes, I was buckled in, and he was firing up the (only one) engine. With a slowly building whir, we lifted off. We had no sooner lifted off and were a few hundred feet off the ground than he said, "Hold the stick right there in the middle!"

I did exactly what I was told, and he then took out a cigarette and lit it up. After he took control, I lit up. We flew at least a thousand feet in the air! It was great fun, and it wasn't quiet. The helicopter was a bubble-domed two-seater. Small.

He said, "We're going to head toward Gatlinburg." It was about thirty miles away. He said, when we got there, "I'm going to buzz my girlfriend's apartment swimming pool."

We did just that and were down to a few hundred feet. What a beautiful way to see the Smokey Mountains. We were back to his hangar shortly, and I didn't even use up my lunch hour.

1979

Around this time, we were members of West Knoxville Baptist Church. We went to Ridgecrest, North Carolina, for summer Bible school. A few highlights were hearing an organ recital and climbing Rattlesnake Mountain to watch the sunrise in the mountains! The organ recital was my introduction to Toccata Finale from Symphony No. 5 in F minor Op 42 No 1 by Charles Marie Widor. Excellent to hear it performed live in a vast auditorium seating five thousand.

There is nothing more refreshing than a brief hike up a mountain in the dark or a very, very early dawn hour. There were no photos taken, but I can still see the sun breaking through the mountain fog and mist. It will always be a unique event. Hiking isn't on my list of things to do anymore, but there will be another hike in Alabama and in Tennessee with Mark.

The following event did merit some photos and news articles—an exchange of letters and a brief bit of fame for our Ms. Julie.

ZERO TO SEVENTY-FIVE

This note made it to a high altitude along with the balloon. *Amazing!*

The note survived being in a tree.

The person who found it was a young person who had the nerve to reply. In today's world of 2021, this reply would probably never be made. Texting is preferable and less personal. We (in Tennessee) were amazed and dumbfounded to get a handwritten response. Our local newspaper agreed!

> December 21, 1979
>
> Dear Julie,
>
> One day me and my friend were walking in the woods. All of a sudden I saw a blue thing caught on a tree. I reached up and pulled down the balloon. I found the balloon on Dec. 10, 1979. I am surprised it came so far away. My name is Peter Steen and I live in Wayland, Mass. It is outside of Boston. I am 11 years old.
>
> Sincerely,
> Peter Steen

Julie Byron, 11, has a map that shows it's a long way to Wayland, Mass., but not too far for her balloon to have traveled. She has a letter from the person who found it to attest to that.

11-Year-Old's Balloon Sails to Massachusetts

When Julie Byron, 11, sent her department store give-away, helium-filled balloon up, up and away, it went way away.

Approximately 860 miles it sailed, from the Byron home at 8905 Barlow Circle to Wayland, Mass., near Boston.

Another 11-year-old, Peter Skeen, found it, a tattered piece of blue hanging from a tree, with the note, and name and address that Julie had attached.

Julie sent it on Veterans' Day, Nov. 12. On Christmas Eve, she received a letter, written on Mickey Mouse stationery.

"Dear Julie," the letter said. "One day me and my friend were walking in the woods. All of a sudden I saw a blue thing caught on a tree. I reached up and pulled down the balloon. I found the balloon on Dec. 10. I am surprised it came so far away. My name is Peter Skeen and I live in Wayland, Mass., outside of Boston. I am 11 years old."

Julie's father, Tom Byron, an engineer with South Central Bell, called Wayland and located Peter's parents, the Barton Skeens, to verify the letter.

Mrs. Skeen said the family received a Polaroid camera for Christmas and will send the Byrons a picture of Peter with the balloon.

Julie, a student at Cedar Bluff School, said she did not have any idea how far the balloon would go. She plans to write Peter a letter in return. They may become pen pals.

A National Weather Service spokesman said prevailing winds from the Knoxville area are eastward and that it is possible, but highly unusual, that a balloon would travel so far.

1980

I became interested in a local annexation battle in West Knoxville, Tennessee. I was a taxpaying citizen by then and decided to stand up politically for my rights and my neighbors' rights. I haven't sat down since! A current US Senator from Tennessee now but governor of Tennessee then, Lamar Alexander, wanted me to run for the state legislature. I was part of a political group that sued a significant city, Knoxville, and would win a multi-million dollar judgment in court. The adage "You can't fight city hall" *is not* true! My future-ex-wife at the time said I couldn't run. "Harrumph!" But I consented. Regrets? Not a lot about the political part of the decision, but I would probably not have gone on to meet my lovely second wife, sweet little Sheila. Life would have taken a different path.

My staff sergeant (my boss) experienced a tragedy in his family. I saw the horrible news on TV, and we hadn't spoken in a very long (20 years) time! I saw the headline in the newspaper about a military C-130 crash at Plattsburgh AFB, New York. His son died in that crash. (He was named a junior, so his name stood out.) It took me a long time to find my sergeant's name using an operator in the pre-internet era! I identified myself, much to his shock, and I expressed my sympathy for his son. We never mentioned his Vietnam duty or my jail duty.

Sometime around this year, I can only say that this happened, just not precisely when! My first wife and I (and someone else) attended a Tom Jones concert in an arena venue in Knoxville, Tennessee. We enjoyed the music, but the longer-term memory happened during his singing. The amount of underwear and keys were thrown on the stage was amazing. Unforgettable!

While we lived in Knoxville, Tennessee, there was a plan to host the World's Fair. It was a fatally flawed plan, as the area would eventually learn! The city planners needed a lot more money than was budgeted to do this. How was the money going to be raised? That was the problem. Citizens for Home Rule (CHR) was organized, and I was heavily involved. We spoke for the area homeowners who also didn't like this tax grab! I have always enjoyed civic involvement. CHR was a grassroots organization that arose spontaneously in West Knoxville, Tennessee. A lawsuit to stop the mayor of Knoxville, Randall J. Tyree, et al., from his city annexing twenty-three square miles of prime real estate in and around our Crestwood Hills Subdivision. Our Byron family and thousands of other like-minded suburbanites resided there and paid reasonable county taxes, no city taxes. Our homeowners' property taxes were projected to increase sharply, but our city fire and police services would not be enhanced. We were paying taxes for services we would never get! When we moved to Louisiana in 1982, they were gearing up for the 1984 World's Fair. We ultimately attended the Knoxville Fair, but not the Louisiana Fair!

As the community pressure increased, our tiny group began to pick up more and more supporters. We were getting noticed by the Tyree crowd! Eventually, as our group grew larger and louder; I was elected to a non-paid leadership role in our little group of rabble-rousers! This led me to be on a TV show called *Good Morning Knoxville*. It was an intimidating event. Fortunately, there was no way to record TV shows, so I've never seen the show. Those TV lights are *so* bright!

An aside here: This photograph was made around this year, and I must include this gem in my autobiography. Yes, Superman (Christopher Reeve) and my little sister Debbie holding her young son Ian! Debbie babysat for Superman's children. Pardon the interruption!

1981

The annexation battle in Knoxville, Tennessee, continued, and the construction of Randy Tyree's World's Fair did too. Randy was our illustrious mayor/PT Barnum. The "show will go on." He will "raise" the money wherever he finds it, or taxes us to get what Mayor Tyree thinks he needs. West Knoxville was where the money was, and obviously, that area was the exact twenty-three square miles for his annexation gold mine target! Our group raised $80,000 and hired a good lawyer. We exposed their scheme (if a Brit is reading this, I mean a scam, not a plan). We ended up in court, and we weren't annexed. Had we lost our war with our mayor, our taxes would have increased significantly, and our police and fire services would not have increased. *Citizens for Home Rule* (CHR) was a huge success.

Due to the above events and the construction boom expected to house the tourists, my telephone workload exploded, as if I weren't busy enough! The construction of inexpensive plywood motels in Pigeon Forge (twenty-eight miles from Knoxville) was one part of my service area. I was responsible for all telephone services requiring new engineering designs. I swore the rain was causing motels to sprout up everywhere! It was typically the tourist season that drew all the crowds and the lost non-locals, adding to the tourists for the World's Fair. The word *nightmare* was not much of an exaggeration.

By finishing this epic piece, I will express my opinions and share my life's adventures for posterity or maybe *prosperity*!

1982

Note: Some states use car tags for multi-years, and only a new sticker is added yearly (multi-year stickers in this case).

I worked for South Central Bell and was transferred to Lake Charles, Louisiana, with Jeff Salyer. Jeff taught me to rely on BDL! (blind dumb luck!) I swore that I was the surplus person; if they had just fired me, the company would have been better off. But I went where they needed me, or sent me to satisfy my existing cohorts. I never had enough time to ponder. Work was always at 100.0001 percent, and I just kept busy. Jeff and I worked in the same engineering office in Morristown, Tennessee. I was relocated several times. The Louisiana Purchase from the year 1803 is involved. It was referenced in the deed to the house my wife and I bought. We owned a piece of the Louisiana Purchase from 179 years earlier. I heard you just now saying, "What are you talking about?"

Here are the details, as noted on our property deed, of our new home in Calcasieu Parish. Louisiana is the only state in America that doesn't have counties. They have parishes, and they don't have county officials. They have police juries! You know them as city councils. As an aside here, several of our fifty states are commonwealths from our British roots. The French influence also runs deep. President Monroe signed and bought the Louisiana territory from the French in 1804 as the Louisiana Purchase. Next, the land was owned by the State of Louisiana. The parcel we purchased 179 years later had been sold to an oil exploration company, and then it was sold to a land developer when not enough oil was found. The land developer then sold a small section to a property developer who built the subdivision and then the home we bought from the first owner of our lot and home! That is five degrees of separation! From the French to us!

Our real estate salesman, David Shirley, told us, "You don't have to worry about hurricanes!" He said this in May. We moved in June and experienced a category one hurricane in September. No problem besides rain. But in our backyard, that played out in a swamp. It became a lake. Thankfully, it did not threaten our house.

In Lake Charles, across the street from my engineering office, there was a movie theater. During lunch hour, the lobby was open, but no movies were shown at noon. A few of us from work went there and played arcade games at lunch, and it became a habit. It was a great distraction from our engineering work! Galaga and Pac-Man, as well as Q-Bert, were available. It wasn't long before my name was locked in as "High Game," and I remained there for eighteen months! Those were indeed idyllic days! I ended up with cataracts a year later. Cause and effect? I don't know, but I have strong suspicions!

1983

Creole Nature Preserve Visit

We were on our way to Holly Beach, Louisiana, and we decided to stop off and see some local wildlife up close. Why we were going to Holly Beach, Louisiana, in 1983 with a population near zero? We could only have been to see the Gulf of Mexico. Who wouldn't want to see a nutria or two (visualize that varmint as a house-cat-sized rat!) or many wild alligators up close!

We parked in a large sandy parking lot next to a bayou and saw several people fishing with wooden poles and string using chicken parts as bait. They were crabbing but entertaining. They were actually unintentionally feeding the alligators. The alligators would eat the bait and sink slowly into the salty water. This was boring, so I went for a walkabout into a preserve area. Mom stayed with the children as I explored the preserve with the consent of a few sleeping alligators.

This would have been what would count as Louisiana cold winter weather in February, around seventy degrees. In cool temperatures, alligators bask in the sun and are very docile, as docile as gators can be. It wasn't too long until I stood right next to these primitive beasties! I gave it a gentle tap on the head and kept walking. It did not move! *I did!* I was correctly told those gators were not active in cool weather. That was accurate, *and* I was lucky. Do not attempt, as the gator you encounter may not have heard what I heard!

I also continued my night school education and enrolled at Lake Charles McNeese State University. Remember, once I start working on a goal, I don't give up easily, nor did the *Cowboys*, the moniker for the school spirit. That is the mantra that drove me to complete this ninety-thousand-plus-word autobiography explaining "who I was or who I am."

The Bell System, as I knew it, along with millions of other people, ceased to be. Its reincarnation was nothing like it was before now ('83) or since!

I can visualize the following extraordinary—unique—event one afternoon at work. One of the areas where I was responsible for telephone engineering work was at the Fort Polk army base. This was an hour's drive north of the office, and it was not on the map. As such, it was in the middle of nowhere. But that's a good place for the military to operate. Except, I've mentioned how hard the GIs work in the states. Not like they do in combat, but anyway, this was unique. I turned south after leaving the base and headed down US highway 171. There, in front of my little puny Ford Pinto, was an Army tank stopped in the middle of the road. Honking my horn wouldn't help! He wasn't moving. The ample (maybe a ton of steel?) metal tread had broken and splayed flat onto the roadway. Calling AAA road service wasn't going to help. They needed a flatbed trailer and a crane to lift this beast onto a trailer and haul the tank twenty miles back to the base! It wasn't like changing a flat. I never saw anything close to this before or since. Having been on that army base another time, looking for the place I was trying to find, I got lost! Much of the base is just piney woods, sand roads, and nothing—until the following sign looming larger than life. The poster was an interstate billboard size: CAUTION LIVE FIRE AREA.

Stop! Turn around! Go in the opposite (180 degrees) direction! The military does things like that. Best to obey the signs!

In a similar separate part of my telephone engineering and military encounters, I was frequently in the middle of nowhere. The road I was on this time was even more remote. I think it was a tree farm paper mill company area. The military liked to use this US highway to guide practice flying, low, fast, and straight! Very low! Very *fast*! This plane was about a hundred feet above me, traveling at least 300 mph! It passed me going in the opposite direction before I heard him. Memorably scary! It was an A-10 Warthog. I'm sure the pilot chuckled as he/she roared past me.

1984

Restoration of the Statue of Liberty began in 1984, and the project was completed in 1986. My aunt Grace (née Byron) Murtaugh and Lee Iacocca from Chrysler Corporation, et al worked on the restoration project of that famous statue. I know she had access to various Byron photographs to create historical images and visualization of New York City Harbor. I was proud to realize that a Byron was involved.

A BellSouth manager/supervisor, Diane Bledsoe (a.k.a. Beeno), came down to Cajun Country, a.k.a. Lake Charles, Louisiana, in May of 1984 to interview Jeff Salyer, and your humble writer, for yet another (the seventh, if you just started reading here) relocation assignment. It was to corporate headquarters in Birmingham. I was interviewed during a solar eclipse! This was an omen, only visible in my metaphorical rearview mirror. A few milestones happened in "B'ham" during my five years there. College graduation from my seventeen years of night school, a divorce, a murder-suicide, a second marriage, my two daughters' (Julie and Lisa) graduation from high school, and my younger daughter Lisa's wedding! We'll get to those events in a bit. I always get ahead of myself, don't I?

Back to my history. This was yet another job-related move, and if you're keeping track, here's how we got there:

1. USAF, KI Sawyer, Michigan-Erlanger, Kentucky
2. Erlanger, Kentucky, to Cincinnati, Ohio (for in-state tuition)
3. Cincinnati apartment to brand-new house in Cincinnati
4. Cincinnati to Knoxville, Tennessee, job transfer and rental house
5. Knoxville rental house to purchase a house
6. *Knoxville, Lake Charles, Louisiana*
7. Lake Charles, Louisiana, to Pelham, Alabama
8. Pelham, Alabama, to Grand Rivers, Kentucky

ZERO TO SEVENTY-FIVE

9. Grand Rivers, Kentucky, to Marietta, Georgia, from where this autobiography is laboriously being put together! I'm not movin' again!

My job in Lake Charles was quite interesting but short. Unfortunately, their economy is driven by a boom-bust-boom cycle due to the nature of the oil business there. We arrived during the end of a boom and left when the subsequent bust happened. As the Cajuns and the French say, "Laissez les bons temps rouler." Let the good times roll!

I had my first cataract surgery with Dr. LaCoste. Yes, I was *only* 38! I got cataracts from all those video games at lunch (remember Q-Bert?) in Lake Charles. I was able to drive again after a short rest and recovery period. As always in my engineering, I was the junior person transferred in and given the "crappy" service areas (telco term) as far from our office as possible. I never worked in the prominent places you might know. I had responsibility, engineering-wise, in towns with five hundred or smaller populations and businesses that didn't show up on most maps and had a lot of trailers moving in and out! People are moving their trailers (a.k.a. mobile homes) from park to park.

This year finds me still attending to the pursuit of my college education. It began in 1970, and I've not missed a quarter (I was not on semester hours). This year, I enrolled at McNeese State in Lake Charles, and I would only stay at this university for two years. Did I quit? Hell no! I got interviewed this year on the occasion of an annular solar eclipse! That's a total eclipse, but the entire face of the sun was not entirely blocked. An annular solar eclipse (https://en.wikipedia.org/wiki/Solar_eclipse_of_May_30,_1984?wprov=sfti1).

See the photo and details in the link above. In the summer of '84, we were on the move again. We headed north to Birmingham, Alabama. No, we weren't Gypsies. I follow my paycheck, and my employer wants me to go! Interestingly enough, there were people from all over BellSouth being transferred to headquarters. We will meet one exceptional employee soon, in addition to Jeff and myself.

As I remember those pre-internet days, it was easy to send a simple message globally. First, you both needed an acoustic coupler to send and receive simple notifications with a variety of tones. Second, you had to have your set up as described. Third, you would place your telephone handset on the coupler and dial the number like usual. You would hear a series of beeps and squeals, as your connection was established. (If you ever used dial-up internet in the previous millennia, it was that same sound.) Fourth, once connected, you could begin typing on the keyboard part of the coupler with your headset attached to transmit all of those beeps. The party across the Atlantic (Paris, France) in our actual trial would see a message typed on their screen. This was amazing back then! Of course, if either party here or there was on the phone, no connection was made! If you were online, in an internet call, the voice party calling you would get a busy signal.

My job was to determine a pricing structure (rate per minutes of use) that made sense and was reasonable *and* met the regulatory body's approval.

1985

I had now transferred all my college credits from Ohio Mechanics Institute to the University of Cincinnati, the University of Tennessee, then to McNeese State. Aside, there was talk that Thomas Edison had an association with this same school. Now I was at the University of Alabama Birmingham. Night school is a long process. *Do not try this at home!* I was currently enrolled at my final college on the journey I began decades earlier in Ohio. I think I ended up with well over two hundred credit hours!

1986

During a training class in northern New Jersey, five of us coworkers decided to visit New York City. Not my first visit, but a memorable visit. We all agreed to have dinner at Delmonico's before the play. I would be remiss if I failed to mention that my great-grand father Joseph dined there often! We had tickets for 8:00 p.m. The meal was divine, but perhaps it was due to me thinking about a predecessor having dined there many times (seventy-five years earlier, give or take a few years). For part of our day there, we saw a Broadway play, but that, as memorable as *Cats* was, does not compare to my first and only visit to the Twin Towers. Later, Sheila and I would see the towers' site at the memorial pool commemorating the 9/11 tragedy in May 2016.

A short cab ride from midtown down to lower Manhattan was fun. There were five of us, so we had to take two different cabs. The traffic was terrible, or average, depending on your perspective. NYC is a noisy, crowded place *all* the time. We separated and got into our separate cabs and got separated (rerouted) by traffic, and each cabbie's route was different. He wasn't using GPS back then, rather his years of driving all over this strange island. It was interesting that both cabs arrived within moments of each other at the WTC site. Both cabs took different twists and turns, and the fares were both the same, as we figured out. We all worked in the BellSouth Pricing Department and thought about life and it's strange details.

Entering the lobby of the World Trade Center was exciting. I love heights, *and* I'm terrified of them simultaneously. The fear amplifies the experience, and as I mentioned earlier, flying is fantastic, especially fast and high in a fighter jet or slow in an open cockpit biplane. Both are unforgettable!

The elevator that took visitors up to the observation deck was fast, and there was room for many people. You could set up a card table and sit around it playing a card game. It would need to be a short game since it didn't take long to feel your ride end and the doors open at "the top of the world" lobby!

I know you readers have been to areas with great views, but this visit will always be unique. There are two reasons—the nearness of the twin building, right across a 1,200 foot chasm viewable from the hundredth floor. But it gets worse. The viewing windows extended about two feet down below your feet with a standard railing to stop your nose from bumping against the window. You can imagine that this allows you to see almost to the ground from this vantage point. You can also see the twin building from the perspective of a bird flying past that building. To add to the thrill, if you stand still and focus on that neighboring skyscraper, you get the bonus sensation of motion, as you sway with the building you are in, moving side to side under your feet. Slowly but noticeable by about, guessing, six inches or so. Gently back and forth. Truly terrifying!

During this year, my last full year of night school, I had a friend from Amman, Jordan, named Muhammed Hadid. He said his father would hire me for a job there after graduation, to which I declined. But then I thought…mmm…exciting position. Too dangerous for my tastes. I said, "Thanks, but no thanks. I can't accept his offer."

Sometime this year, I hiked Cheaha Mountain, the highest point (2415 feet) in Alabama. It is near Talladega, Alabama. A little adventure with Mark was exhausting for a non-hiking forty-year-old smoking dad. Trying to keep up with a twelve-year-old boy was an adventure in itself! The trail was steep, and there were great views of the area below occasionally. It was heavily wooded but exciting. At the top, there was an old concrete block building. Unfinished? Finished and then abandoned? I don't know, but the view was lovely. You could see the Talladega racetrack. I didn't become a NASCAR fan until I married Sheila!

My son was always adding some excitement into my life. He was a very active youngster! One summer afternoon, around this period, Mark rode his bike in our Chandalar South, Pelham, Alabama, neighborhood. The main road through our subdivision was *very* steep. Something went seriously wrong on one of his trips down that road! He parted company with his bike, and after he was tended to by paramedics that a neighbor called, he was airlifted to a hospital in Birmingham. Scary times raising boys, but girls were nearly as difficult. In retrospect,

I had a severe bike wreck in 1977 in Knoxville, Tennessee. Like father, like son. Isn't that the old saw? (See pages 150, 151)

29 November 1986

To close out the year on an upbeat story, I met Tim Chapman. There is a "21–17" reference in my private notes (somewhere) that must be a Bama reference. Yes, I looked it up! It was, and it was a crushing defeat for every Bama football fan. Their arch-rival, Auburn, had recently won the Iron Bowl game. He married my daughter, Lisa Dawn, and turned my granddaughter Lauren into Bama fans! Rabid fans at that, but my Sheila turned me into a diehard/rabid UK Wildcat basketball fan! Sports will always reign supreme in the South, if you didn't know that!

Timothy Ray Chapman is an attractive young man. He is a salesman like his dad, Cecil. Heather and I met his dad and his wife, Linda, for a sit-down interview at the Chapman residence before their wedding. We must have passed the interview!

1987

On a hot afternoon, sitting on our screened-in back porch on July 22, I had to make a life-altering decision! It was time to go over the metaphorical Niagara Falls! Scary but survivable if you were very, *very* lucky! It had to be a drastic decision, since I had pondered and fretted over it for a *very* long time! In more ways than you could ever imagine! It was not a sudden decision. I had thought about what she'd say, which was "Okay!" not "What?" or "No way" or "Are you kidding me?"

I told Heather, "I want a divorce" as we sat on our back porch.

She immediately said, "My dad was planning on giving us $5M." (My best recollection, but it was a *lot* of money.) Not *"What?" or "Why?"*

I calmly replied, "And?" And then I knew it was over.

I didn't know that the rock I had just thrown into that pond would have such a widespread and rippling effect on so very many, many lives and families! It had to be said that I was only prepared for her anger. There was none! You should know she was not an emotional person to begin with. I was ready mentally for a fight! Nothing, was what I *hadn't* considered! In my decades of retrospect now, I shouldn't have been surprised. Providence changed that entire scene about five weeks later, at least as best as I can recollect. Divorce was the *only* thing on my mind. I was not prepared for the results of my decision!

There are life-altering times in all our lives. Some we understand immediately, while some we never understand. This event I'm about to relate to is both. The finality of it was sudden and extreme and was evident and immediate! This experience of mine has never been told widely and in public until now, as I write this, thirty-two years later. Some events are best left in the past, but a few other people should also know. Finally! They are my thoughts that have been locked up and kept in the darkest recesses. They are rarely even thought about, much less written about. On the date of this writing, the thirty-second anniversary of this epic failure which impacted many lives, I will write about them and place them in those days. They are a part of me, and they will always be the nadir of my life's experiences! The impact was both horrific and miraculous. It *was* life-altering!

As you, dear reader, and I have heard during our time here on this earth, there are good and bad things that happen to everyone. Some deserve them; some do not deserve them. There are heroes, and there are villains involved. There are angels and demons always present and walking among us, and they are at war with each other. We cannot see the battle in *that* realm, but we have heard about and seen the destruction those evil forces leave behind. The angels try to comfort us, and I know who the archangel is who rescued me from this pit that I would be cast into. Some know her as a mom, or later as Nannyshe, or Sheila, as I do. We don't usually see the work of angels, but I, along with a few others, have. This evil that I experienced is hidden from us by the demonic forces of evil. Those who witness it can sense these forces, and the lady in these two articles did. Sin took her away. I was there with her just moments before this event became public and in newsprint. I did not sense the depth of the sin!

ZERO TO SEVENTY-FIVE

Woman fatally shot in head in parking deck attack

Wife-slaying suspect apparently kills self

She sensed the danger. She never said anything. On this afternoon that would be her last, she said, "We need to leave here *now*!" *Here* being our BellSouth desk jobs. We left work and took the elevator down to the parking deck level. She walked to her car and I to mine. When and where we were going to meet was a blur. Much of that entire Tuesday was and will always remain a blurred memory. Or perhaps just buried as she is.

When I drove past her car, I saw that she was held at gunpoint. We did not make eye contact. I do not remember the exact sequence. I do remember the fear. It was palpable. I could taste it. The chaos! The raw emotions. Abject terror!

Then my next recollection was sitting on the garage's concrete floor, a hundred feet away. I saw the police! The paramedics! Many other people were unknown to me, standing and kneeling next to her car. I caught a glimpse of her lying on her back on the concrete with several paramedics tending to her. An angel most certainly kept me from seeing her face. No one came to me to ask me anything. Was that odd? I don't know... I had never been an intimate witness to a murder. Few of us are.

Eventually, I would be accompanied by someone (a cop, a priest, a stranger?) in my continuing state of near shock—an angel. I was helped to cross the street to buy another much-needed pack of cigarettes. He was an older Black man. He seemed to come out of nowhere. I was reflecting on this (that Black man), and I've not thought about this person for over twenty-five years. I walked out of the parking deck, oblivious to anything external. Did an angel appear in the form of an old Black man? He arose and then disappeared. Was I in shock? No one told me anything! That's the best I can do with recreating this event. I was baffled. No one asked me any questions. "Who are you? Are you all right? Do you want any water? Do you know that lady?" Nothing. I was in extreme panic, dazed, in shock, perhaps sitting on that cold concrete, leaning against a hard concrete wall.

Eventually, time went haywire. I got in my car and drove out of the garage. Dumb move. Where was the shooter? The wooden entrance gate to the parking deck was in splinters and scattered into the parking area. I went to the nearest hospital. I knew where the ambulance had taken her. Who told me? Did I ask? How I knew are forever lost. God only knows since he must have been driving my old gold-colored 1970 Maverick to the UAB Medical Center!

When I arrived at the ER desk, I asked about Mrs. Templin. I was pointed to a door leading to another smaller and more private area. My senses didn't say, "This is where the family is." Their collective look must have mirrored mine, and they immediately knew who I was. *I was the devil* to them!

I quickly and silently left the emergency waiting room and saw the horror on her family's faces, and I dove deeper into despair. Their collective voice was echoing in my head!

What are you doing here? GET OUT OF HERE! I thought to myself. But I was directed to this room. I gave someone the name I wanted to know about. My mind just shut down.

How I ended up at Tim and Lisa's apartment that evening and slept on their sofa, I don't know. Any other details are gone. I did get invited that weekend to stay with a coworker, at the lakeside home of Roger Frederickson and his wife, Arlene, near Birmingham. They took me in like a wounded animal. I was a total and absolute wreck. I remember watching *Top Gun* on his big-screen TV with surround sound. That was amazing. That was a distraction. That was just exactly what I needed.

I recall amid the aftermath of that September day. At some point, I was taken by telephone security to the twenty-eighth (top) floor of BellSouth Headquarters. I was debriefed and even allowed to smoke. Or, they didn't *stop* me... Questions and answers for about thirty minutes of my discussion of whats, whys, and whos. Somber. Scary. Horrible. Sad!

When did I return to work? No memory. I don't remember what sweet and recently divorced Sheila Brown thought about or discussed. It was significantly and warmly welcomed. She understood my soul. She understood me. She is still my archangel!

My second life began when I divorced (September 18), remarried (December 1), and I finally graduated from college (back in March 27 of '87). My oldest child, Julie, had graduated from high school, and her younger sister, Lisa, was married this year. Mark moved to Ohio with his mother and repeated this move between Ohio and Kentucky, back and forth. It can safely be said, and I do say, it was a year that divides my life into before and after, more precisely than a surgeon's sharpest scalpel!

Witnessing the murder of anyone, let alone someone that close to you, is ultra traumatic. It is not like the Hollywood depictions—*ever*! I don't talk about this because it is kept in the deepest reaches of my mind, like in a catacomb, there but rarely disturbed. It is a coping mechanism I learned from childhood. Partition and leave alone. Divide and conquer, if you will! Over the years, I did this to my childhood, and much has been locked away in a catacomb of my mind and irretrievable. Is that good? Is that bad? Do I want to find out? Sadly, our divorce date was made final on 8 September 1987. I'm sorry, Lisa.

Sheila and I were married on my uncle Clarence Francis's birthday, December 1. He was born in 1888, and we were married in 1987 on his ninety-ninth birthday.

Beer for Breakfast in Andalusia, Alabama

9 November 1987

The person reading this knows who they are, so you being that person, you are being asked not to divulge your secret and to remain anonymous. Your choice. It was an early morning trip to rescue you, and it was still evening for Sheila and me, so when we were finished with our rescue ($$$), we enjoyed a few road sodas on our way home! Glad to have helped, and "I felt obliged to include it in this autobiography. It is now the *perfect* autobiography!" H/t David Allan Cole (https://youtu.be/s4pZFsEdP3Y).

25 June 1988

Judith Ann Byron Olivieri married John Almond in Tucson, Arizona, poolside. It was around 120° in the shade but low humidity (that's the standard line about the *warm* weather). This part of America is a beautiful desert area and hot, but extremely dry. Very dry means little when it is 120° in the shade during the wedding it *was* friggin' *hot*! I was the photographer and took some snaps. In a few more years, I would be doing precisely that. Professional wedding photography. I was the photographer of record at 500 weddings!

During this visit, Sheila and I also took a day trip to Nogales, Mexico. Quaint, hot, and scary. Hot? Yep! We were lucky we found a vendor selling ice-cold Corona beer from a Coca-Cola display case now holding a beer! Refreshing does not adequately describe how great they tasted!

As we left Mexico, legally entering the United States at a border-controlled section, we were followed. Two guys (we never turned around to look at them) were behind us, asking us if we wanted to buy drugs or something that meant drugs. We were both too scared of becoming victims right there on the spot! We ignored them and walked fast, but not entirely running. We got to our car, about five miles away. Actually, it was a few hundred feet into the US! We drove away, without noise, posthaste! We will never go back. *Ever!*

Back home and later in November, we went to a UAB (my university) lecture and met the person the movie *Good Morning, Vietnam* was about. It was an exciting evening (https://en.wikipedia.org/wiki/Good_Morning,_Vietnam?wprov=sfti1).

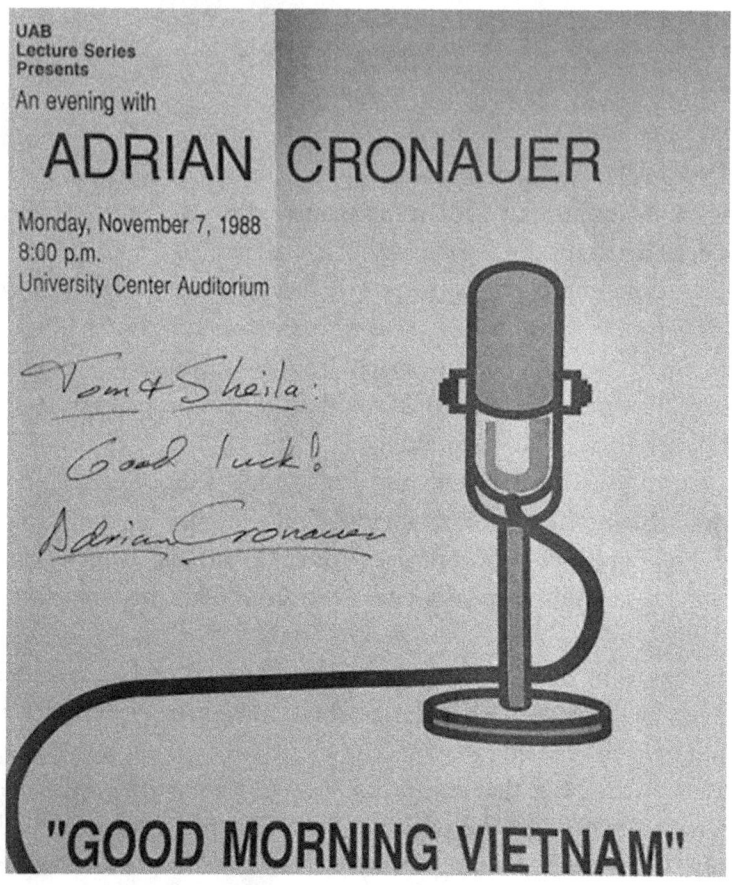

At another UAB-sponsored event, we met an American citizen who became that former Iranian hostage in Iran released after four hundred plus days as a hostage (https://www.history.com/topics/1970s/iran-hostage-crisis-video). It was interesting and educating to see and *meet* someone from an historic event in American history. The details are better explained in the link.

I remember a visit to Cincinnati, Ohio, in August of this year, the *eighth* precisely—8/8/88. At the same time, we were driving on *Eight* Mile Road along the Ohio River. We *ate* pizza for our dinner. At 8:00 p.m. Weird factoid and an insight into how strange my mind works.

1989

In June, we moved to Grand Rivers, Kentucky. Sheila and I got significant positions (jobs) in our new life. She was a business office supervisor, and I was an outside plant (telephone) engineer. We would never miss Birmingham (or Pelham, either). We were never city folk. What a significant change from the big cities we'd both been around and didn't much care for. It was a place where you could see the stars at night and listen to the local wildlife! Julie moved with us, and Mark moved in with us. But if the truth is told, they both preferred the city life. Mark ended up in Cincinnati, and Julie ended up in Atlanta and then Covington, Kentucky, across the Ohio River from her brother.

Several years later (15) in 2004, Sheila and I left Kentucky, and moved to Marietta, Georgia. When we got moved in and began to look around, we noticed our place was one block from where Julie used to live. One of those strange coincidences listed at the end of my life review!

My daily commute from Dover Road, Grand Rivers, to 305 S. Main Street, Madisonville, Kentucky, was sixty miles one way, every day, for three years. This assignment permanently set my biological clock to awaken at 5:00 a.m. CST. Since there were occasional snow emergencies, I set the standard for my coworkers ("locals" from Madisonville) promptness. I was never late, no matter what. I "let" the local coworkers show up late. I wasn't the boss. This always bugged me! But they *were* nice people to work with!

Once I arrived at my office, I typically (more likely than not) got into a company vehicle and spent all day driving as part of my engineering duties. My area of work responsibility (Muhlenberg County) was almost an hour's drive, on local two-lane roads, from my office. When I was in the office, I sketched out design plans for the construction people to install the cable type, where it went, and specific splicing of the wires. It is as tedious as it sounds! Otherwise, I drove a hundred miles to various small towns in Muhlenberg County. It was never dull.

In September, Mark, myself, and Sheila traveled to Frankfort, Kentucky. Among other places we saw was Daniel Boone's grave, overlooking the Frankfort River. This sundial points to each veteran's death in combat since the sun's inclination changes a little each day. Quite clever, if I do say so.

Vietnam Memorial Frankfort, Kentucky October 1989

© Byron

1990

In 1990, we saw where the Cherokee Indians had been led through Livingston County along the Trail of Tears, a natural rock formation called Mantle Rock, which sheltered their overnight westward journey. Also, near this spot, there is a small but stunning waterfall named Mandy Falls. The entire county is very rural and largely undeveloped. Quiet. Peaceful. No doubt, much like it always has been. And will always be.

How the West Was Won opening scenes were filmed in Smithland on the street leading up to the Buzzards Roost nearby. The opening scene of that adventure shows Smithland fixed up to include a nicely done recreation of dirt streets and appropriately aged for the early 1800s.

We did spend a lot of time exploring our new surroundings. Lucy Jefferson Lewis's (President Jefferson's sister) grave was up on a large hill (I have a photograph of that in my files. Specifically, Rattlesnake Hill, not a "mountain"). No sign pointing to it along the road then. We were told about it by locals, and then I hiked up the trail to see it. I even volunteered once to go caroling in Smithland. Or was it wassailing? A relaxing time could always be found sitting at the Buzzards Roost, watching the traffic on the Ohio River.

In 1992, during our Livingston County days, I was in a Christian movie produced and directed by Livingston County native Mr. Ish Teitloff. I was cast as an old-time photographer. I have the VHS tape for proof. I had no lines. I was merely a human cameraman prop! I placed my folding Ansco view camera on a tripod, and I looked like an old-time photographer! Completed with a black focusing cloth. I bought this Ansco camera at a flea market item in Smithland a few years earlier!

One afternoon, we were going to take the ferry across the Ohio River at Cave-In-Rock, Illinois. The date has been forgotten. There was an old-time river baptism taking place as we waited on the ferry across from our destination. It was the first and probably the last time we'll ever see that type of specific church service. Cave-In-Rock, Illinois, on the north side of the Ohio River, which was a robber's roost during the early 1800s. It is an exciting place to visit. The scenic view at the top of the bluff along Ohio in the river is alone worth the visit. The cave is filled with graffiti burned into the ceiling with torches. Around 1912, the Ohio River flooded as it rose to historic levels, and you could barely get a raft into the cave. But those that did, left historic black and sooty graffiti on the cave ceiling. I have an interesting photo of this cave in my collection.

A Few Road Trip Adventures

Here, I think, it is as good as any time to relate a collection of our many road trip adventures. It has been a habit of mine to explore places I've lived. How many, you ask? Ten states were called home in my long and winding life's journey. I have lived in Ohio as an adult and was born in Ohio, then moved to Pennsylvania, entered the military, and was in Illinois (briefly), Texas (for a few weeks of basic training/"schooling"), and Illinois (also a few months of hydraulics schooling). Michigan, over three years, exited the military (honorably discharged) and moved to Kentucky, in two towns and two different lives, Erlanger and Grand Rivers. Then to Tennessee, Louisiana, Alabama, and finally today in Georgia!

During my time stationed in Illinois, during my three months of Air Force Training at Chanute AFB, I was trained to be a hydraulic repairman. I took a weekend train trip adventure in July on "The City of New Orleans," the original Woody Guthrie song that named this train between New Orleans and Chicago. I met my first wife, Ms. Heather Ann Houston, on the Chicago subway. On a second excursion, I also visited Springfield, Illinois, and saw President Lincoln's tomb. Film and a camera weren't available then. Poor as a "church mouse" aptly describes my financial status, which it would be my status for decades. That's why there are no photographic memories of this period of my life. My parents met on public transportation, namely the Staten Island Ferry, sometime in the mid-thirties. Later, with Sheila, we rode the AMTRAK train, City of New Orleans, to *New Orleans, Louisiana*! The most lovely Southern City, but as I finish reviewing this autobiography, sadly I can say that New Orleans is currently the murder capitol of America. I met her son Blake on that trip. We had a wonderful meal at Antoine's.

A little more about traveling by train is added here since I love to travel by train. I do love to fly, as I mentioned already, but my second favorite way is by train. Back in 1986, I had a training class in New Jersey and chose to go by train, from Birmingham, Alabama, to New York City via AMTRAK. I had to prove to my superior that, since this was a company-paid trip, the costs were nearly the same for train or plane. Being convinced and simultaneously confused, he approved my voucher. It would be my unique visit to the World Trade Center and "the Top of the World" observation deck. Voilà! Memorable and very sad in retrospect. Sheila's son Jason lost a colleague, Sullivan, on 9/11. Her grandson William Sullivan Adams carries that name!

When Sheila and I moved to Kentucky in 1989, and stayed there for fifteen years (thus far), we made many road trips. I've figured out that that's always a good idea when you move to a new place. You should check out the local attractions and I've never regretted that habit. In no particular order or date, we went to Memphis a few times: Elvis's home, Graceland tours, Bad Bob's Vapors, a nightclub run by Elvis's horse veterinary doctor. We saw many Elvis impersonators in an annual contest at that nightclub. We did this at least three times, and we once went to Tupelo, Mississippi, on a side detour on our return home. Sheila met Patsy Presley once at Bad Bob's, and they had a long conversation, and they ended up moving to the lady's room lounge for a very long "girlie" chat. I took many photographs of the singers then, and had them developed overnight and returned with proofs and the best image as an 8"x10" the next night. That alone made enough to pay for our meals and refreshments.

Patsy and Elvis were double first cousins. (https://familypedia.wikia.org/wiki/Double_first_cousin)

Elvis's father, Vernon, married Gladys Love Smith, and Vernon's brother married Gladys' sister. Two brothers and two sisters from two different families married brothers and sisters from another family. It sounds odd because it is also legal *and* acceptable. It's just hard to explain!

On another one of our road trip adventures, we visited two *real* places: Mummie, Kentucky, that only had a Baptist church, and Egypt, Kentucky, which was on the map but with nothing there anymore. On a separate trip to far west Kentucky, we went to Monkeys Eyebrow, and the only building there was a TV antenna tower. Separately, we visited the famous Moonbow waterfall. A moonbow is a rainbow, but only when a full moon is seen from this waterfall. Unusual but beautiful.

We had heard about a rather unusual restaurant, and it wasn't that far away. We headed out for breakfast one morning but didn't realize it would be *very* memorable. We still have our two souvenir coffee or iced tea mugs: *Lambert's Home of the Throwed Rolls, Sikeston, Missouri.* "Throwed" isn't a misspelling.

The first sign we had, that this was a very different but very popular place, happened before we entered this restaurant. A tour bus in the parking lot discharged forty or fifty senior citizens (we weren't elderly back then, not just yet). The menu and prices were easy—one price menu for "All you can eat." I can't remember what it was, but I can remember two things: worth it and still unforgettable. This memory was from 1990, more or less thirty years ago as I write these memories down.

The waiter traveled to each table with a pushcart loaded with your food: bacon, eggs, sausage, toast, grits, biscuits, pancakes, coffee, milk, etc. Like a mobile breakfast bar. Did I mention those yummy rolls?

If you ate the one from the waiter and wanted another one, they had that handled. You stood up by your table and got the attention of the "Roll Thrower". They would throw you one, and if the roll ain't caught, they "throwed" you another one. You would see it hit the floor, while also noticing many other rolls on the floor. They were eventually cleaned up and taken (I suspect to the trash, but maybe as food for hogs). The food was excellent, and the service was "hands up" fabulous!

We enjoy visiting weird places. There is a place, not that far from Lambert's Restaurant, in Kentucky but *not* accessible from within Kentucky. That's not a typo. We've been there, and we've seen the lone house surrounded by cornfields on all sides. https://en.wikipedia.org/wiki/1811%E2%80%931812_New_Madrid_earthquakes This event changed the Mississippi River's location.

Here's a map:

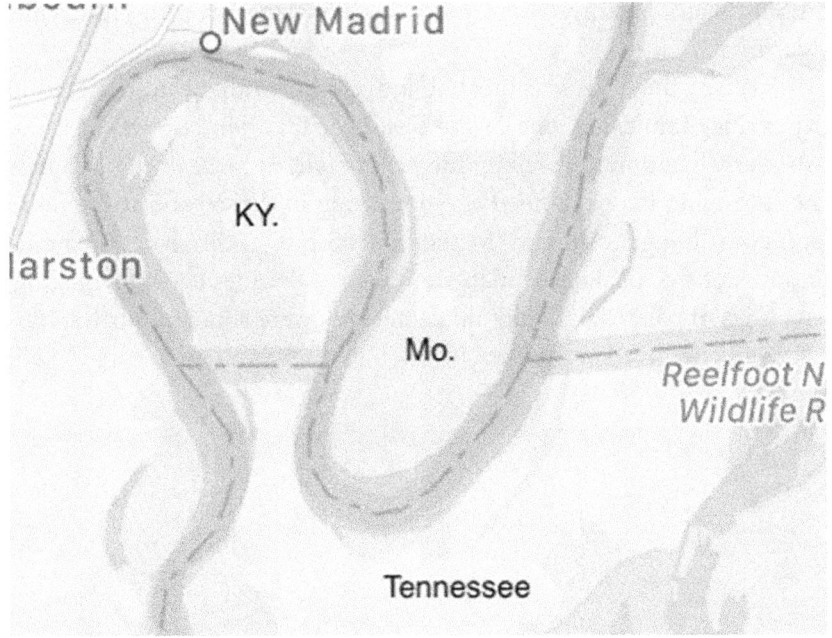

Kentucky LBL (Land between the Lakes) is a national recreation place nestled between the Cumberland River and the Tennessee River. When my first wife and I lived in Knoxville, that was the beginning (headwaters) of that river, where the Clinch River met the French Broad River. The Cumberland and Tennessee rivers empty into the Ohio River near Grand Rivers, Kentucky, and Ledbetter, Kentucky, a few miles downstream toward Paducah. The Tennessee River runs very close to Lisa's former home in Huntsville, Alabama. She later moved to Tuscaloosa and her daughter Lauren met and married her sweetheart there. My great-grandson Chapman lives there as well.

As an aside, and my references to rivers, consider the following. I was born in Cincinnati, Ohio, along the Ohio River. For a brief period, I lived in a Pittsburgh, Pennsylvania suburb, and that is the mouth of Ohio River. When we lived in Grand Rivers, Kentucky, many years later, that is very near the terminus of Ohio River. So what you say… when I lived in Knoxville, Tennessee, that was the mouth of the Tennessee

River, and a few miles west of Smithland, Kentucky, is the terminus of Ohio at the Mississippi River. The Cumberland River's terminus is also in Smithland. Lisa lived very near the Tennessee River in Huntsville, Alabama!

When the TVA was created and subsequently headquartered in Knoxville, Tennessee, one of the results of that flooding was to abolish every abandoned dwelling the people left, because of the two new lakes to build hydro dams. Everyone living in those soon-to-be flood areas was "bought out" and "forced out". Progress. Still a bad taste in the mouths of the local descendants in the area decades later! Picnicking, sightings of bald eagles, and old cemeteries were some of our wanderings while we lived in the area.

1991

Northern Boulevard, Tipperary Arms

Sadly, there *was* a marvelous Irish Pub, a gem in Queens, New York, that could just as well be in Dublin, Ireland! Breeda was the barmaid there, with a lovely Irish accent from Dublin. Charlie and Peggy were quite the senior regulars we got to know. (p.s.) We are now like those seniors from "the tip" in New York, now at *our* local pub.) They were pleasant folk who had reserved barstools at the end of the bar on your right as you enter the front door. We now seem to have our reserved afternoon table at our local bar. Some Irish music was the only music on the jukebox at that Queens pub. Children around three or four years old play on the floor where there are people nearby. We were fortunate to visit there twice, and then we found out it was sold and torn down. Sad! I should mention two other favorite bars in Marietta years later that were torn down. Los Bravos was removed for "growth," so we moved to the Rose and Crown. Five months later, it was demolished! In 2020, we located another watering hole, Delkwood Grill, formerly known as Bimbos, where my daughter Julie used to visit often when she lived in Marietta. Walking distance from where we now live as I type this. I have to add "as I type this" because I've always been moving. Fortunately, more moving is no longer much of a prospect.

Setup piece: There is a famous event in our family, here's that story about *"the Bessemer Salute"*, an Italian reference to placing your open hand, palm down, and then brushing your hand forward under your chin briskly.

The scene: After four or five hours on a sweltering July afternoon in Bessemer, Alabama, we had just attended an air show. I was sitting in the hot sun and enjoying the noise and the planes. I was hot. Did I mention that? Ninety degrees plus the ghastly humidity! We walked to our car and parked in a field with one thousand other people after the show ended. We were finding our car and getting in line to move to the dirt and gravel road, and it was hot! I already said that, but this is part of the story. When you get hot, you're *hot*! And cranky.

The story: My daughter Lisa was driving, and I was seated behind her with Sheila to my right and my son-in-law, Tim. We finally ended a long, long, tediously long line, and our driver was overheated, mad, and confused. Did I mention that we were all very overheated? The cop directing traffic had been out in the hot sun too, with no wind, no shade, directing traffic. He was a large fellow and was impatient with us. The cop got agitated, and as we were near him, he blew his whistle and barked an order to "GIT MOVIN'!"

As we proceeded cautiously into our left turn to go home (should we be making a left or a right turn was on our minds), the cop was behind me, waving his hands and yelling at us. We were merely driving too slow in his mind, and he didn't enjoy his assignment that day! I was sitting in the back seat, and I turned around. The time now would be mid-afternoon, in the Alabama heat, and Lisa said, loudly and upset, "What's that cop got his lights on for?" She slowed down and pulled over. She waited for a ticket or a chewing out. None of that. Watching all of this from the backseat, I gave him the soon-to-be-famous "Bessemer Salute" as she was stopping the car! (That would be your humble author/correspondent)

"You! GET OUT OF THE CAR! said the traffic cop to me, in the back seat.

"I'm not getting out. I'm not driving!" I said in a polite but low and pleasant voice.

He said, "OUT OF THE CAR! NOW!"

I explained that I was not going to get out. Lisa was as nervous as a w——e in church! "What's going on?" surely that was what he was wondering.

She later asked me, "What did you do?" She was sure I gave the cop the bird or something obscene, but he was bumfuzzled. She saw the gesture before but was confident the cop didn't like it.

After much jawing, he told us to get "*Outta* here!"

No ticket!

I explained this to Lisa as she closed the window and cranked up the AC. Did I mention it was hot? It was! He was! We were all *hot*!

1992

We decided to drive down to Florida and visit my parents in Ocala. The visit was okay, but it's not the memorable part of this home vignette. Before I leave this page, I should point out an interesting sidebar.

My parents moved from Florida to Vermont to be close to their daughter, my sister Debbie. Their Florida apartment, we visited briefly, was a mess. My father was a bit forgetful (dementia in both of them) at age seventy-eight. They were sorting out stuff to go in the dump, to be given to Salvation Army or Goodwill, but in and among these piles were two heavy brass bookends. I asked my father if it would be okay for me to have them. I became the owner of a beautiful set of very heavy bronze bookends with the scene of *The Gleaners* on each of them. Why do I give you readers so much detail on a pair of bookends? Because I recognized them from an old family photo (1935 era) taken in the Staten Island home me and Sheila and Patty visited and mentioned earlier here in my life's story.

Yes. We are strange. We decided not to take I-75 north (no comments, please) on our return trip. We chose the local two-lane road that ran parallel to the interstate (sort of) US Hwy. 41. We followed it north through Atlanta, Georgia. And finally, in Nashville, Tennessee, we lost signs for US 41 North. After scrabbling around and generally wasting time *and* patience, we found US 41 and headed north to Ft. Campbell and the Kentucky area. Now one more oddity to US Hwy. 41. If one were to continue traveling north, you'd get to Madisonville, Kentucky. And then after another one (?) thousand, you'd end up in Marquette, Michigan. Unless you are skimming around in this autobiography, you missed that tidbit. I was stationed a few miles off US Hwy. 41. It was an exciting experience! Then twenty years later, I had a telco job placing me off US 41.

The last legal hanging in Kentucky was seen by my friend Robert Rayburn. My unusually quirky friend in Smithland, Kentucky, told me around this year about how he and his friends spent one memorable night, that being the night before a high-profile verdict of murder was carried out. I was visiting him and his wife, Mercedes, at their Ohio Riverfront home. Many years back, he related it as if it had happened last week. In 1935 (then sixty plus years in the past), the intro to this event started at Branstetter's Tavern, when drinking at public houses was legal. Taverns and alcohol in Livingston County are now a faded memory. Robert and his friends drank to be awake and alert to be eyewitnesses to history. Willie DeBoe had raped, many years later, a lady who would become our new neighbor's mother. I figured that out independently from Charles Johnson (also in heaven with his mother now).

Robert was buried in his pajamas when he died, per his very, very unusual wishes. "I want to be buried in what I'm wearing when I die!" He did, and he was!

June 1992

Later this year, Harry Lynn's brother David Johnson, in the same family as our neighbor Charles just mentioned, was charged with murder. The trial centered around a murder victim found along the banks of the Ohio River upstream from Smithland. I was hired to take some photos (after hours) at Ginger and Pickles Bar to explain this event. The legal stuff... I just ignored that stuff and made great trial photos. I photographed the scene where the preface to the murder occurred with his lawyer. They *found* a body (not *the* body). Also, my son Mark worked for Harry Lynn and his sweet wife, Betty, at his antique shop in Paducah. We still have a small brass-capped chest we bought from him.

Sometime this summer, as I was serving on our county school board, I flew to New Orleans for a school board conference. Routine stuff here that is not going to merit much discussion. But the keynote speaker was very involved in children's education and ideas on improving schools. His speaking ability was stellar, not dull, and unscripted! He knew his topic. When it was over, several of us decided to go on a short walk over to Bourbon Street. This would become my third visit there, and a few years later, we visited Sheila's son Blake in New Orleans while he attended school at Tulane. I digress. We were walking along Bourbon Street and relaxing when one of us noticed two huge men walking toward us along the sidewalk with a much, much shorter gentleman betwixt them. You're ahead of me. Yes! It was our guest speaker, Henry Winkler, the Fonz. We, all five of us, stopped and chatted. He was friendly and polite to us strangers, and it was the most enjoyable odd meeting/encounter of my life, except for meeting Sheila Faye Ryan in the tariff room at South Central Bell Headquarters, a.k.a. "the Seventh Floor."

The Long-Anticipated Elvis Stamp, Issued 08 January 1993

Everyone who was anyone was there! Memphis! It was my first time being interviewed by CNN. I never looked at the video, so I can't include it here. Our second CNN interview will be seen in the 2012 chapter.

For the stamp event, I waited in line for hours and hours! Eight hours, more or less! I was the first person, actually, and my wife, Sheila (major Elvis fan) was second, since we wanted to be seated down front to see Priscilla Presley and maybe, according to rumors, Lisa Marie. Earlier in the week, we met Patsy Presley (Elvis's double first cousin photo of her and Sheila is on page <<see P. 191>>) at Bad Bob's Vapors nightclub and the annual impersonators show.

The rain and the fates were not aligned that chilly night of 06 or 07 January 1993. Persistent rain fell all afternoon. The celebration was a tent event, much like a Southern Gospel meeting, including music. Are you aware that Elvis's only Grammy Award was for gospel music? It was for "How Great Thou Art." Back to my story. Sheila and I were seated in row 2. The front row was for the dignitaries—Post Master General Marvin Runyon, the governor of Tennessee, and the mayor of Memphis. Their names escaped me. I'm too lazy to google them!

As the festivities began, a large group of singers came on stage. The mood was festive. Within moments after the show started, I heard an odd sound behind us, to our right. Nothing loud, nothing scary, just out of place. Back to the music. The five or six Hume High School girls' chorus sang something from the fifties. Elvis was the theme and the focus. It was grand. Not five minutes after that first noise, there was a second noise. Louder! Sharper! It was followed immediately by low murmurings, which continued to grow louder. As I turned my gaze from the singers on stage, I looked back where I had looked a few minutes ago. The folding chairs used for this event were on their sides, and people were standing. Uninjured but dazed and confused. The music suddenly stopped as the emcee came to the mic.

"Your attention, please." Firm but not panicked. "Will everyone please calmly and immediately proceed to the exits?"

The seating area was built on plywood sections raised above the ground about four feet. As I said, it had been raining. *All day!* No one knew that the cinderblock pillars holding up the flooring had been slowly sinking into the ground as the rain continued all afternoon and now into the evening.

We were the last ones out since we were the first ones in. No one was happy, except the big shots who got to stay seated and watch the show where we'd have been to see the presentation and unveiling of the Elvis stamp. Not to happen for us to see! As a final insult, Elvis's wife, Priscilla, *and* their daughter, Lisa Marie, showed up. The rumors were precisely spot on! A very, very rare public appearance, and we missed it!

Spring 1993 Floods

There was a horrible flooding event in Kentucky and southern Illinois. I spent one afternoon working alongside state prisoners brought out of Eddyville State Prison (very near by to Smithland) as laborers. Their freedom for the day was in exchange for shoveling sand into bags and toting those hefty bags to their place on the hastily built flood control dam! These men were mostly much larger and better built than me. They looked tough, but outside, working to help a community, one couldn't tell they were prisoners! They did tend to test me a time or two by throwing hefty bags at me! *Phew!*

Later this month, we would visit Ste. Genevieve, Illinois, north of Smithland, about fifty miles. We stopped for lunch there. We went to an Illinois town *west* of the Mississippi River, actually in Missouri, but named Kaskaskia, *Illinois*! An old, ancient (early 1600's) Catholic Church and two mobile homes comprised the town (https://en.wikipedia.org/wiki/Kaskaskia,_Illinois?wprov=sfti1).

> A historically significant village in Randolph County, Illinois, United States. In the 2010 census, the population was 14, making it the second-smallest incorporated community in the State of Illinois,

behind Valley City (pop. 13). As a central French colonial town of the Illinois Country, in the 18th century, its peak population was about 7,000 when it was a regional center. During the American Revolutionary War, the town, which had become an administrative center for the British Province of Quebec, was taken by the Virginia militia during the Illinois campaign. It was designated as the county seat of Illinois County, Virginia, after which it became part of the Northwest Territory in 1787. Kaskaskia was later named the capital of the United States' Illinois Territory, created on 03 February 1809. In 1818, when Illinois became the 21st US state, the town briefly served as the state's first capital until 1819, when the capital was moved to more centrally located Vandalia. Quick Facts: Country, State... Most of the town was destroyed in April 1881 by flooding as the Mississippi River shifted eastward to a new channel, taking over the lower 10 mi (16 km) of the Kaskaskia River. This resulted from deforestation of the river banks during the 19th century due to crews taking wood for fuel to feed the steamboat and railroad traffic. The river now passes east rather than west of the town. The state boundary line, however, remained in its original location. Accordingly, if the Mississippi River is considered a break in physical continuity, Kaskaskia is an exclave of Illinois, lying west of the Mississippi and accessible only from Missouri. A small bridge crosses the old riverbed, now a creek that is sometimes filled with water during flood season. Kaskaskia has an Illinois telephone area code (618) and a Missouri ZIP Code (63673). Its roads are maintained by the Illinois Dept. of Transportation, and it's few residents vote in the Illinois elections. The town was evacuated in the Great Flood of 1993, which covered it with water more than nine feet deep.

Historic French settlement. The site of Kaskaskia near the river was long inhabited by varying Native American indigenous peoples for thousands of years. The historic Illini peoples lived in this area when European encountered and traded with the early French colonists.

French colonists named the town after the Illini word for the Kaskaskia River. Historically it was referred to with many spelling variations, such as Kasklas, Kaskasky, Cas-casks, Kasquskias, and Kaskaskias. In 1703, French Jesuit missionaries established a mission to convert the Illini Native Americans to Catholicism. The congregation built its first stone church in 1714. The French also had a fur trading post in the village. Canadien settlers moved into farms and exploited the lead mines on the Missouri side of the river.

Favorably situated on a peninsula on the east side of the Mississippi River, Kaskaskia became the capital of Upper Louisiana, and the French built Fort de Chartres nearby in 1718. In the same year, they imported the first enslaved Africans, shipped from Santo Domingo in the Caribbean, to work as laborers in the lead mines being developed in Missouri.

"One Summer Night" by the Danleers

1993 in Paducah, Kentucky

(https://youtu.be/QT4LJxBBaF0)

On another exciting evening of dining with my wife Sheila, we returned home (twenty miles) from a lovely restaurant. I had two shots of JD, and we shared a bottle of wine. The steak dinner (Stacy's Restaurant) was superb! I was tired. As I was driving, perhaps ten minutes into the trip, Sheila said, "You need to stop weaving." I agreed after much back-and-forth (arguing is another version). We pulled over where, at the time, there was a buffet-type restaurant near where Mz. Gayle, her first name, sold us our beer at her store, Drive-By Liquors. This was an open parking lot to stop in. It was around 10:00 p.m. and there weren't many cars parked anywhere. I decided to pull in so we could change drivers. The cop behind me was about five seconds from turning on his lights, or he did after I stopped. As I stopped, he came up to my driver's door, and my window was already down. He said something about, "Are you okay to drive? I've been watching you."

And I said, "I was stopping to let my wife drive. We just had dinner and a few drinks." I was very polite and spoke clearly. My first fib was "I decided to let my wife drive."

He asked if she was sober, and "Yes, she is" was my polite answer. I don't think she was sober, but she sounded firm when she warned me about *my driving*! We were home safe. No ticket. No accident. Primo lesson learned!

In the early nineties, I was the wedding photographer for my friend Judy Fulks, who booked a wedding in Madisonville, Kentucky. Of all the five hundred plus weddings I photographed, this one, as I will relate, was unique. I found out that this wedding had an Arabic groom and a Kentucky bride. There were two events I witnessed that stood out in my mind. One was the wearing of the Palestinian headscarf (excuse my lack of knowledge of that culture). I was told it was a combat ribbon/symbol for killing an enemy soldier. It's the same headdress you've seen Yasser Arafat wearing. It is the iconic black-and-white checkered scarf. It is equivalent to an American combat ribbon worn on your dress uniform.

One never knows where and how history will be taught. I was told all of this when I noticed a few groomsmen were wearing that scarf.

The pièce de résistance was the groom's discussion with the officiant. "We want to fire our guns in the air…"

He was immediately cut off and firmly told, "*No!*"

Yet another vignette from Atlanta involving multiculturalism.

City: Atlanta, Georgia
Restaurant: The Majestic
Date: Forgotten, but the event was memorable

Sheila and I were having lunch at this restaurant/diner. Our waiter was Greek. While our waiter talked to another customer at the lunch counter, we were seated twenty feet away at a booth, waiting for our meal. It was a busy Saturday morning. Not long after we were seated, we heard raised voices, and a customer was berating our waiter's very thick and lovely Greek accent. It stopped the conversation in that area of the restaurant. This Greek fellow was getting mocked and ridiculed. We could sense the waiter's fear. It was nasty and getting nastier.

After what seemed like an eternity, the Greek fellow stopped what he was doing and began yelling at this insulting customer! Everyone was watching, not eating. Finally, this ruckus got the manager's attention, who immediately entered this fray. Immediately, he told him, in a loud and firm voice, "Get out of here! Now!"

The entire restaurant immediately erupted into applause and cheering approval. I forgot what we ate. I forgot if it was even good food, but I remember that incident! Not the food. I also learned how vicious and mean people could be!

Back row: Ron, Tim, Patrice, Tom, Sheila, Tracey, Terri, Nikki
Middle row: Julie, Lisa, Mark, Jason, Blake, Craig
Front row: Lauren, Alex, Zach, Sully, Macy, pet Chloe, Belle, Ryan, Tessa.

This is the only photograph of our blended family, which your humble author/photographer/retired engineer made for the permanent record. Thank you very much!

1995

(TIME / DATE OF WEEK / ... WHO CARES) JAN

GANG:

MY "RETIREMENT" CAME OUT OF THE BLUE; MOON OF KENTUCKY AND CERTAINLY WAS AN IMPOSSIBLE DREAM COME TRUE. I'M GLAD I CHOSE TO DO IT MY WAY. THANKS FOR THE '57 CHEV CORVETTE, ROOT BEER AND PHOTOS, THEY HAD ME ALL SHOOK UP, BUT THAT'S ALL RIGHT MAMA! THE ONLY IMPROVEMENT COULD HAVE BEEN A LONG BLACK LIMOUSINE FOR THE LUNCH, OR A PINK CADILLAC.

HOW GREAT THOU ART FOR KEEPING ME FROM HAVING A BLUE CHRISTMAS AT HEARTBREAK HOTEL. NOW THAT I'M IN THE GHETTO, I MISS ALL THE FUN WE HAD. WHAT A GROUP YOU ARE — I HAVE LOTS OF GOOD MEMORIES AND I WILL NOT GET MOODY BLUE. I HAVE BEEN A LITTLE WILD IN THE COUNTRY AND A LITTLE BUSY WITH MY NEW CAREER. AS LONG AS THERE IS NO KENTUCKY RAIN MY CAMERA AND I CAN GO ANYWHERE WE WANT, MAYBE EVEN TO GRACELAND. DON'T BE CRUEL BY NOT KEEPING IN TOUCH, YOU KNOW YOU CAN CALL LONG DISTANCE INFORMATION, GET ME GRAND RIVERS KENTUCKY AND REACH ME ANY TIME.   THANK YOU, THANK YOU VERY MUUCH...

Tom

P.S. PLEASE ROUTE TO MDVL GROUP

We were in Queens, New York, and my cousin Patty's friend had a car. We decided to go Irish bar hopping over in Brooklyn. We rode in the back, and Patty told us her boyfriend was a licensed livery driver for Mr. Paul Newman and his wife, Joanne Woodward. When Sheila heard that one of Joe's regular customers was Paul and Joanna, as in *Newman*, you could imagine her reaction! She said to the driver, "Am I sitting where Paul had sat...years ago?"

My dear Aunt Grace Murtaugh passed away (23 May 1912–09 August 1995). Her husband was George Bart Murtaugh (23 July 1913–31 January 1955). My mom died on 17 January 2003. This would be my last visit to Queens on Northern Boulevard and the Tipperary Arms Irish Pub, right next to the funeral home and across the street from my cousin Patty Murtaugh's apartment she shared with Joe. It was a short cab ride from LaGuardia airport to the pub.

"Cabbie, take me to the Tipperary on Northern Boulevard in Queens."

He knew instantly where that bar was. Then to the funeral home. Then back to the pub for a wee pint of Guinness. Charlie and Peggy were there sitting at the end of the bar, just as if they hadn't left since our last visit to Queens in 1991! The funeral and memorial gathering was a very low-key event. I didn't know anyone there.

Eventually, Deb would give me some of our mother's cremains. In 2014, we visited Norn or the Northern Irish pronunciation or Norn-Iron and then Giant's Causeway. I privately scattered her ashes there. Rest in peace, Mom, near the green, green, grass of home in Norn Iron.

Belle Adams was born 22 May 1995. I photographed her birth while standing right next to the OB-GYN. Oh my, and holy *bleep*, what an experience! My concept of birth was forever altered. 'Nuff said about that. Mom (wife of Sheila's son, Terri) was pleased. I was left in a slight state of agitation and mild shock. Brides and children are more fun to photograph.

Jason and Tracey's wedding was on 10 June 1995, and I hired an assistant photographer, David, for the only wedding of the five hundred I covered that I typically covered solo. I wasn't taking any chances on a family wedding! We ate our rehearsal dinner at an open-air pizza restaurant in Buckhead. The owner and friend of Jason's, named Rocco, was murdered later that same year. (Aside: my opinion of Atlanta isn't very nice!) It was a vast, boisterous, and happy gathering! The wedding, from my perspective, was very formal but very stressful for me. It was a grand wedding, a gala party, and a joyous celebration of weddings, youth, life, and fun!

1996

January 11, 1996, was a day I cannot ever forget. My few and only moments with *Tyler Edward Byron*. I went to the hospital immediately after Mark called me. Mark and Melanie Gage's son did not survive birth. Holding this infant for a moment was the saddest day of my entire life! If a day is ever more miserable, I am sure that I won't tell you about it! He never drew one breath. So, so sad. He was wearing that tiny knit cap on his head. It looked like he was sleeping, only he was asleep in heaven. Unbearable.

In October, in Livingston County in rural western Kentucky. A short walk down the road from home was the closest point I could see the northern sky with fewer trees, and it was my favorite place to watch the stars. In 1996, I was able to view the Hale-Bopp Comet. This was a comet that history said helped the Norman Conquest in 1066 at the Battle of Hastings. Whenever I get a chance to see anything periodic in the heavens that is viewable without a telescope, I'm game!

Atlanta Summer Olympics

A visit to Sheila's son Jason made for an inexpensive holiday to see some Olympic events. There were so many countries represented here in this Southern city of ours. *Gone with the Wind* was filmed here and depicted a more violent era in the Deep South, so a few days of sporting competition between former enemies (Russians and Cubans) was a pleasant diversion.

We attended at least two days, all day, well into the night. As history would expose our memories of this time and to us, standing out dramatically, to me in particular... we'll get to that.

I was then the family historian in that pre-cell phone era. My photos of the Olympics would result in a visit to our Kentucky photo studio by the FBI.

There was a lot of walking involved every day of our two-day visit, but we were all a lot younger. Sheila and I were not even yet fifty!

Fortunately, in the heat of the Southern summer, there were beer gardens! We watched a volleyball game from a corporate box that I remember vividly. A family friend, Gregg "Radar" Sharpless, had a fine corporate box! Somewhat dull game for a non-fan, but the foofaraw was entertaining. Gregg was like Radar O'Reilly from *MASH* (TV show). He could procure anything. Sadly, he died very suddenly at home several years later. Too young and so vibrant. RIP.

Mostly, for myself, it was all about people watching. A photographer's mecca, with lots of different cultures everywhere. Lots of random candid images, the people, the buildings and flags, the signs and lights.

On the event's last day, I found myself waiting on stranglers, or stragglers, not that it matters. I was near a group of policemen (to be PC, I didn't see any police ladies) chatting and maybe even covertly watching the crowd. My camera, as always, hanging by a strap right on my shoulder, was convenient. Why not a few last-minute clicks with my Nikon *film* camera? I hadn't entirely gone to digital yet, as I recall. People of all stripes are legit subjects for candid photography.

As I finished taking crowd photos, and it was getting later, I was finally getting a bit tired. The rest of the group showed up. It was still a fifteen-minute walk to the car. We would fight the local traffic and, then slowly merge onto an even slower I-75 northbound traffic! I remember President Clinton having attended the Olympics, and in a leap of logic, it was his fault his motorcade had screwed up the traffic! It takes very little to bring Atlanta traffic down to foot speed, so Jason turned on the radio for music or news.

In seconds, the music was interrupted by a news bulletin. It was just after 1:20 a.m. "There's been an explosion at the Olympics!" That caught our attention! We listened to the radio reports while were stuck in heavy and prolonged traffic. It was determined that a bomb was placed in a crowd in a backpack and set off with a timer. Fortunately, no one was killed. The local, state, and FBI people were investigating this horrific terrorism!

I told the group in the car, "I was taking photos as I left. I will have photos developed and printed in my [photography] studio to review as soon as I get home!"

Sheila processed the film negatives, and I did the printing.

As I kept hearing the news, I learned they had not caught the bomber. "He" already had a news name, the Centennial Park Bomber.

My photographs were interesting when I printed them. As I looked at the pictures, I noticed the last ones I had taken—crowds, the police standing around, and a figure sitting by what looked like a backpack. Mmm… I began to wonder. I had heard the requests on the radio and TV. Call the FBI if you have any information, tips, or pictures. My grandfather Percy Byron taught me, "Never refer to your work as pictures if you're a photographer! "Amateurs take pictures while professionals take photographs!" His words, not mine. Always. I've followed this advice since 1957 when he, Percy, corrected my reference to what I'd seen as his work.

"CALL FBI." *Ring! Ring!* "Hello, how may I help you?"

I told them what I just told you above, dear reader. They were very, very interested.

"What is your name, address, phone number, etc.?"

About a week or so later, they showed up at our photography studio, 100 percent business. No small talk. I didn't tell them they looked like *Men in Black* as in the movie, you know, as they asked me all about the event, the times, who I was with, why, and all manner of questions. "Where are the [cringe] pictures?" I didn't explain what my grandfather's advice was that I just told *you* about! No chitchat.

They proceeded to take dozens of pictures of me. Naturally, I was curious. "Why all these pictures of *me*?"

Their reply explained why. "We need to know what everyone at the bombing location looked like. We want to know your names, and the pictures we took of you can be compared to other pictures we find when we visit other informers like you. If we see you in the background of other's pictures, we know who *you* are."

I said to myself, "Duh!"

Several months later, I received a package from the FBI with a standard form reply. "Thanks" was all they said. If I had been any help, then or later, it was not known then or twenty-three years later as I recount this event. Richard Jewel was wrongly arrested and charged. He was never found guilty, but his health was destroyed, and he died early.

Heart attack, I think. They did find the actual bomber, Eric Rudolph, hiding in the mountains a few hundred miles from Atlanta a few years later. He was sent to prison for life.

1997

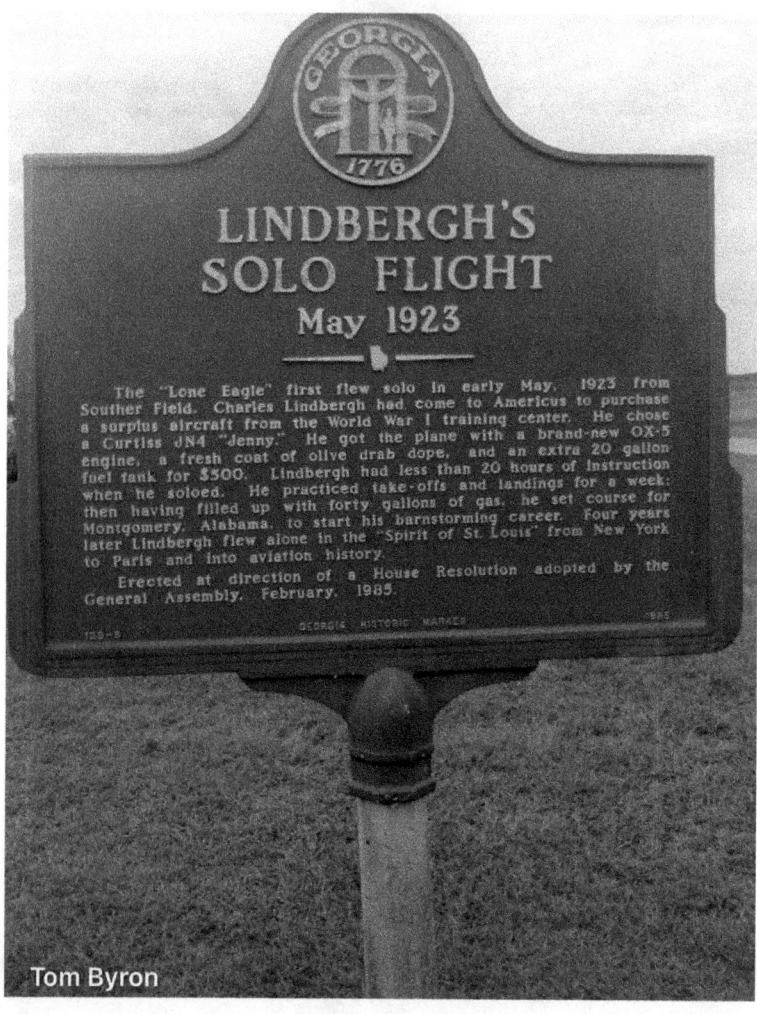

We discovered this historic gem on a wandering trip around Georgia, where we learned of Mr. Lindbergh's Georgia connection. Just the sign, not his plane, but the airfield office was still there and in use, or so it appeared to us.

The Great Basement Flood

15 February 1997

It was just a typical Saturday. Sheila went to a basketball game at Rupp Arena on a Bill Scott bus trip with her two sons. I was booked to photograph a wedding that same day. Neither event could be canceled. I don't remember the wedding, since it was one of five hundred in my career. Now I could pull out my list of marriages and find more than one dual event (a wedding and a UK game), but why? In Ledbetter, Kentucky, one notable conflict/wedding situation like that *did* arise.

Allow me to digress. I was scheduled to photograph a wedding in early March during tournament time, and either the bride or the groom were not *extreme* Wildcat fans. For those not familiar with Kentucky basketball fans, we are rabid. We are loyal. We literally follow our team! Why anyone would schedule anything—even a funeral—during a game is nearly a mortal sin!

The game, in this case, was nearly over with a very close score. "Win and advance, lose and go home!" As the wedding began, I noticed many people still gathered outside near some cars and listening to the game. I had to do my job. No replays! The wedding went off without a hitch (pun intended), and I was nearest to the reception area. I poked my head in and saw a TV on. I saw the score. What to do? I turned and faced the attendees, and since I was wearing a UK tie, I gave a two-thumbs-up, and everyone knew the UK had won. This was not the UK game Sheila and her sons were at. Just an example of how rabid UK fans are! I photographed this wedding, probably a 30 minute drive away from our home, a lovely country home with a, swimming pool, a tennis court, and a separate photo studio building.

Back to Sheila and her sons at a UK game. I returned home, alone. I walked in the backdoor and felt a *squish-squish* sensation under my shoes! It had been raining for a few days, off and on. It was not unusual, but three inches of water over the carpet was *not good*! The timing was also horrific. We were already remodeling the upstairs and had moved a lot of things *downstairs*! It was time to use the phone and place a much needed "lifeline call!" I needed help immediately. Job one: move as much back upstairs as I could. As fast as I could!

A few friends came to my rescue. When did Sheila get home? I do not remember if it was the next day or that night. It was a total disaster. We learned later that the uphill side of the house did not have proper drainage to channel rainwater around the foundation. Several months and tens of thousands of dollars later, everything was normal. It will never be forgotten!

And now for something completely different—the fascinating Hale-Bopp Comet. Earth's closest approach was on 22 March 1997. Only since we lived in Kentucky, were we able to see the blackness of the night sky. Being in a remote county gave us minimal light pollution and an excellent ability to see this comet. A telescope wasn't necessary. I could view it clearly from Morris Cemetery, only an eighth of a mile away.

Following an anonymous tip, police entered a mansion in Rancho Santa Fe, an exclusive suburb of San Diego, California, and discovered thirty-nine victims of mass suicide. The deceased—twenty-one women and eighteen men of varying ages—were lying peacefully in matching dark clothes and Nike sneakers and had no noticeable signs of blood or trauma. It was later revealed that the men and women were members of the Heaven's Gate religious cult, whose leaders preached that suicide would allow them to leave their bodily containers and enter an alien spacecraft hidden behind the Hale-Bopp Comet (https://www.history.com/this-day-in-history/heavens-gate-cult-members-found-dead).

My brother-in-law was a Harley-Davidson biker. A Harley Owners Group (HOG). He passed away on 16 June 1997. He and my sister and family lived in rural Vermont. My sister Deb still does. They were, and always will be, Vermonters! Tim's father had committed suicide previously in the garage next to their house. Devastation fell on their home. Again!

Deb's account follows in her words:

> Wasn't in the garage, though he tried, and survived that attempt. I was not at home when he made another attempt, and I arrived home and found him

unresponsive and called the rescue squad. I believe he was trying, once again, to affect me feel sorry for him. He was in his car, upon the grassy knoll, trying to make me feel sorry for him, but he had a "friend" who gave him some pills after he spent three days on a biking trip and was exhausted; the drugs took over. I will always believe he did not want to die, but exhaustion was strenuous. Pa did not die in the garage; he blew his head off, up under the pine trees. ☹☹☹☹

My sister was there. Her third family member died violently by their hand, including our youngest brother. You'd think there was no love anywhere. But peace, tranquility, camaraderie, and loving sympathy can be found where you'd least expect it.

The funeral was arranged, and I made my way 1,044 miles up to Vermont. Lovely place. A quirky, quiet, and quaint group of folk live there. The funeral service was conducted in a small country church, a Vermont postcard, if ever. We sat quietly in the back in this very small white Rockwell-esque steepled church. It was set near a pine tree–cleared area and evoked a long-forgotten era.

His funeral, with all the bikers, was memorable! The services were held at 11:00 a.m. at White Oakes Congregational Church in Williamstown, Massachusetts (I kept the church notice and the sequence of the service), and a significant number of attendees were elderly. The stark contrast between the bikers and the church members was fascinating.

After we were out of our car, at the top of a hill at a lovely cemetery, we were about to experience two more unique events. I was chatting quietly with a mourner and thought I heard an unusual sound. I paused to listen. "What is that?" I asked myself.

My answer came to me as the first of many bikes came up the hill near where we were gathered. The low rumble of many HOGS was a distinct sound you'll never forget. The riders brought my brother-in-law's bike on a trailer. His helmet was on the seat. Backward. No words were spoken. The service lasted a few minutes, and we witnessed, next, the last piéce de résistance.

It wasn't a long ride from the cemetery to my sister's old family place. No talking. She was now the lone occupant of the house. Her two boys were grown and living independently.

She knew how to cut the firewood she used to heat and cook and make hot water with. She damn near lost her thumb when her ax took it off. She managed to have it re-sewn onto her hand!

We assembled in the yard. There was no place for all the visitors who arrived by car and bike. It was summertime, and a few of us were thirsty.

I noticed to my right a biker fellow *opening* a bottle of Jack Daniels. He opened it like he'd done many, many times before. With a quick sharp twist and in a well-worn routine motion, he took a sip and, as if choreographed, passed it to his left. Sip, pass, sip, pass... Then I held the bottle and took a drink and gave it again leftward. It was soon at the end of the arc of bikers. Empty. Amazing. Powerful. Unforgettable. I had never sipped JD in a group manner like this, but now I have, and I felt a kindred spirit there. My mother had taught me to drink my whiskey straight. She sipped her scotch straight too. It was *a family tradition*.

01 December 1997

Maui, our tenth wedding anniversary and America's fiftieth state/heaven. It was a vacation and celebration that was beyond excellent! Sun. Rainbows. Ocean views. Friendly people. Sightseeing. Kentucky Wildcat basketball. We hated to leave, but we were anxious to print up all of our films. It was not the digital age yet!

The Road to Hana (a paperback book in my library) was the trip of a lifetime. Five hours to drive fifty-two miles. Hundreds of (620) blind curves you went at two miles per hour. Steep 500' drop-offs to your left heading toward Hana ahead to the right. Even more challenging to see the road's edge to farther away on your right, heading north on your exhausting trip home! Not one guardrail! Mostly forest and mountain terrain with eucalyptus trees, beautiful trees. On the road *to* Hana, we stopped at Baldwin Beach and ate sandwiches with deli meat and cheese from the local and only grocery store. What a Thanksgiving that meal was!

Charles Lindbergh's grave (1902–1974) is in Hana. We knew approximately where he was buried, but afterward, some research proved enlightening. Interesting factoid: the kidnapping of his baby son was investigated by none other than Gen. Norman Schwartzkopf Sr. Norman Schwartzkopf Jr. was Stormin' Norman (https://en.wikipedia.org/wiki/Norman_Schwarzkopf_Jr.?wprov=sfti1).

There were lots of basketball games to watch in Lahaina Stadium (open unassigned seating much like a high school gym), and we even ran into Sheila's cousin, Betty Washer, who lived in Nashville, Tennessee. Tom, eagle-eyed, saw her walking across the court's sideline at halftime. *If that ain't about as random as you can get, what is?*

1998

It was sometime around '98, but it's challenging to be specific because it was an annual event. If anyone doesn't remember the empty keg being thrown in the pool or Mark's potato launcher, they weren't paying attention, or they weren't there! Both of those happened in different years at our July Fourth party at our country estate. It was two acres with a pool, plenty of parking, and a lot of beer and music. Once darkness arrived, the fireworks were set off. There were no neighbors to annoy. The closest place was a church, and they never complained. I photographed a wedding at the small church next door and snapped a wedding in San Diego, California. They are almost three thousand miles apart. It's difficult to remember all of them as I was hired five hundred times! Typically, thirty to forty people attended. It was always a great extended weekend we all looked forward to. There was partying, food grilled, and water fun!

The pool was the central place where we all hung out, and everyone enjoyed the music. Karaoke (with our machine) for several years is firmly in my memory. How's yours? Remember, Sheila and I dressed up as Sonny and Cher's "I Got You Babe" (https://youtu.be/HKGjCPBSG38). There's a Rick Holland video on a cassette tape somewhere.

One wedding among the five hundred that I remember, as if I were there as I type, this wedding involved *too much* Jäegermeister. A very potent liqueur that should be consumed in sips. Small sips! As the event began, I went outside with the boys to smoke. The conversation during their smoking session was about how great Jäegermeister tasted!

"Why don't you go get some at the liquor store?" someone was asked.

He left to run that errand, and my five-minute break was over. I was out on the dance floor's perimeter, watching the bride and groom having the time of their young lives. The venue was in West Paducah, which I remember...including what follows.

I heard some talking in low voices and noticed a slight disturbance, minor at best, to my left. As I gathered my senses and re-shifted my focus to a small group heading toward me, I saw something odd. One of the three gents wasn't walking! He was the middle part of a trio, and he was gently but slowly and quietly being "escorted" or dragged (his legs weren't moving) to his truck. His truck was parked right outside the reception/dance hall. He could not walk because he was in a stupor. He was dragging his feet, soles upward and toes facing rearward. He was numb/blind drunk. He was heading toward his truck with help. One of his friends reached to the truck door, gave it a quick tug open, and deposited this lad into his truck's passenger seat, a temporary sleeping area to sober up. I turned to go outside, where I was occasionally smoking with the guests, and saw the answer to my private question I was wondering. There was an empty bottle of Jäegermeister on its side on a table. I guessed that very few drank all of that bottle, but the passed-out fellow had his share!

In October, still in Livingston County in rural western Kentucky. A short walk down the road from home was the closest point I could see the northern sky with fewer trees, and it was my favorite place to watch the stars. Always a place near a cemetery and an amazing place to watch for shooting stars, and feel closer to the stars.

It wouldn't be until 06 November 2021 that I photograph an actual UAP. See page 320.

1999

I traveled to Breckenridge, Colorado, to photograph a high school classmate's winter wedding. It was a long and exciting trip and my first visit to the Rocky Mountains, and it was a fantastic experience! The Eisenhower Interstate Tunnel was at 11,013 feet at the East Portal and 11,158 feet at the West Portal and passed through the Continental Divide. We would cross that famous landmark called the Continental Divide several years later, in a different climate, in New Mexico to visit my brother Paul in Farmington, New Mexico.

I had never driven this far to cover a wedding before, but for an old high school friend, why not? I created many memories for many people, and I got a paid-for-trip for my first visit to the Rocky Mountains! It was a beautiful little drive. The wedding was not very elaborate, but the couple's venue was gorgeous! Several years later, I would watch *Christmas Vacation* and be stunned to see the scene from that movie showing the same road where I had driven along to this wedding! Watch the film where they go to get their Christmas tree. Trying to visualize this road? Watch the opening few minutes of *Christmas Vacation*. Chevy Chase and family buy a Christmas tree. They live in the Chicago area but drove to Breckinridge, Colorado. I had been there, so it didn't fool me! A little farther past Breckinridge is the *Beavis and Butt-Head* series, South Park (Colorado).

2000, Y2K

This was the year everything was supposed to collapse! The end of the world! That didn't happen because it wasn't on the evening news. Since programmers didn't think much about the thousand-year decimal place changing (i.e., 1999 to 2000, duh), everything would crash! Banking would cease, wars would commence, or it would be just another Sunday night. Monday morning, 01 January 2000, would be expected! It was. Yawn!

2001

11 September, 2001, Tuesday, our generation's Pearl Harbor moment occurred. We had already experienced a presidential assassination in 1963 on Sheila's seventeenth birthday. We saw the first man walk on the moon in 1969. We watched President Nixon resign in 1974. We were eyewitnesses to two failed impeachment efforts. We will see more political upheaval in 2016 concerning President Trump! Due to TDS (Trump Derangement Syndrome), there was a second impeachment attempt. *That* failed, and someday, we may learn that a secret plan to steal a future election was conceived. We boomers have had our share of firsts and tragedies! A day that would never end and would touch everyone deeply. Much has been written about this moment that is still not over fifteen years later as I write these words. Fifteen years before this day, I was in New York City and made my only visit up to the observation deck of the WTC, the World Trade Center. Stunning. Their brochure said, "The closest some of us will ever get to heaven." Irony. Tragic. We commemorated this date in our family now, from 2002 onward, my grandson Zach's birthday, September eleventh! We also celebrated my step-grandson Sully being named after his father's college friend, Patrick Sullivan, who died there in those towers on that beautiful and clear blue-sky morning.

    I spent the *entire* day with Sheila watching this nightmare unfold. I didn't know a tenth of what we all know now in 2020 as I edit this biography. It's hard to think of this as *my* autobiography. That sounds like a step beyond my reach. I am now only "one of three" in my family of eight. This narration now falls to me, or no one, to gather this together for unknown generations to read. It is a formidable task! It was as big a task then, for those of us alive then, to watch our country under attack as it is now for me to write this all down. I watched the City of New York, where my father spent his youth, where his father and my great-grandfather spent twenty years documenting their enormous record of NYC growing up, sort of what I'm doing now. *Once Upon a City* was my grandfather Percy's book title showing their photography of New York

City over the turn of the century, eighteenth to nineteenth. I watched the fire department and the police and paramedics try to save lives amid so much horror. Never in America will this scene repeat itself, and if it does, I pray I'm long since dead and forgotten!

© John Almond (Judy's husband). This is the last group photo with the five of us Byron kids together. No one else can say what date this was taken, but I know I flew to Arizona when the US Army was guarding all activities at the airport. That situation never happened there like that before, or since!

October 2001, Tombstone, Arizona visit

A few days or weeks later, when I flew from Huntsville, Alabama, to Arizona, it was pronounced that the US was still on high alert post 9/11. There were heavily armed military members in uniform, ready with assault rifles at the entrance to the airport terminal!

On 26 October, I was in Tombstone, Arizona, with Sheila, Mike, and Laura White. This just happened to be the actual anniversary that put this place *on* the map! This date was exactly 120 years since that famous shootout! It was spooky knowing that we were randomly in this town on the same date that made the city famous. The Boot Hill Cemetery had all those names in old Western movies—those B&W ones in particular. My memory of dates and events is a bit screwy. Here are my recollections of that visit, and I apologize for my sloppy memory. Tombstone, Arizona, is well worth the time, and this quaint town is both famous and remote. When my sister lived in Tucson, I made the trip to see this iconic place. A few family members (forget which ones) and I went into the famous bar where they treated a gunshot victim on a pool table. Remember that movie? We each had a shot of whiskey. The only part of the furnishings of that bar that was original was the ornamental ceiling.

The streets were not dirt anymore, and when movies were filmed, they covered them with dirt. Boot Hill Cemetery is accurate, and if you pay $5 at the gift shop on your way into town, you can "walk amongst the dead," as the wooden sign beckons. The famous and mischaracterized film about the shooting at OK Corral is played out daily for another small fee. When we saw it, a Hollywood actor (unknown to me since I'm not into "Hollywood" stuff) was doing the reenactment of the movie. There are a variety of different tales about who, what, why, who shot whom, etc. The acting was well done. It was memorable and lucky that I was there on the same date for the 120th anniversary (my best memory). A few of the actual people are buried up on Boot Hill behind the gift shop, so named the "Boot Hill Gift Shop".

It's a real town with a storied past, twenty-five miles off the interstate highway. Quaint. Worth it if you're in the area. Souvenir stuff and a few photos are in my old office filing cabinets in this tiny apartment I now live in. I can still picture the town and the legend of the Old West while walking around town. We left before dark. It might have gotten weird and dangerous if any ghosts showed up. Just sayin'…

2002

This year, two grandsons were born, and the flowering of one very long-awaited plant. In 1982, I was given a cutting from a night-blooming cereus houseplant in Lake Charles, Louisiana. On 23 October, the blooms that were anticipated finally came to life. Chalk up that coincidence to my long list of coincidences (see <<p. 321–326>>). Twenty years of patience and moving the plant from Louisiana to Georgia and then to Kentucky paid off! It was a short but sweet event. The bloom lasted a day or so, and the aroma about as long. It was a lovely event. I still have this same plant, and it is thirty-nine years old (as I typed. It was a gift cutting in 1982 when we lived in Lake Charles, Louisiana!

This year is more accurately remembered for the dates of the births of Zach Byron, who was born on 11 September, and Sully Adams, who was born on 23 October of that year!

2003

I'm not sure when I received the following note (See P. 236-237). It shocked me to my core. I will share it with you since she was justifiably angry with her husband. Their marriage began as a sham to cover up the out-of-wedlock birth of my older brother, Paul. It never got much better! Paul hated his father for his entire life.

My parents had decided to move from Florida to Vermont to be with some family in their final years. They had alienated four of their six children, and the fifth had committed suicide. One daughter lived in California, one in Arizona. My brother lived in New Mexico, and as I said, my little brother, Ricky, had committed suicide—his means of escape from whom he perceived as a tyrant.

My dear mother died at age eighty-six in Vermont on January 17 near my youngest sister in Pownal, Vermont. I never received advance notification of her impending death. I was told (years later) that in her final days, she was being fed meals at her nursing home, and she didn't *like* the food our father sloppily prepared. My uncaring egomaniacal father refused to comfort or love her. Here's where I get my stubbornness. *She refused to eat!* She died by suicide, self-induced starvation. This was her final and fatal decision—not to eat until she caused her own death! I can *respect* that! I was told she just laid down her eating utensils and refused to eat! That was typical of her strong-willed spirit. She was never a middle-of-the-road person! And then there were six of us (21 October 1918–17 January 2003).

2004

Georgia road trip: Warm Springs, Georgia, was worth our visit. The Summer White House was President FDR's summer retreat and a place for treating his, largely unknown at the time, polio.

Georgia road trip: Andersonville, Georgia, was a massive confederate prison camp. It's notable as the birthplace of a common word in the English language—*deadline*. It has its etymological roots there. Crossing the double-layered parallel wooden fort-like fence to escape found you in the wrong place, the kill zone, if you attempted to escape from that compound. It was called the deadline." You'd be shot on sight there! The "pain" of escaping triggered my memory thusly.

I never kept track of my history of dentist appointments, but this one I'll review is permanently etched in my strange brain! I remember his name, Dr. Mike Smith in Paducah. It was a root canal procedure. As he was working hard to remove the root of a lousy molar, the process took an exciting turn. He suggested I might need another injection of novocaine, which he figured was wearing off. He said, "Do you want another shot as it will take longer than planned?"

I declined and listened to the music being piped into the room. You might be thinking, *What music?*

"Comfortably numb." (https://youtu.be/_FrOQC-zEog) I got amused with the lyrics and began to laugh. It distracted me, and I laughed even harder as Dr. Mike kept drilling. I seemed to be releasing endorphins as I laughed. This was nature's way of eliminating pain. It worked as he finished. When he cleaned up, we went into his office, and we both sat in his office and had a smoke. I never knew he smoked. I never knew how strong endorphins could be!

On 27 March 2004, my dear sister Judy passed away in Arizona. She was too young to leave at age sixty-two. She waited for me to arrive from Kentucky. It was so, *so* sad to see someone survive lung cancer, only to succumb to a superbug caught in the hospital. Her husband, John, told me at the hospital she died from MRSA! I've heard others say differently, but I'm going with John's statement to me! She was the person who introduced me to politics! She was a significant influence in my life! I have two scars on my left arm. One from a potato peeler she was using while fixing dinner and my getting a glass of water!! The other one farther up my arm was her fingernail. She scratched me with her "Knox Gelatin" nails drink she took as a teenager to harden her nails. Her plan *WORKED*! She waited for me to travel from Kentucky before leaving her hospital bed and this earth to "go with the Death Angel." And then there were five of us as a family (13 October 1941–27 March 2004).

It was 1956 when Judy bought me a large box of Reese's Peanut Butter Cups for Christmas. In 1965, I was at her apartment in Philly, on Delancey Street, 2100 (?) block something, and I got drunk for my first time. Gin and Schweppes tonic! I can say that after our fun evening I walked to the train station to get home. It was about 13 City blocks to the train station! I must not have been drunk or I was lucky. *Or both!* A the *sweetness* of youth!! There were six children in my family. She was my older sister, and I also had an older brother and two younger sisters. My younger brother, Ricky, died in 1964. When she moved to Arizona, she said she had been "reborn" and discovered the desert was her home. She was free of the trees and the pollen and the congestion of city life in Philadelphia, near where we all had grown up. That was the fifties and the sixties.

It was 2004, and my sister Judy lived in Arizona. I was married and lived in Kentucky. We occasionally visited in Arizona. She never saw me at my home, but it *was* an 1,800-mile trip. The phone call I received when she thought she had cancer was scary. I was in my mid-fifties. She was in her early sixties, five years older than I am, and she was my pseudo-mom. My birth mom had six kids to raise, so it was a joint effort for the older kids to help with the younger kids. I heard what you said about this cancer, and both of our mortalities hit us hard. Secretly. We don't use the D word. The C is bad enough! But I talked to her, and we went through the details. She explained her progress as time passed. Her surgery was very successful. Lung cancer was always a demon in our lives because we both smoked. It was there, ever present and lurking.

"The surgeon had never seen a tumor this early in its growth," she told me. But she *whipped* it! She was brave. Hell, she even twirled fire batons in high school. That was a long time ago. She is and was and will be always locked in my familial memories!

The game my sister (and Sheila and I) love is basketball. She gave up attending basketball games (particularly her Arizona Wildcats. Oddly, we are **Kentucky** Wildcat fans, and she refused to go out for fear of colds and germs. She was under postoperative treatments, which weakened her immune system. MRSA was now her unknown enemy. MRSA, or Mer'*sa*, as it is pronounced, was ever present in her mind, though not mentioned. MRSA infection: https://www.mayoclinic.org/diseases-conditions/mrsa/symptoms-causes/syc-20375336

I received a phone call from her husband saying she was in the hospital for her regular follow-up treatments, but was not feeling exactly right. She and everyone else assumed her treatment was the blame. Everyone was wrong, very wrong, to ignore this deadly superbug, mutated and immune to antibiotics! Now she had an enemy that was worse than cancer. It was untreatable. It was fatal. Always.

The next phone call I got was much more urgent. Tom, my brother-in-law, said, "You need to come to visit your sister soon! *Very soon!*" As I got airborne on the next flight from Nashville, Tennessee (2 hours from our home), to Phoenix, Arizona, I was pretty anxious. I didn't know how serious it was. The flight was three hours, but it might have been an eternity. I rented a car and drove to the hospital. It was now twenty-four hours since the phone call. It was scary. Driving this distracted was worse than drunk driving, but I made it to the hospital. I entered her room. I barely recognized her! As I saw her there, not conscious, lying there in the safety (?) of a hospital with her beloved John (husband), I realized what would happen in only a few hours. Or minutes. I spoke to her. She could not see me or respond. But I know for 100% certainty she heard my voice. I watched her chest slowly rise as she inhaled, and a long, long pause. I went to a nearby waiting area and made my arrival known to her daughters, Cris and Steffie, and I told them they should come to her room. Now! I left for her room, and as I returned, I again watched her breathing. Another long and slow, silent breath. Maybe two? I watched, hoping for that next breath… It **never** came…

    She truly *had* waited for my spirit! We said goodbye on that higher plane.

    RIP Judy.

Left to right: Joe, Betty, Paul, Judy, Tommy, Ricky, Laura, and Debbie.

The Post-Judy Period of My Life Begins

The 2000's weren't starting too well, but they would close with moving to Georgia and having a new president later. Some retrospect about these seventy years before I end my life's rambling(?) story:

- Politics was always, and still is interesting (h/t Judy). For the first time since Presidents Adams (no. 2 and 6), father and son, we had another father and son presidency. History rarely repeats like this, let alone witnessing it. Presidents Bush, no. 41 and 43.
- George H. W. Bush was the first sitting VP since President Van Buren (1837) to be elected president. History was continuously being made, and it was interesting.
- I saw the first presidential impeachment since Andrew Johnson in 1868. That impeachment spectacle was riveting, and I hope we never go through that mess again! I saw the first president resign in 1974, and before that, VP Agnew resigned, only the second since 1832, when John Calhoun left after serving only sixteen days.
- I remember before VISA™ and MasterCard™ when I could tell who the rich were and the poor were very quickly—by the car they drove. New vehicles are now $25,000 plus (as I type) and can be financed. New cars dominate the roads. Since 1966, credit cards have replaced cash, and interest payments have become a significant revenue stream for banks.
- I witnessed two impeachment attempts against Donald J. Trump that did not result in a conviction either time. The Democrats sure hated that man! (Look up TDS in your favorite search engine.)

Now we have a large amount of wealth being created by businesses that produce no physical product, no factories. Sports franchises produce games or events and billions in revenue. Hollywood makes billions in revenue and produces only images on a screen. The music industry makes digital songs, nothing physical, without records or albums—just downloads. Factories are fading from America, and we import too much from *China!* Skilled trades are declining. We have no repair shops for radios and TVs. Everything is thrown out, and better models are bought. We hire cheap labor to fix things around our home, if we even do that. I remember people who could fix almost anything they used that eventually broke. Products were sound enough to wear out and could be repaired! I became one of those home handymen borne from living in or very near poverty. Even since we have lived in an apartment, I am (in my very late sixties) still repairing our washer and dryer myself. At around six years old, I began taking things apart. My mother was always after me: "Stop that.!You'll never be able to put that watch back together!" My children and grandchildren never do that.

It would be no surprise to anyone that I ended up as a telephone engineer, designing phone systems and where to place poles and cables. I got to see the physical results as I figured out what was needed for customers who requested telephones. Those days are mostly gone now; all cellular phone service (well over 90 percent is my guess) today. A foreign company makes and launches a satellite, and a person in China makes the phone I use. My old job doesn't exist. When I was growing up, there were no satellites and no computers, and color TV was still years ahead, as were seat belts in cars, but I survived. We all survived by following a set of rules. In a functioning society, following the rules is essential! It's a shame not everyone agrees with my last sentence!

On Sunday, 30 May 2004, we moved into Powers Ferry Plantation Apartments. Now we're in Georgia. Next move… I'll let you guess. Hint: no visitors allowed. What a change from this:

© Byron (leaning out of plane window)

2004

Dear Ja,   Jim.

I have something to say to you — it's about your affair — it's been nearly 3 yrs now. I had thought it would have been over ages ago.

I'm ~~telling~~ asking you that it's time to end ~~of~~ it — forever! But if you'd ~~rather~~ have him to write to, ~~tell~~ see, then so be it. We'll just be two people sharing a house & nothing more — after

> all it's just a house —
> a home is built on
> love & trust.
> You've promised lots
> of time. It was once
> but it isn't.
> This will be your
> decision — If you do
> mean for it to stop
> I won't say another
> word. —
>
> Betty

On 03 July 2004, Sheila's son Craig and his betrothed, Nikki, were married on the beach in Providenciales, The Turks and Caicos Islands. I was the photographer of record. The flight was not very long from Atlanta, out over the ocean to a tiny spec of sand. We found it pleasant but a bit pricey for our income range. We had grown up going to the Jersey Shores summer after summer, so what's another beach? Answer:

another beach! If I do say so, I did a decent job covering the wedding and staying sober when needed. Craig and Nikki moved to "Cali" some years later, and I hear it's a beautiful place. But not my cup 'o tea! I've never been to visit them. Sheila flew to San Fran once and visited their house, and a second visit to a home with a view of the Pacific Ocean in the LA suburbs.

This was my first and only Byron photography assignment that was an international wedding I had ever attended or photographed. It was several days of drinking, surf, sun, and beach. The setting was terrific, and I worked very hard. Several families kept an eyeball on my work to capture the perfect island moment. Sunset, paradise, and the newlyweds!

2005–2011

Some Lifetouch Adventures, Year by Year The Bay of Pigs Invasion, Cuba

As a means of transitioning from retirement, I took a full-time stop gap job—a place to hone my photography skills, or a job that pays me to become a better photographer. My plan was a success, albeit a tedious way to improve my talent, and I don't enjoy being idle for very long. It was a place to learn formalized lighting and portraiture techniques. During the few years which went by swiftly, I'll take the liberty (it is my story, after all) to place all of this in one chapter. I worked for LNSS (Lifetouch National School Studios) for six long and tiresome years. The hours were long, and the job enjoyment was limited, but I always found a way to provide income for my situation!

On one occasion, my van was stolen right under my nose! I worked at a *middle school* dance for thirteen- to fifteen-year-olds. I drove home late, not suspecting I would be followed by kids (future thugs). The following day, when I woke up and went out to my van where I kept my cigarettes, this event unfolded! I parked in my usual place and walked over to that spot before I even looked to see that it wasn't there. WHAT THE —— HAPPENED TO MY VAN! Gone. And *no* cigarettes! The van was also loaded with a lot of LNSS gear! I called my supervisor, Bo, immediately and told him. I also pointed out that *my* laptop was in my apartment and safe.

"All the tripods, company camera, and lighting equipment were gone! So was my van! with all of my equipment in the van! I won't be able to work today. Sorry, Bo." My boss, Bo Kinsey, was not happy. I said excitedly, "I was at middle school last night." It was only then I realized and remembered several young kids were watching me load my van! I told Bo, "You know what I think happened? Some young ruffians followed me home!"

I would be correct because Bo got a tip about where the stolen gear was later that day. The kids realized they couldn't use these professional cameras, lights, etc.! An observant and kind citizen noticed the equipment thrown out in a field. They saw the company ID tags with an 800 number to call "if found."

My employer was luckier than I was! I called my insurance agent and explained that my Chevy Astro van had been stolen. I think it was a few days later when I got a call from an impound lot (in a sketchy part of downtown Atlanta): "We have your stolen van!"

When I got to the "impound place from hell" and went up to the clerk behind a barred and caged area, I presented my ID and insurance card with VIN and my van. It would not be a pretty reunion. My van was sitting among wrecked cars, stolen cars, and sketchy people. The guy in front of me in a line produced a large wad of cash from his pocket and slid it under the bars to the clerk as I watched from my peripheral vision only. It was *that* kind of place!

My van was trashed. The steering wheel had grown a "goatee of wires" where my knees would have been, had I been sitting behind the wheel! I called my insurance agent and told him. The rest of the sorry details have faded away. I went to my insurance company's lot a few days later and retrieved my few personal belongings. My nice camera vest jacket from the Banana Republic was gone too! And, as I went home after all this, I recalled that only a few days earlier, I had spent a few hundred dollars (unsuccessfully) trying to get it to pass Georgia emissions. I was going to register her and place Georgia tags on her. It was not to be! I learned that I would *never* drive straight home from any assignment ever again!

One other LNSS event that galled me nearly as much as my van episode was trying to get a $100 bill, a Benjamin or C-note changed for smaller bills… You can't go to a Royal Bank of Scotland (RBS) bank in Dekalb County Georgia and get smaller bills from a $100 bill! Not in a Dekalb County, Georgia, bank. UNLESS YOU HAVE AN ACCOUNT WITH THEM! Oddly enough, this was needed for a photo session in the same area where the neighborhood kids went to high school! That stunned me, and for some reason, I didn't make a scene! Only later did I do some research on RBS bank's company president. Mr. Nixon was his name, and there were plenty of complaints I noted on the website for his bank. I "stormed out" of the bank and found a branch for my bank [redacted] and told them I needed some smaller bills. I was politely given two 20s and five 10s and two 5s in change. All was right. Now I could go back to that school to be sniped at for ten hours by many brats! *(School name always remembered but not spelled out here in my autobiography.)*

In a different area, I was locked in a high school for several hours during a gun sighting incident. That was both very stupid and highly annoying. I entered an unguarded open rear exit into the building that got into the habit of using. This was my usual entrance to sign in and work on their campus! Can we revise that now, to an *unorganized* campus? The epitome of unorganized, sloppy, and dumb can be referenced here.

Warning! I'm about to relate an actual, ugly, disturbing event that happened at a local high school (fifty miles away). It was summertime when photos were taken of sports teams. More about this in 2009.

Being delicate here, I'll try to describe *another* event with euphemisms that I will never forget! *Ever*! When I had some free time, or perhaps I was early ("regular" was my middle name) for my assignment, I took a potty break. The restrooms were next to the gym and near the concession area. I strolled into the bathroom, and upon entering a vacant stall (they were *all* vacant), I noticed no toilet tissue. Bang. Open door. Look in. None here. None anywhere. What to do? This was near the concession area, and as luck (or bad luck) would have it, several non-English-speaking ladies were working, cleaning, and socializing around the concession area.

In a whispered voice, I said, "Do you have any toilet paper?" After a few attempts, I received a brand-new, unwrapped, unopened, fresh roll. *Relieved* (he just used an appropriate euphemism) at the possibility of *being* relieved, I entered a stall. In a little while, you'd find (or *not* find) me finishing my business and unwrapping my brand-new and unused fresh roll of TP!

But wait! There's more! Hundreds of *more*! *Roaches everywhere* in my crotch, pants, shirt, the floor! I still can see those bugs as if I just ran out, pulled up my trousers, and nothing else. I have allowed my mind to block that part. Now it's here for future generations to read and laugh their pants off! *Pun intended!*

2006

I have never been to Stonehenge in England, but there is a similar stone carving here in Georgia that resembles the real Stonehenge. The Georgia Guidestones is a granite monument in Elbert County, Georgia, USA. Sheila and I visited there one afternoon and were amazed! No fanfare. No one there to explain this or charge admission. It's just there in the middle of nowhere! In an open field, no sign along the highway saying, "1 mile Georgia Guidestone." A message in stone, clearly conveying a set of ten guidelines, is inscribed on the structure in eight modern languages. A shorter message is cut at the system's top in four ancient language scripts: Babylonian, Classical Greek, Sanskrit, and Egyptian hieroglyphs.

On 06 July 2022, an explosive device exploded at the site. Destroyed totally!

Georgia Guidestones. ©Byron circa 2006. (http://en.m.wikipedia.org/wiki/Georgia_Guidestones)

2007

<<pages 236–237>> for the note my mother gave me. Before this year expires, *my father makes his (final) exit on 02 November*. That November came earlier than he'd planned since he always said he'd get shot by a jealous husband at one hundred. He fell seven years short of that plan, though I was told by my sister Debbie that he did not have dementia. But he did have Amy! *Who's Amy?* We were never introduced, nor did I even meet her. I never met any of my father's paramours that I was aware of. He did bring too many people too much grief, and I can say that with *authority*! My father died at ninety-three (04 October 1914– 02 November 2007). Finally, after a lot of pain inflicted on our family, many of his "friends" and their wives, and slowly the generation he now had left behind, began to heal. And then there were four of us as a family. It was lung cancer that he could not "bullshit"… (sorry for swearing, but he evoked that type of language!)…his way out of. He did smoke Chesterfield, non-filtered cigarettes, for decades. Though we (the remainder of my family) are too old to recover fully, but we have learned a lot. We understand manipulation and being mentally abused—with alcohol, tobacco, drugs, verbal rants, and the resulting suicides are the all too common escape mechanisms surrounding the "old man". I would also include running or moving away from home. I chose both, in my way, and I have no regrets.

Footnote: In my personal effects, I have the original copy of his lengthy poetic autobiography. I hope my copy of his autobiography is kept in the same place as my copy of this autobiography.

2008

I began working a ten-year part-time job in Marietta, Georgia. I was a low-paid volunteer poll worker. A great place to watch the grittiness of people voting (waiting in interminably long lines) and an eclectic group of determined citizens. The strange questions they ask and the frequency of not filling out a simple form boggle the mind, at least mine! Working from 5:30 a.m. until 10:30 p.m. (including unpacking and setup time, plus the tear down and load up the equipment) was a pain and a pleasure. More of the former than the latter, all for $100.00 and a fifteen-minute break. *Wow!* Intense. But I was doing my civic duty, and my coworkers were generally the same age. Younger people couldn't or wouldn't handle the tediousness and constant attention to details that were always required at any moment. My last "tour of duty" ended when I thought I was having a heart attack on the way home. It was only my frazzled nerves, but the entire experience was an eye-opener!

The following event is from 11 November 2008, in Dekalb County, Georgia, post-Lifetouch job. While our photo team was having a late after-work dinner at Applebee's, I saw many, many customers celebrating Obama's election victory. The restaurant was mainly African American, and we were all a bit unsettled at the possibility of alcohol adding to the party. Atlanta does have a history of violence and race-based issues turning ugly. That is a fact-based statement! Since this was typed, there have been several severe racial incidents in the city of Atlanta in 2020.

My Lifetouch duties required me to travel all over the state of Georgia! During my tenure:

- I had a school confiscate (permanently) my new gift from my son, Mark, an excellent Leatherman knife.
- I had the opportunity to interview students and see a lot of ignorance, with rare flashes of brilliance.

ZERO TO SEVENTY-FIVE

- I saw the cops arrive at a basketball game, and I heard (as I exited the gym) that a gun was found.
- I typically worked twelve-hour shifts!

October 2009

I have to return to my afternoon in 2009 (a close guess) to answer this question. I remember the afternoon quite well. It was a unique experience that made me wonder. *Are schools doing all they can? Are our staff members aware of a threat?*

Here's what happened one afternoon. I went to this particular school regularly (as I did at hundreds of schools) as a school photographer. I had a photo company ID (not a school ID badge). I was supposed to photograph a swim meet this afternoon in the natatorium adjacent to the main building. I used the convenient rear entrance, not the main entrance, because the parking area was next to the swimming area. Not the first time I'd been to this sprawling school complex. Entering the building, I passed a few staff members routinely going up the same stairs as I was on as I went to the lower level where the administrators were. I said "hi" as I passed one staff member. "Hi" was the standard reply.

As I arrived on the ground floor, having come in via a closed and unlocked upper level door, I immediately wondered why it was very dark in this area (I had been here before, and it was usually lit) on the lower level. But not seeing police or panic anywhere, I approached the desk area and announced my arrival.

"I need to sign in to take photos of—" I was stopped mid-sentence.

"Who are you?" I explained my visit again and was asked, "Don't you know we're on lockdown now?"

"Really? Huh?" I replied, "Your back door isn't locked. What's going on here?"

"We are locked down, and you *don't belong* here!"

I replied politely, "I'll just go back out where I came in and—"

They cut me off. I was told to go with another person who came around the counter from the sign-in desk.

"Come with me." And I was escorted quickly down a short hall and was told, "Wait here. We're under lockdown. There's an active shooter event going on." She opened the door leading to a small waiting room, suitable for four or five people.

I sat there, in silence, for at least an hour. Alone. No update. No news. Very weird and unsettling.

I had some prior experience with a school shooting several years earlier. We were in Hawaii on a wedding anniversary stay. Turning on the TV, I saw a funeral on the news. The deceased was from our hometown. I recognized the name as I saw her photo on her casket—my photo. *Unfathomable!*

The Vermont Traffic Stop

Mark and I were with my nephew Ian Wright, my sister Deb's son. We had dinner at Chili's. Each of us had a beer (one beer) and a (one) burger. We left the restaurant and headed to Ian's. After only a few minutes, Ian yelled from the backseat, "THERE'S A POLICE CHECKPOINT AHEAD!"

I saw it right in front of me. "Thanks" was my immediate reply. When I approached the cop, I had my window down.

A rotund policeman leaned in toward me and asked, "Have you been drinking?"

Politely, I responded with, "Yes, sir. I just had a beer and a burger at that restaurant behind me."

Pausing for his reply, Ian let loose a long and loud *gasp!* While he was inhaling rapidly! "Thank you, sir. Have a nice evening!"

Ian asked me, "Why did you tell him *that*?" He was scared and confused!

That same local Chili's was also in the news after another adventure. Someone tried to steal the neon sign from the front of the store! Bizarre stupidity. 'Nuff said.

2010

While watching mall people, I play mental games quietly to predict what people's body language may indicate they will do.

> Will they walk past a store or go in it?
> What does their pace tell about them?
> Are they shopping or buying?

I hold as my tenet that "women shop and men buy." There is a difference! People behave when not aware that they're being studied. Watching teens interact and behave is interesting as well. Their alpha member usually is apparent through physical and nonphysical interactions. Body language speaks louder than voices. You can tell who's shopping, buying, or just hanging out. At least I can!

I can spend hours as my wife shops while sitting and people watching. Airports are also good places to do this. Fellow drivers on the highway are well worth watching closely as well. I always expect the unexpected while people/car and driver watching!

This was the year of one of the few visits I made to Ambler. It was a mini high school reunion. I finally visited 313 Heckler St. where I grew up. What a déjà vu experience! The new owner, Bob, was quite receptive and welcomed me into my old house / his new house.

2012

Titanic Memorial Cruise (TMC)

Sheila and I would visit *the* actual sight where the real *Titanic* sank. The same place in the ocean. That ocean was blacker and scarier in person than you read about than seeing it at 11:40 p.m., a hundred years later. In person. In the cold! In the night ocean air! *Unforgettable!*

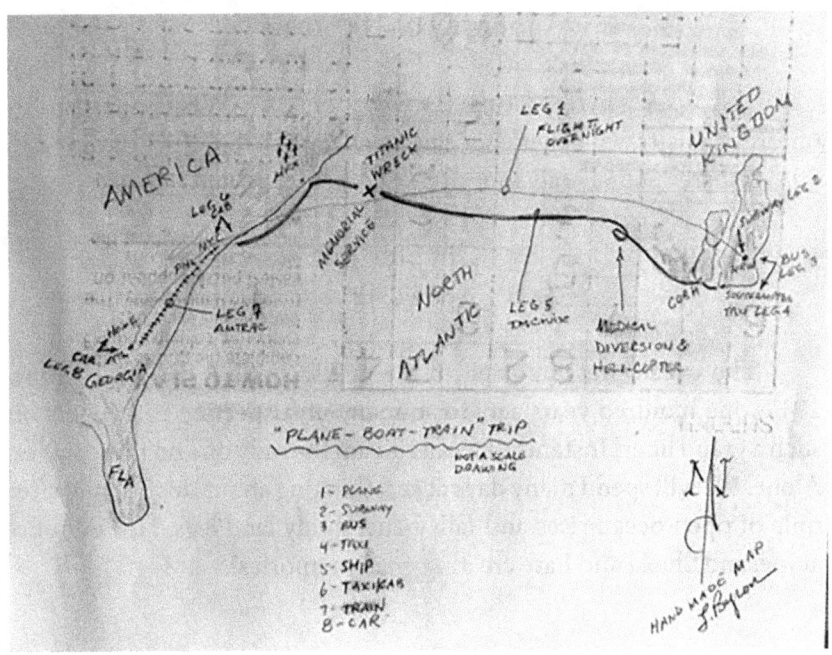

https://norybmot.wordpress.com/about/

    The following paragraphs may become one of the few focal points in my life, aside from births, marriages, and deaths. (*A Journey of 100 Years*, which follows.) Here is my novelette about that memorable trip. Sheila and I were two of the total 220 people from the US to travel to the *Titanic*'s resting place on the exact one hundredth anniversary of her sinking. Accurate, to the minute!

Here is our interview with CNN. We were celebrating our twenty-fifth wedding anniversary by going on the Titanic Memorial Cruise.

Note: it may be slow to load due to a commercial preceding the video if you'd enjoy seeing your author and his lovely spouse! (https://www.cnn.com/videos/us/2012/04/07/pkg-somra-titanic-memorial-cruise-couple.cnn)

*****

A Journey of 100 Years

Also, see here: https://www.quora.com/Whats-your-rmost-unforgettable-travel-experience/answer/Tom-Byron?ch=17&oid=2367059&share=56d5c71a&srid=3JBw&target_type=answer.

Chapter 1
April 2012

The ocean presents itself to me as I imagine it did on 10 April 1912, one hundred years ago, to so many unsuspecting passengers on such a grand liner! Instantly, I feel as if I am the only one on these waves. Alone. We will spend many days at sea, thinking about this, as mile after mile of open ocean rises and falls beneath my land legs. No! I am *not* alone, and Sheila and I are creating *great* memories!

ZERO TO SEVENTY-FIVE

INITIAL BOARDING & DEPARTURE CONDITIONS		
DAY	SUNDAY	
DATE	APRIL 8TH 2012	
LOCATION	SOUTHAMPTON	

TIME LOG		
OUR BOARDING TIME	April 8, 2012	11:04
PILOT ON BOARD	April 8, 2012	14:35
GANGWAY SHIPPED	April 8, 2012	15:31
LAST LINE AWAY	April 8, 2012	16:10
PILOT AWAY	April 8, 2012	18:05
FULL AWAY ON PASSAGE	April 8, 2012	18:26

CONDITIONS AT TIME OF FULL AWAY ON PASSAGE				
MAGNETIC CO	259	DISTANCE TO COBH		382.00 N.M
GYRO	259	ETA AT COBH		13:00 9TH APRIL
SPEED	13.25	DISTANCE TO WRECK		2,210 N.M.
WIND	WSW	ETA AT WRECK		
FORCE	6			
AIR TEMP	12 C	SOULS ON BOARD	STAFF	521
SEA TEMP	10 C		PASSGRS	1250
BAROMETER	1008	FUEL ON BOARD		1,143.74 M.T.
WATER DEPTH	51 MTRS	DIESEL ON BOARD		197.61 M.T.

We are sailing out of Southampton at 4:10 p.m. or 1610 hours (local time) from the dock precisely next to where *the Titanic* left on its maiden voyage. Too many hopes and dreams of hundreds of immigrants' exhilarating trips that would end in a disaster, and the world would shudder to learn about it! Many of the world's most influential and wealthy returned home with their servants and maids on "the ship of dreams." Our journey takes us back to those on this journey one hundred years, and I know that 1,496 people back in 1912 will never see land again. Seven hundred twelve survived, and we will meet some of their relatives. Millvina Dean was the last of those 712 survivors from that horrific night to pass away. We have her autograph. She signed 712 books, and we have one of them. Her signature is precious!

We are given a celebratory send-off with a band playing joyously. Everyone was waving goodbye as the crowds did in 1912. They shared our anticipation as the ship's propellers increased their power, and we entered the main shipping channel. The similarity is haunting as I think of those faded black-and-white photos we have all seen. The tugboat pushes us in the right direction, and we are underway.

The following day is foggy as the sun rises to warm the cold morning air. We didn't stop at Cherbourg, France, across the English Channel for reasons we never figured out! The seas are calm and serene, at least from the deck of the *Balmoral*. It is hard to imagine how close death can be, maybe only a few feet. I know *this* modern ship will not sink, and the *Titanic* passengers knew *their* ship could/would not sink! The difference between what can be and what will be is a haunting reminder as this day unfolds.

A warm cup of coffee is a welcomed treat in forty-degree air as day 2 begins. The seas have turned angry overnight, reminding me and many others that we have not yet earned our sea legs as quickly as possible.

The *Balmoral*'s arrival in Cobh, Ireland, one hundred years after the *Titanic*, is celebrated by this community. This port was known as Queenstown in 1912. We were a bit behind schedule, but there was plenty of time to make that up. If anyone had ever heard of the Irish story of leprechauns and the proverbial pot of gold at the end of a rainbow, as the rain stopped and I looked toward the east, they became believers. The day ended on a very hopeful note, both literally and figuratively.

We didn't sleep well our first night out on the open ocean since the seas had gotten very rough as night fell. Trying to sleep at sea was a chore. We would adjust!

The following day: The announcement comes over the ship's intercom suddenly and unexpectedly. From the bridge, our captain, Robert Bamberg, tells us that we have an emergency. The collective gasp of the passengers is palpable! We memorialize a disaster on a state-of-the-art ship, and *we have an emergency*? Certainly not! Over the comforting sounds of the powerful diesel engines carrying us over the ocean at seventeen knots, we are told the devastating news. Heart attack on board. This is a frightful statement, but over a hundred miles out on the open ocean, it is your worst nightmare! You hope you can survive this event if you get to a hospital in a few minutes. Modern techniques and medical treatments are amazing in 2012. In 1912, you would likely not survive. With the nearest hospital a hundred miles away, this would be serious if you had to travel by ambulance. But if you had to wait three hours for the medical team to reach you and then had to ride three hours to the hospital, terrifying. Now imagine your ambulance is a helicopter. Here's my friend Craig Lee's excellent video. Get a cuppa or a "wee nip o' whisky." As our Cap'n Bamberg says, "A diversion."

ARRIVAL COBH

TUESDAY

APRIL 10TH 2012

AT SEA

TIME LOG

April 10, 2012	15:08
April 10, 2012	16:05
April 10, 2012	18:48
April 10, 2012	19:11

MEDICAL DIVERSION DATA

VARIABLE	DISTANCE RUN		
VARIABLE	HOURS RUN		19.83
14	AVERAGE SPEED		VARIABLE
NW	DISTANCE TO WRECK		1,618
8-Jul			
12 C	SOULS ON BOARD	STAFF	521
12 C		PASSGR	1,253
995	FUEL ON BOARD		1,041
4,054 M	DIESEL ON BOARD		189.71

https://youtu.be/XD6SXve_tO0

As the Irish medical helicopter arrives several hours after the captain's announcement, Sheila and I and our 1,300 fellow passengers are given our instructions. We are all involved in this "rescue operation", as our Cap'n referred to this emergency over the intercom.

"*Attention! Will all passengers and crew please leave all outside deck areas and remain inside the ship until further notice.*"

Roaring and whirling helicopter blades are heard as the rescue chopper approaches us on the open ocean. We all watch anxiously as the rescue team approaches, all heads craned upward to watch as the drama slowly unfolds. Others undoubtedly share my thoughts as we watch silently with our ideas. Will this be successful? Is it too windy? We have stopped here with no land in sight. With no backup plans. This is success or failure—*right now!* As the red chopper hunts overhead for the correct approach, the downforce of the blades on the glass ceiling is protecting us from a potential catastrophe, but the chopper is mere feet above us. We all wait. The attempt is slow, noisy, and meticulous. The medical team is lowering a basket that swings precariously above us. Everyone who has a camera is clicking away as the seconds pass for the patient. We know little or nothing about his situation. Is it life or death? As quickly as the basket is lowered, with only a brief hesitation, it lifts, and this substantial red invader of our ship's tranquility steals away and out of our line of sight.

After only a few seconds, we assume the mission here is over, and the patient is headed back to Ireland. No! No sooner is there a collective sigh of relief and chattering about "Did you see *that*?" than a second chopper approaches the ship from the clear blue sky above us. No. Is it the same helicopter taking on yet a second patient? We are not given details, just a warning to stay undercover inside. We cannot see what is happening. We all have to guess. The chopper again descends toward us with a rescue lift basket dangling perilously close to the ship. Rumors suggested that the first try was a failure. After maneuvering and adjusting to the pilot's commands from a slightly different angle, down comes the basket! The medical team, over our heads, out of our sight, guides the rope dangling from the chopper to the proper position and quickly raises the basket for the second attempt. We cannot see what is going on since the thick glass sheltering us is covered with salt spray. This is not where we usually look. We want to see the ocean, not the skies overhead. *Success!* The chopper is rapidly angling up and away toward a hospital in Ireland and medical help. It was a "Titanic" effort. *Now* we can relax.

It is still five days until we reach the ocean grave of the most famous shipwreck. The marking of time becomes confusing. "What time is it?" and "What day is it?" becomes a common question. For these next few days, we all have various plans on how to spend each day. The choices are varied between sunning out on the decks, attending lectures, reading, or eating and drinking more than we do back home. But all the while, our conversations evolve to *Titanic* discussions: "Did you know that…" and "Have you seen this or that photograph?" Every day my knowledge about this ghost lying over twelve thousand feet below the surface grows.

Chapter 2
April 2012

I awake today after a night of somewhat calmer seas. The bed and the floor are moving? Oh, I realize I am at sea! I learn later that the waves last night were around thirty feet high. No wonder sleep was elusive. My alarm clock is now the TV. Since our cabin is much like the size that the *Titanic* steerage accommodations were, there is no porthole view. I do not know the time, since we are under "ship time". The TV in the cabin has a channel that shows a webcam feed from the bow, so a glance at this tells me if the sun is up or not. When finally I come out on the aft deck, I immediately notice two things. Sleep was better last night, and the haunting comments made in every *Titanic* story I have ever read are related: the sea today is "as calm as a millpond." Now I have this eerie feeling of coming out from my steerage cabin and seeing how peaceful and inviting the sea is today. When there is any free time, which there is plenty of, my time is spent just watching the sea. The wake from the ship, trailing behind us, is a deep blue with white foam. Quite hypnotic. No birds. No ships. The clouds and the waves have become my skyline.

Today's sunrise is typical of the remaining mornings, with broken clouds and fog. As the sun rises higher, I can capture some pretty photographs. There is no smog to ruin my view. Part of my time on my second cup of coffee is whale watching. We might see them, so I would like to get at least one chance to take this photo—if I am super lucky! After several more days toward the wreck site, I have another photo goal shared by other photo hounds aboard: *icebergs*! There are plenty of lectures to attend every day. Today, it is Mr. Littlejohn, the grandson of a first steward on the *Titanic*. He told us his own story from his family, and it was pretty enjoyable, but the idea that he was an actual living relative was my main reason for listening to him. Nothing specifically informative. Just being a little closer to a few of the passengers' families who were on board *the* Titanic was exciting enough.

Of the 1,300 or so of my fellow Titanic Memorial Cruise passengers, one chap deserves special mention. There are hundreds of Brits, Irish, Australians, and many people on this trip. John Strachan, from New Zealand, is among those many other foreigners (German, Japanese, Australians, Scots, Swedes, Canadians, etc.) traveling on the *Balmoral*. John is also using two canes to walk, but again, there are other wheelchair users and disabled people. John Strachan did tell me something shocking. He is traveling alone, *at the age of eighty-seven!* Every time I passed him on my trips around the ship, he always had a big smile and was having as good a time as the younger passengers.

I have realized one item that will increase my sense of the *Titanic's* journey and foundering. I have learned that the ship's construction number was 401. When we stayed at the Grand Harbour Hotel in Southampton, our room number was 410, and the cabin on the *Balmoral* was 4010. Mmm?

Chapter 3
April 2012

Another lecturer spoke to a large gathering of perhaps two hundred of us who are always interested in another *Titanic* story. Mr. Haisman, age seventy-three, did not disappoint. He told us about his mother, Elizabeth, among the 705 passengers who finished her trip to New York on board the rescue ship *Carpathia*. She was fifteen when she was placed into the lifeboat and was rowed away from the *Titanic* as it slowly died. I can now understand, at least partly, how this experience must have felt. The North Atlantic is so pitch-black. So cold. I can hardly imagine how terrified that must have made her feel. Having personally stood at the railing of the *Balmoral* and looked out into the ocean at night was scary. I realize it was much clearer that night in 1912, but since I have not seen any stars yet, I don't know how much light they added. It couldn't have been much, if any! If I have one regret on all my days at sea, it will be that I never saw those stars that were out that night. "A Night To Remember".

Mr. Haisman is the youngest of ten children his mother bore, and to sit and listen to him talk about someone who told him about that night was mesmerizing. A connection to that night, one hundred years ago, was stunning. This is one of the reasons we took this voyage.

Whales! Finally, my time spent staring at the ocean is rewarded. Do you think five seconds of seeing two orcas was worth the four days of hunting for them on a vast ocean? It was, even though this was probably a mother and her calf. Once I yelled out, "Whale!" a small group gathered next to me and saw these visitors. Or were *we* the visitors? I told them I had seen a spout of mist, then another next to the first one a second or two later. Then I saw large black fins simultaneously rise above the surface and immediately disappear. Mother and child? There was zero chance to aim my camera, focus, compose, and take a photo!

There are still three days remaining before we will reach the location of the *Titanic* wreck. Our captain gives us a daily report at noon, which concludes in his Norwegian accent: "And from za bridge, all… ees…vell!" This saying is said in unison by all the people around me as he speaks. It is uplifting to know where we are, and our Captain keeps us informed. We know our location, heading, speed, distance, sea depth, and air and water temperatures. The excitement builds as we make our way westward since his report also tells us the distance remaining to the wreck site.

There is always a group on the lido deck to chat with and exciting stories whenever I ask, "How did you become interested in *Titanic*? What country are you from?"

Jane, from the UK, is an excellent example of one of those answering these conversation starters. Jane has been interested in the *Titanic* for a long time. She collects what she can that is *Titanic*-related like we all try to do. She tells me that she recently found something on eBay that caught her eye. Like most of us, we have all seen those iconic photos of the *Titanic* at the dock in Southampton. She was lucky enough to find an ancient *Titanic* print. When she receives her photo, she notices two things immediately: it is ancient, and it is water damaged. (For those photographers here, I think it is a silver-gelatin print.) Jane's question is simply whether this is the *Titanic's* or the Olympic's. Where else to get a reasonable opinion but here on this cruise? It is determined to be the *Titanic*, and it is also realized that this photo was probably made on 02 April 1912, maybe after her return from fitting out and sea trials. It is known that a dinner was held on the ship for VIPs that same day. The print is not in 100 percent condition, but it is a professional and very sharply focused photograph.

Plenty of minute details can be seen. During her handling of this hundred-year-old photo, tragedy befalls her prized *Titanic* photograph. The print and the cardboard mat it is mounted on breaks in half. The irony is gripping! Here is an original photo, not a copy, of the *Titanic* being shown to fellow *Titanic* enthusiasts on this memorial voyage of the breakup and death of this ship of dreams out on the same North Atlantic as in 1912.

Chapter 4
April 2012

After a week at sea, I have become friends with many people who are now regulars on the lido deck 7. We drink (coffee and beer) together, discuss our shipboard experiences about all things *Titanic*, and spend our time between lectures and meals having a relaxing trip. I am still trying to understand my three Scotsmen—Ally, Nigel, and Henley. It might be my DNA that I share which allows me to understand the Irish and the Brits including the Scots. These my DNA percentages, now. They've been refined in the last ten years. I now know I'm Irish 65%, Eng & NW Eur. 21%, Scottish 14%. When the Scots have had a lot more to drink than me, well, it is all English... but huh? For three days, I am on a team putting a jigsaw puzzle together. Claire is a true puzzle fan, and she even has a large carrying case on which to assemble a puzzle.

The scene for this giant puzzle (thirty-by-forty inches) is the *Titanic* debarking from Southampton in 1912. I helped Claire and was joined by Lauren and others. It became a team effort for many hours there on the aft deck! Smoking and building, puzzle piece after puzzle piece, a scene of the *Titanic*! Slowly, the picture came together, and we had others watching and helping with this process. We all enjoyed finishing this and knowing that there were no missing pieces among the one thousand we had. Claire would later tell me that this puzzle was given to the servers at the Lido Lounge.

Every evening at 8:30 p.m. is a formal dinner on deck 6 with three other couples—Kris and Kurt from Alaska; Susie and Gary from Ventura, California; and Karen and Susan from Santa Barbara, California. At our first dinner, Gary asks, "Are we all Democrats?"

Oh my! If he had only known. I raised my hand, acknowledging my political leaning to the right. It was seven Democrats and one Republican, and it was interesting for the rest of *that* dinner. There are now **TWO REPUBLICANS!** The next several dinners did not involve any political talk because I didn't mention politics, and Gary didn't. I learn that our Alaskan friends are in the Merchant Marine service, and they share their ship experiences with our cruise experiences. Kris and Kurt enjoy living in "the middle of nowhere," Alaska.

I am ready for our arrival at the wreck site tomorrow evening, and while I am listening to (music see end of chpt. 6) Anthony Stuart Lloyd sing, my mind is dwelling on how all this will go on the fourteenth. I am confident the cruise will organize a memorable, respectful time. Today is "Friday the thirteenth", not a good time or place to be a superstitious person. Tony, as we call him, has a vast bass-baritone voice and sings opera, mostly. Fine with me, but not so fine for some. Tony is a fellow smoker, and along with many other regulars, we swap stories and drink long into the night! Tony is Welsh, as well as being about six five, and is the only person I have ever heard speak Gaelic and Welsh. As we retire, I am aware, from the captain's report, that the depth of the sea is over two thousand meters, and the air and water temperature is below twenty degrees Celsius. I hope the sea stays calm.

Chapter 5
April 2012

14 April 2012, Saturday, will be *the* day of this voyage. We are on the seventh day of *A Journey of 100 Years*, and it is rough sailing after a long calm stretch of open ocean. The day's talk centers around the events happening at 11:40 p.m. tonight. Our captain tells us we have set the ship's clock back one hour and twenty-seven minutes. What? Where did the twenty-seven minutes come from? In a later one-on-one Q and A with the captain, I am told it has a little to do with leap year and a little to do with "historical" time. "Way too complicated for me to explain," he tells me. I will figure out this twenty-seven minutes issue later.

I am told that the ship's people and the *Titanic* people disagree some on this point, but Captain Bamberg has the final say! Twenty-seven minutes. The captain tells everyone in his noon update what to expect tonight when we are at the same wreck site:

OFFICIAL TITANIC MEMORIAL SITE CEREMONY				
DAY	SATURDAY	TO	SUNDAY	
DATE	APRIL 14TH	TO	APRIL 15TH	
LOCATION	LATITUDE	41 - 43.57 N	LONGITUDE	049 - 56.49 W

TIME LOG		
	DATE	TIME
ARRIVED TITANIC SITE (EOSP)	14TH APRIL 2012	23:56
COMMENCED MEMORIAL CEREMONY	14TH APRIL 2012	23:40
COMPLETED MEMORIAL SERVICE	15TH APRIL 2012	2:20
RETURN TO NORMAL STEAMING (SOSP)	15TH APRIL 2012	3:07

MEMORIAL SERVICE AT TITANIC MEMORIAL SITE DATA				
MAGNETIC CO	VARIABLE	DISTANCE RUN		1,908
GYRO	VARIABLE	HOURS RUN		124.6
SPEED	ON STATION	AVERAGE SPEED		VARIABLE
WIND	VARIABLE	DISTANCE TO WRECK		ON SITE
FORCE	1 (LIGHT AIRS)			
AIR TEMP	10 C	SOULS ON BOARD	STAFF	521
SEA TEMP	15 C		PASSGR	1,253
BAROMETER	1016	FUEL ON BOARD		1,041.14
WATER DEPTH	3,026 MTRS	DIESEL ON BOARD		189.71

41 43' 32" N49 56' 49" W. There will be two minutes of silence at 11:40 p.m. There will be three wreaths dropped overboard from the aft deck 7, and there will be a brief Christian ceremony led by the Reverend Canon Huw Mosford, director of chaplaincy, the Mission to Seafarers, Halifax, Nova Scotia. There will be a song by Tony Lloyd. There will be tears shed, hugging, and people staring blankly off into the abyss. Am I ready?

Our formal dinner tonight is in the Ballindalloch, named after the Speyside village and castle in Scotland. The *Balmoral* is named for the Scottish home of the UK's royal family. The dinner was the same dinner served on 14 April 1912. There are seven courses. *First*, Poached Salmon with Mousseline Sauce, or Quail Eggs in Aspic with Caviar. *Second*, Consommé Olga, or Cream of Barley Soup. *Third*, Asparagus Salad with Champagne Saffron Vinaigrette. *Fourth*, Punch Romaine. *Fifth*, Baked Haddock with Sharp Sauce and Buttered Green Peas and Boiled Rice, or Calvados Roast Duckling with Apple Sauce and Roast Potatoes and Braised Cabbage. Or (my selection) Filet Mignons Lili and Sliced Baked Potatoes with Roasted Cherry Tomatoes and Baby Carrots. Or Roast Pork with Sage and Pearl Onions, and Boiled Potatoes, Creamed Carrots, and Minted Pea Timbale. Or finally, Vegetable Marrow Farci. *Sixth*, Waldorf Pudding, Peaches in Chartreuse Jelly, or Chocolate and Vanilla Eclairs (my other choice). *Seventh*, Assorted Fresh Fruits, or Selection of Cheeses. After dinner, tea and coffee. I could never eat a selection from *all* seven courses at 8:30 p.m. But wow! Grand dinner!

We return to the lido deck to digest and reflect on why we booked this cruise and drink and smoke. You could, by now, begin to sense the emotion of the night. It was chilly, perhaps thirty-nine to forty-three degrees. Not cold, but indeed a lousy night for swimming about in the blackness of this ocean. I cannot imagine the terror of that night based on being warmish and dry on deck. There are no stars to be seen or when the clouds parted, nothing like a hundred years ago! As the time approaches, the second ship arrives at the site. The *Azamara* comes from New York. This second ship was added late in the planning of our trip due to the high booking demand for this one-time memorial on this night.

There is no way, no words, no photos to convey the sense of what I am witnessing. Hundreds of people gathered on the aft decks (7, 8, 9, 10, and 11) with no room for one more person. The minister, the soloist, and three young men dressed in 1912 sailor suits are gathered at the edge of the aft deck 7 with three biodegradable commemorative wreaths and three candles to be lit. It is challenging to jostle into a position to view everything happening. After the candles are lit, the wreaths are thrown overboard into the ocean. There is a brief participatory ceremony, and Anthony Stuart Lloyd approaches the microphone. Cue the music, linked at the end of this chapter. He starts singing in his lovely deep, rich bass-baritone voice, "Nearer My God to Thee." And if there were any dry eyes, they are not now. Powerful, haunting, sad, gut-wrenching. To realize that a hundred years ago, as the *Titanic* sank below the waves, as the survivors rowed away from her, these were the words and melody they heard. My imagination cannot get there. Time is frozen. We are one mass of humanity, weeping and hugging.

We recognize several people in this video whom we have held reunions with in the UK. The ship in the background is the *Azamara Journey* that sailed east from New York City. You can also see her in the ending videos of our arrival in New York City on 19 April 2012.

You may need to find a tissue before watching this: Anthony Stuart Lloyd sing "Nearer My God To Thee" https://youtu.be/Hig7XAfUKCY.

Chapter 6
16 April 2012

Halifax, Canada, is where the *Carpathia* took passengers (then deceased) who did not find a lifeboat as the *Titanic* sank. As we head for that very same safe harbor, I am on the lookout this morning for any sign of land, and the appearance of a seabird should tell me we are getting closer. We spend all day Sunday, 16 April, on a calm and cloudy sea. Now it is not as cold as when I was on this deck. I am entirely not sure if the cold air is solely to blame for feeling cold last night. My thoughts are still of being in a wooden lifeboat and on this morning, as the 705 survivors were, while they were hoping and praying for rescue. Everyone was a little tired from staying up until 3:00 a.m. and were struggling to process the events of just imagining where we were, stopped in the North Atlantic. *We* are looking for land. *They* were looking for salvation from the ocean. On the sixteenth, as the mist cleared and warmer air returned, it brought some sense of how those who were being rescued at this same hour must have felt—onboard a safer vessel.

As I sit and look at the ocean, my attention is drawn to a sound I have never heard before. A Japanese man is standing at the railing of the aft deck, at the same place where the last passengers on the *Titanic* stood, as eight hundred and eighty three feet of iron and wood and safety sank beneath their feet, leaving them in the twenty-eight-degree water. I should point out there was one particular survivor from this situation—the ship's baker. He was very drunk, having unceremoniously and alone finished off a whole bottle of scotch(?). In a stupor, he has carried off this same part of the ship where I now hear this music coming from. *He survived!* I will learn later that the person playing the ocarina was Mr. Hiroshi Otomo, and when he finished this lovely song, I thanked him for sharing this haunting music with me. I will never know if this was his commemoration to all those who died a hundred years ago or just a tune he liked. Was it a coincidence he was playing on the aft deck by the railing? I must point out, though, that this was the first and only time I saw him on the *Balmoral*. I am glad he permitted me to take several photographs. We still exchange messages and compliment each other's photos on Facebook! He is a kind and good friend!

I am excited to spot a seabird, perhaps a tern. The land is still about a hundred miles away, by my rough calculations, but it will be good to feel the earth beneath my wobbly feet. It won't be until later today (the sixteenth) that we reach Halifax, Nova Scotia, Canada. I finally see more birds, a few tankers, cargo ships, and land around 3:00 p.m., but it won't be until 5:00 p.m. that we are in the harbor. As I wandered around the ship this afternoon, I discovered a wedding on deck 11, the observatory deck. The couple, from Ireland, are dancing their first dance and are accompanied by a lovely singer playing something (I wasn't listening, just watching) on the piano. Lauren Casey and my wife, Sheila, had met earlier in the dining room. This was the first wedding I have been to after retiring from being a wedding photographer. Odd to sit and watch.

By 6:15 p.m., the ship is tied up at the dock. Solid feeling, no rocking, and I know sleep will be peaceful and restful finally. Tomorrow I will be on "terra firma" and visit the cemeteries.

Chapter 7
April 2012

Halifax's cemetery trip is going to be very interesting. Considering that this is the only place I have ever seen photos of what can be visited, I am ready to go on this tour. The security getting on and off the *Balmoral* is very efficient. Just a card swipe of your ID, and you can hope they will not sail off and leave you behind. Their system has all your info on a magnetic stripe on a credit card-sized ID. As much as I dislike being driven around with a tour director announcing this or that, but I have no choice. The tour covers other interesting places between our ship tied up at the dock and the three cemeteries: historic mansions in the $10 million range, military installations, old churches, and several places related to Halifax's connection to the *Titanic*.

The first stop is the most famous and most viewed cemetery, Fairview. The *Titanic* section is an area within a large actively used cemetery. There are 121 graves here, including a number and other obvious information (of what was known). The number is a grim reminder of the enormity of this tragedy, as their bodies were recovered on to the deck of the *Carpathia*. They were numbered, 1 through 334. The stones, mostly just inscribed with the name "Died 15 April 1912," stand forever to remind humanity that when we think we are indestructible, we learn humility.

Every grave is decorated with flowers, and it is a time for quietness and remembrance. Different groups in Halifax feel a loving sense of connection to these souls. The stones placed by the White Star Line are simple and uniform in size and shape. The black starkness of their plain shiny granite is also a stark reminder to all who visit this resting place for so many families. These rows of monuments are laid out to form the outline of the bow of the *Titanic* and silently remind us of all of the lives lost a hundred years ago.

Chapter 8
April 2012

We conclude our brief tour of Halifax and re-board the *Balmoral*, ready to sail away around 6:00 p.m. and back on the open sea by 7:00 p.m. We spend the eighteenth starting to realize our memorial cruise will soon end. There's a "Queen tribute" (as in the rock group) concert for our last night on board. Gavin does an excellent job, but Freddie, he is *not!* A few pints of Guinness and our last night on the ocean ends, but tomorrow will be unique. As I leave the lido deck very late, I notice that even though NYC is over a hundred miles away, there is a faint but certain glow on the western horizon. *The* city.

By 6:00 a.m., the next morning, I have my coffee and a place in my regular location on lido deck, and the crowd grows. My hope for this harbor sight of New York is rewarding, as the morning darkness changes into a heavy mist, which the sunrise quickly burns away. By the time we pass under the Verrazano Narrows Bridge, there are not many free places to stand at the railing, but I get a few photos of us arriving in America. This massive two-mile-long suspension bridge, at dawn, with the orange sky and the droning of the ship's engines, is something to behold! Immediately after this comes Lady Liberty, the focal point of America that every immigrant knows. Its symbolism is a proud invitation to go to the USA. All those steerage passengers surely thought about this sight as they left Southampton and now lie eternally at Fairview Cemetery. As we sail into New York City, I see the Freedom Tower under construction. It is yet another symbol of hope and resurrection. My journey of a hundred years is ending, and I will always feel a slight sense of understanding of all that I experienced.

We arrive in New York Harbor. Thoughts of ours, at the time, were of those who never saw their dreams becoming real and seeing what you'll see in this video with a musical soundtrack!

https://youtu.be/Zr9B9W5P36c our arrival in America
https://youtu.be/CC700Bo2QSk our arrival in America

As we part with our newfound shipmates/friends, it was said more than once, "Have a good life." We know these goodbyes could be as final as the *Titanic* ones. Farewell and RIP.

*****

This lengthy section above, covering a memorable trip, was the progenitor of this autobiography. I found an answer to my search question about learning to write better—on Quora. I stayed there for about five or six years, and the above story was my first product. Now this autobiography is my second product.

23 July 2012

A memorable decision was made, on this day, after much thought! My teeth had to go. I was going to wear dentures. In retrospect, it was a grand idea. The day after my surgery, and after a single dose of OxyContin, I was oblivious to pain. I realized as my dose wore off, I was still in control of my pain. But my troubles were both ending and beginning. Two different ideas in parallel—I quit smoking the next day, and my forty-six-year-old Zippo lighter went missing. I became a "deranged case" looking in my recliner chair, in my bathroom, in my car, everywhere. No luck! *Zip*, nada, zilch! I became possessed. Eventually, I gave up. It must have fallen in the toilet.

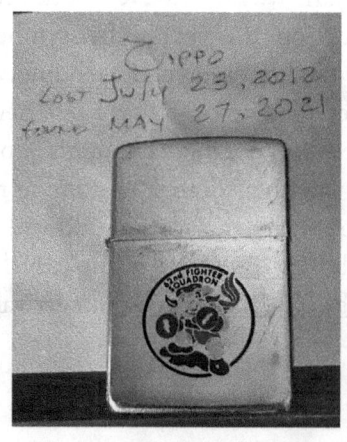

2013

I have been on my favorite site, Quora, for about a year now. I'm still working on help with my writing skills. A new ambition, perhaps? I answered a question that led me to write down a few random events. The list grew as I wrote and probed my memory. Here's my list in your hands right now. I decided this could become part of my autobiography. As it grew, it would no longer be just a list. It would serve as my life's story, and I became an accidental author! I kept a log (as it were on Quora) of these experiences, prepared just for a question like this. Here it is for you viewers to consider. While I was newly retired, I was asked if I'd like to be in a movie. I was an extra this year in a movie in Savannah, Georgia, called *Cracker Jack*. I don't think it was a huge hit, but I had to watch it. My scene was cut. No wonder it was a flop! At least I was paid $75.00 and hung around the set from 6:00 a.m. until 11:00 p.m. It was tiresome, and I decided that Hollywood was not for me.

2014

Belfast and County Antrim Adventure and TMC Reunion from Cruise

Belfast trip https://norybmot.wordpress.com/2014/04/

The above highlighted version contains all the photographs from this visit.

Chapter 1
2014

TMC Reunion 2014, Belfast, Northern Ireland
Friday, 18 April 2014

It was with heavy hearts and much sadness, with a long goodbye, that we left Northern Ireland just now.

Leaving Belfast

As the wheels went up on our plane, leaving George Best City Airport, we looked back on those few days with many, many warm memories. We could never have imagined this trip as it now lives in our memory. We were thinking back to when we arrived at our new international terminal, where we set out on 09 April 2014, in Atlanta, Georgia, ready for a lifetime adventure. It was 6:00 p.m., and the security and ticketing were much smoother than expected. Time for dinner, and then wait to board our British Airways flight to London.

It is never easy to sleep on a plane, but we tried. It reminded me of Christmas Eve. You fight sleep thinking about what the morning would bring.

I woke up somewhere over the North Atlantic, several hundred miles before we saw land.

The Irish coast was as pretty as we imagined. Green open pastures and small farmhouses. We were going to flying be over Ireland for a little while as we headed for London.

London Heathrow Airport was noisy and crowded, not as new as Atlanta's airport. Very much like any airport in the US, except they all drive and walk on the left. We never got used to doing or seeing that. After some shuttling around through a rat maze of buildings and tunnels, we got from our arrival terminal to our departure terminal. More waiting.

Leaving London behind, we headed north back over some of the same terrains we had just traveled over, but with anticipation growing as we got closer and closer to where we would spend the next ten days. Claire (remember the lady with that Titanic puzzle from our ship?) met us and made our short trip to our temporary home very easy. After a few hugs, we were ready to head to the Ramada Encore in the heart of Belfast. Again, as I got in the front seat, it felt awkward to see the steering wheel on my right as I sat where, in America, I sat when I drove. Weird. But we were in Belfast and didn't even care that it was raining just a little. Northern Ireland is the rainiest part of Europe, so we felt lucky that we never had to use our umbrellas. The rain does make Ireland as green as you can imagine, especially in early April.

Sitting in the bar at our hotel, listening to someone singing Bob Dylan music, was not exactly what we imagined. I drank my Guinness and Sheila drank her Stella (no Bud Light), we could finally relax. The music was good enough, though, especially after listening to the whine of those jet engines for eight hours over the Atlantic and one and a half hours over England and Ireland. Now our ongoing chore we would never complete was the five-hour time change! I kept reminding Sheila that as we drank our nth beer, it was only 9:30 p.m. back home while it was 2:30 a.m. in Belfast. We were told to stay up as late as possible the first night (or until they ran out of Guinness, which didn't happen) to get on local time.

Chapter 2
2014

Thursday, 10 April 2014

Our first surprise met us in our room. It was dark, and the lights would not turn on. A trip to the front desk made me feel stupid. I forgot to use the room key to activate the lights. But your room key could not help the bathroom situation. The shower and loo area were all common! No shower enclosure separated the bath from the loo, but a nice hot shower in the morning still felt good, even as I wondered if I was missing something as I missed about those lights earlier. Lovely people, the Irish are. I am proud that my mother's parents are from Ireland.

Off to sleep. Too tired and had too many pints to battle this odd shower. This is off to bed for Sheila and me. Tomorrow is an off day, but about sixty "Titanaracs" (like the word maniacs, but altered and getting more common) will be arriving. On Friday, 11 April 2014, we have until 3:00 p.m. to relax and get unpacked and sorted out, and our first adventure begins. What time is it? Should I be sleeping now? Why am I tired? I am watching people in the Encore Restaurant and looking at people as I drink my third cup of black coffee. Sheila's sleeping, but since I don't know if I recognize this couple from the *Balmoral* or not, off to the room with coffee for Ms. Sheila and to get ready for our first tour on the River Lagan. It is not real warm, but it is damp and overcast. We didn't come here for the sunshine and beaches. *Titanic* is on our brains, and we expect there is no test when this trip comes to an end, so we will listen and pay attention.

River Lagan tour boat

There are about eleven of us leaving the hotel at 2:30 p.m. to find our way to the statue of a fish near the River Lagan and where our tiny boat will carry us up and down the Lagan to see several *Titanic* landmarks. It is exciting, but the wind is biting. Did I dress warmly enough?

After some confusion (no one would admit they were lost or where the building was to buy our tickets), we made it through some construction and detours, and it was nice to get inside. The boat we climbed aboard on was about fifty feet long, with all outside seating. Our cap'n navigated and explained the sights we were chugging past. We made our way past the Belfast Titanic Centre, the H&W cranes, the reconstructed bow section of the *Titanic* (for the Discovery Channel TV show), the pump house, and docks. All these would be visited individually over the next several days. This was an incredible boat tour and lasted a little over an hour, giving everyone a preview of our upcoming adventures. Our "den mother," Claire, and her two assistants, Maureen and Susie, would see that all of us were organized and on time for each of these trips down "memory lane." Photos and excitement enough to last forever were in store.

Back to the hotel for more refreshments for most of us and a nap for others. Our adventure had begun. I was snapping a few photos and trying to sort out the myriad of sights, where we were, and pausing to think, *We are here in Belfast after waiting so long for this reunion!* The meet and greet begins at 8:00 p.m., and we will then realize this trip is underway! The name tags are a great idea since we didn't meet everyone on *Balmoral*. Even though we were on the same ship, it was quite an enormous space. Lots of fun meeting people and putting names with faces and hearing their accents: German, Australian, Danish, Irish, British, Canadian, American, and Scottish.

On Saturday, we will be on our first bus trip, but for now, "All eez vell from zee bridge." Time for a pint and off to bed by midnight. We are leaving early tomorrow morning.

Chapter 3
2014

Saturday, 12 April 2014

Today is another early trip out and about. We better be assembled in the lobby by 8:45 a.m. for our briefing and instructions for visiting Thomas Andrews' home, Dunellen. This is our first venture away from the center of Belfast.

Mr. Andrews said goodbye to his wife, Helen, and his daughter, Elizabeth, on 02 April. The sailing date was delayed one day due to weather. He assumed he would return to his family after a maiden voyage to New York City. He was only thirty-nine and had just recently celebrated his last birthday, February.

We were greeted by Thomas Andrews (Mal Stocker-Jones as an impersonator), who explained that our visit to his home was poorly timed. He was headed off to board the *Titanic*, which he explained to us was a fantastic feat of engineering! He was pretty charming but showed us a video, and he said, "This might explain it better." After about forty-five minutes, we were back on the bus. The next stop was Comber. What a beautiful ride through some country we were treated to before we arrived, taking the scenic Kings Road, A22. Several schoolchildren greeted us at the Thomas Andrews Memorial Hall. This lovely old building was now being used as a school and was immediately across from an old linen mill. The Andrews family owned this, where they earned their fortune.

The Andrews Mill papers comprise 544 volumes relating to the flax spinning mill in Comber, Co. Down, and fifty-five about the various Andrews family farms and estates, Cos Down, Cavan, and Kilkenny. Once the volumes had ceased to be of administrative use, they had been placed in the attics above the mill offices for safekeeping, and there, they had remained relatively undisturbed. The archive was uplifted from the attics during 1997 and transported to PRONI in two van loads. This massive business archive, perhaps one of the biggest in PRONI, provides a unique insight into the life not only of a significant manufacturing company but a whole community.

The archive has been divided into two principal sections: records of Andrew's flax spinning mill, Comber (D4189/A-D), and farm books (D4189/E). Before describing the archive and the wealth of information recorded within it, it may be helpful to give a brief introduction of the family which created it. The Andrews family loom large in the history of the mill and of the town of Comber, which, to a large extent, is a mill village, dominated by the spinning mill which was the primary source of employment in the city. (See my blog post here: https://

norybmot.wordpress.com/category/titanic/). We will visit PRONI in a few days, but for now, we shall return to our visit.

The children were dressed in costumes representing various settings—a soldier, a bride, and a groom (two girls as they didn't have enough boys). They had also made drawings and paintings. They had just performed *Joseph and His Technicolor Coat*. The children also made drawings of the *Titanic*. The very delightful welcome they gave us was something special!

Back on the bus and a trip to Thomas Andrews's church, the Comber Non-Subscribing Presbyterian Church. It sits a short distance off the main road overlooking a lovely valley. The view spread out along and in this valley was so pastoral and serene that I hated to leave. The patches of different shades of green and the sheep grazing in those hedge-lined fields were photogenic. Typical of what anyone who has not been here would see in a photo of Ireland. I am glad I had the opportunity to see this with my own eyes, feel the wind on my face, and smell the earth. Beyond description. On the vista side of the church, downhill, is the Andrews family cemetery, with the memorial stone to Mr. Andrews, who was lost at sea when the *Titanic* sank. It is a peaceful place next to this quaint and small country church. The church does not tell the story of its famous congregants by merely looking at this modest building. Upon closer examination, the observant viewer is rewarded with several beautiful stained glass windows depicting scenes of the Andrews family. After a few more photos of our group for the local newspaper, the ladies and gentlemen of the church served us tea. The custom of an afternoon tea is quite lovely, and I could get used to this practice. We were soon back on the couch after a short walk.

We arrived at the Ulster Folk and Transport Museum for our final day stop. The museum was dedicated to the *Titanic*, old cars, and trains. Lots of walking here. Several levels are needed to house all odd displays. We all went past the trains and cars. The *Titanic* was our focus. Wow!

We all enjoyed the *Titanic* displays, but we had already done a lot of walking, so I knew Sheila and I were tired. The scale model of the *Titanic* sinking, which showed how many perished and how many survived based on classes, was fascinating. A shame Conor Clarke (our very own expert on all things Titanic!) will need to call them to discuss a few things. He said the bow was too high out of the water in the sinking, and there was not enough starboard list to the ship. It was still a dramatic depiction of that event where we all sailed together twenty-four months ago on the *Balmoral* out on the cold dark North Atlantic. Time to get back on the coach and head back to the bar and the hotel.

Chapter 4
2014

Sunday, 13 April 2014, 9:15 a.m.

The coach left for the Belfast Titanic Centre on time. First was on our agenda was a three-hour-walk-around and then tea at 1:00 p.m., followed by the Belfast Titanic Centre. I must relate that by this point in our visit, everyone knew that we had better be on time. Ms. Claire gave us our orders, but Susie reported around midday, concluding, "And from zee bridge, all ees *vell!*" (Sans the Norwegian accent, "From the bridge, all is well!")

The Belfast Titanic Centre is a fantastic piece of architecture depicting the bow of the *Titanic* as the four corners of the building. There was already a crowd here touring this collection of *Titanic* memorabilia. There are nine interactive galleries. https://www.titanicbelfast.com/

Walking all over this place was a real treat, which we were told would conclude at 12:45 p.m. sharp on the fifth floor. There would be a group photo and many selfies on the grand staircase. The clock always read 2:20 p.m. and was the center of many pictures. We had a group photo made here, and then we had lunch, but not before several surprises.

I was told by Maureen, "Someone wants to see you!" This fellow sticks a video camera in my face and asks me something. Before he gets very far, I realize it is Craig Lee! What the! He could only attend our reunion for two days, and he sneaks into our tea, hiding behind a video camera. It was great to see my photo-running mate from the *Balmoral*. He had already surprised Claire. The video is on the TMC 2014 Facebook video page. Very well-kept secret and a very pleasant surprise.

Some tea, pastries, and sandwiches were very delicious. My feet needed some rest too. Then we were all ordered to gather on the staircase for a group photo. Sort of like herding cats, they say, but we behaved long enough for several snaps. Now time for all of us to photograph each other on the staircase, take some selfies, and generally clown around.

Now to go back out and get on our tour bus. It was a short ride to the Hamilton Dock at 3:00 p.m. for a tour of the SS *Nomadic*. https://en.wikipedia.org/wiki/SS_Nomadic_(1911) This was something many were anxious to see. The *Nomadic* was built as a tender ship for the *Titanic*. The ports were not designed for ships as massive as the *Titanic*, an H&W-made beauty. Nearly the same age as the *Titanic*, her keel (no. 422) was laid on 22 December 1911, while the *Titanic*'s was laid on 31 March 1909 (no. 401). This was like being transported back in time—some of the people on Titanic's maiden voyage, for example, Molly Brown were on this ship (tender to be precise). The H&W Drawing Offices. More touring and another iconic photo event. This was another "time travel moment." Walking into this cavernous building and visualizing all the drafting tables in place and the design of the *Titanic* being put into construction plans. From this room came the life of the *Titanic* as those workers from Belfast would put iron and steel to life into Thomas Andrews' ideas. Back to the Encore. Claire gave us our briefing for the next day. We better pay attention and report promptly. She would call names and check her list ... counting noses, so she had all her "peeps." It was a perfect day, as Frank Sinatra once sang!

Chapter 5
2014

Monday, 14 April 2014

We all knew the drill: wear comfy shoes, get a good night's rest, and eat a good hearty breakfast.

We are going to the H&W dry dock where the *Titanic* was fitted out. Remember, this ship was over 882 feet long, so the dry dock is a massive piece of construction. Everything about the *Titanic* is gigantic. It was the largest ship ever built, so imagine this ship floated into a port and set down on steel and wooden blocks to be made after the hull and keel were constructed. We walked from one end to the other, staring in wonder and amazement at the scale of this dock! We were shown photos taken from where we were down in this cavern and could most visualize this ship.

With this physical labor (non-mechanized) that was done to build this ship, the sheer muscle power was staggering. But as the T-shirt says, "She was okay when she left *here*!" She was an engineering marvel, grand and opulent like none before her, nor since. We made a short drive to visit PRONI (the Public Records Office of Northern Ireland). Not just any public government office but a very secure (and as it happened) and a fascinating repository of documents. They are all searchable and printable. You can find out about the property, marriages, deaths, and public information galore, but also an abundant amount of *Titanic* memorabilia. Stunning glimpses into the letters, news articles, photos, and *everything* you ever wanted to see about this ship. It was built not far from this beautiful building. You can see the H&W cranes (Samson and Goliath) from the building. Their images reflect on the glass of the building I'm in.

Before getting into the secured part of the records area, we had to lock up all our belongings in a locker. No phones, cameras, pencils, erasers, pens, etc. are allowed near the documents. We filled out a form and got our photo taken by a polite clerk, just like you were getting a driver's license. The document tour was great, and we spent over an hour here. Exciting!

A short walking tour of downtown was our next stop for some who didn't have enough walking. Aidan McMichael, chairman of the Belfast Titanic Society, was very informative. We saw where Thomas Andrews went to college. The sight of the Europa Hotel concluded our tour. This hotel was ground zero for the Troubles in the recent past. We are all grateful and hopeful that such deadly history is never happening again. We spent about an hour or so looking at landmarks and statues and places of interest all around the City Centre. Great history lessons and decent weather, no umbrellas needed.

The evening was dinner at a lovely place, Robinson's Pub (across the street from the Europa), and some pints of ale were had by many, including your humble author. To cap the evening off, we left the pub around 1:30 a.m. and walked to city hall for the memorial service. It was a short walk but leisurely. We were tired by now. We spent our time eating, not drinking. The memorial service was respectful, sad, and tearful.

We experienced the loss of *Titanic* this night, 102 years after the tragedy, as we did two years earlier on the North Atlantic. Tears and a song with the most profound respect. There was a small chorus singing and a small group of drunken young people milling about across the street. Not much different than the screaming that must have been heard from the lifeboats in 1912 as survivors rowed away from the *Titanic*. The darkness and the cold waters drowned so many lives and dreams. We took a cab to the hotel around 3:15 a.m (10:15 pm back home—made me feel a wee bit less tired). We would return later this morning for another official memorial ceremony. It was a long day, and part of the next day before we were finished paying homage to so many lost souls!

Chapter 6
2014

Tuesday, 15 April 2014

We have a public ceremony today at city hall. There will be press coverage, politicians and photogs, reporters, and the general public watching this event. Time for flowers, wreaths, and more tears.

The Belfast City Hall encompasses an entire city block. It is a magnificent building, and we will see only a fraction of it. What we do see is opulent, *Titanic-esque*.

There are a few treasures to be seen here, but not until after a public recognition of the contribution and lives that Belfast people have invested in the memories of *Titanic*. Here, at the center of Belfast's government, is the heart of *Titanic*'s story. Her citizens, who built this ship, created her in steel and rivets. They spent nearly three years building and equipping her for what turned into an extraordinarily brief lifespan. The first gathering of our band of Titanoraks until today was almost as long as *Titanic*'s time in Ireland and on the North Atlantic. Her memory will live on well beyond our descendants' years, on into generations as yet unborn. We will do our part to strengthen and uphold this bond we feel toward Belfast and her *Titanic*. Forever. There are interviews, photos, prayers, proclamations, politicians, and clergy involved in setting aside this day to honor those lost in peril on the sea that night in 1912.

Chapter 7
2014

Wednesday, 16 April 2014

A few things to take away from this visit to "the Emerald Isle." Memories of friends, the *Titanic*'s legacy, and the world's fascination with her and her birthplace. *Titanic*'s womb was in Ireland; her birth was magnificent. The lovely people, the lovely country, and the Antrim Coast. I have been to Hawaii also, and I now know where Hawaiians go when they die and go to heaven. Ireland. What a fantastic place we are about to cap off with this visit, when we climb aboard our tour bus this final morning.

Tired and with little sleep after a long day, Claire rounds up her charges. We are going to live to tell about seeing heaven. Stupendous. *Supercalifragilisticexpialidocious*. The roots of the word have been defined as follows: super "above," cali "beauty," fragilistic "delicate," expiali "to atone," and docious "educable," with the sum of these parts signifying roughly "Atoning for educability through delicate beauty." According to the film, it is defined as "something to say when you have nothing to say" (Wiki). We will see scenes that defy our previous definitions of nature's gloriousness. The green spring of Ireland is beyond description. We see tiny nameless hamlets, dotting the landscapes, as we are transported in our comfy bus up the northeast coast of Ireland and County Antrim.

It was these waters we notice the Irish Sea out the right side of our coach windows. That body of water carried the *Titanic* away from her birth home to Southampton, and into history and everyone's hearts. Joy and sadness commingled. Bonney before Northern Ireland is stop no. 1 (http://www.discovernorthernireland.com/Andrew-Jackson-

Cottage-and-US-Rangers-Centre-Carrickfergus-P2801). The view would allow a glimpse of Scotland across the Lough, but not today. A wee bit misty and hazy. Getting back on the bus, we would continue to notice spectacular coastlines, rocky sea cliffs, and fishing boats in harbors. Cameras were abuzz, and our guide would describe memorable scenes. I continued to wonder, "like the school kid I was decades and a lifetime earlier!"

We passed old churches, rugby fields, pubs, and shops. We saw firsthand, with no scripts, exactly how these simple people lived. No huge mansions or estates but tiny row houses and cottages along the road. We arrived at a place to pull off the road and take in the Irish Sea's coastal view. We were near a town I forgot the name of, but we (me, anyway) shall continue. Photo ops. We all got out our smartphones and took loads of photos that would be shared around the world. There are nine countries represented on this bus. We continued westward along County Antrim's coast, and it was approaching mealtime!

Bushmill's Distillery was granted a license to produce whiskey in 1608 (406 years ago, at our visit). I tasted their whiskey, and I know why they are still in business. Yummmm-*eeee*! This was our lunch stop. They had a restaurant here, and the food was as good as their whiskey. The dining room was not fancy nor large, but it was a lovely break to enjoy and build up our strength for the rest of our afternoon walk.

The legendary Giant's Causeway! If you haven't seen it, the photos don't do it justice. Rocks! Huge boulders and oddly shaped stones. It was sprayed about, as if by a giant. The walk from the parking lot to the sea was about one-fourth a mile. All downhill. I am wondering why such beauty is so hard to get to. I can walk down this hill, but can others walk back up? For £1 each, the problem is solved. A wee bus runs back and forth, up and down this hillside. I decided to save time and ride back up the hill, but not before seeing unbelievable ocean views. Fortunately, nature was not cluttered by any buildings or pasture fences. It was just like it had been for millennia. It was undisturbed and not destroyed by man. I left my mother's ashes there. Now at peace, she is home where her roots are—Ireland. By the seaside for eternity. RIP, Mom.

We had heard how the giant of lore had created this place in a battle told by those who had listened to the story passed down by generations whose bones are not even dust now. Fascinating place, but we had two more stops to make before we would rest our weary bodies—a fourteenth-century castle and a rope bridge over rocks and water. The Irish are clever lads.

The Dunluce Castle was old before the colonists settled in North America. It fell into the sea in 1639 during a storm and has been abandoned ever since (http://www.discovernorthernireland.com/Dunluce-Castle-Medieval-Irish-Castle-on-the-Antrim-Coast-Bushmills-P2819). The Carrick-a-Rede rope bridge is scary but beautiful. (http://www.nationaltrust.org.uk/carrick-a-rede/.)

For a few pounds, you can risk life and limb and cross this contraption. Pray that your knees don't rattle your bones right off this device and into your demise and oblivion. Photos as proof were made by all (all the others) who dared to cross. Some made their photos, but all made it across and back, "shaken *and* stirred," by the adventure, to quote Mr. Bond.

Back to the Encore for libations and stories and posting photos to the internet. What a way to end a great visit. Well, not quite, but the organized part anyway. Thursday, 17 April 2014, was our day off. No travel plans, just a time to relax. We decided that even though it began to rain, we should walk next door to take a peek inside the cathedral next to our hotel. We saw the back of the church from our room, and we went to take a look to see.

What a place! This cathedral was built in 1904, but the church dates back to 1776. It was a work of architectural wonder. Vaulted 125-feet high ceilings, stained glass windows, and candles lit. Time for my last selfie. Why not? (https://en.wikipedia.org/wiki/St_Anne's_Cathedral,_Belfast?wprov=sfti1.)

Chapter 8
2014

We were safely home. It is both sad and joyful. We had an almost uneventful trip home. The "almost" was what nearly happened, and I did confirm it with the aircrew as we disembarked the plane in Atlanta. It was a bumpy ride almost from Upstate New York flying south to

Atlanta. As we approached Atlanta Airport, we descended through the clouds we were in, and the bumping was over... almost. We were going about 150 mph (the 777 had a display at each seat), and the runway was in sight. As we touched down, it was apparent we were not landing level. The right wheels touched first, and a second later, the left wheels touched. *Then* it got interesting very fast. We veered about ten to fifteen degrees from straight down the runway. There were audible gasps and mumbling conversations heard as the plane shook and as the crew fought back and bounced and quickly turned the plane back straight. We had briefly begun a skid heading off the runway. Everyone must have wondered if we would have a bad landing. What we *had* was a scary landing!

As I passed the crew a few minutes later on exiting, I remarked to the three crew members, "Nice *save* on the landing!"

One crew member nodded toward another and said, "Thank *him*!"

I said, "*Good* job!"

He sheepishly grinned knowingly that I was correct. We skidded unexpectedly, and he recovered nicely.

Home safe. Home sad. Home with a lifetime of memories. Good night, Claire, Maureen, and Susie, wherever you are. We are home but ready to return.

Chapter 03–05, June 2014

My last reunion, with all of us together, with my three siblings—Paul, Laura, and Debbie. Also, Delores Wilson (Paul's companion), Mike (Laura's husband), Ian Wright (Deb's son), and Rachel White (Laura's daughter) all met in Bennington, Vermont. Lots of meals together, lots of stories retold, and likely a fib or two was told.

17 October 2014

My fiftieth (as in five-oh) high school reunion nearby my hometown, Ambler, Pennsylvania. Much anticipated, but that's about it! Nothing memorable beyond seeing old classmates after 50 years and telling or hearing a few lies! A few photos and nothing else! I suppose I wasn't part of any clique then…

22 November 2014

Again, a death on Sheila's birthday. The year 1963 was sad for our nation. This year, it was sorry for a coworker of Sheila. The funeral was in South Georgia, south of Warm Springs, where President FDR summered in his last days. The cousin of Sheila's coworker's, Stephanie (née) Terry Wilson (a NASA astronaut), was attending. Sheila and I were the only White people in this church, or this area, as a matter of fact, for miles and miles. It was a unique life experience. We were glad we attended! My photograph was used on his funerary notice to those attending his funeral. It was from a wedding anniversary event I had recently photographed.

Later, in 2016, our downstairs neighbor died…on Sheila's birthday!…

To conclude this exciting year, we pieced together a coincidence. Yet one in my long list of "how'd that happen?" We had made friends as regular customers at a local establishment that sold alcoholic beverages. She said she immigrated to America with a boyfriend. Interesting, but a few years later, we were at a different restaurant, and there was a handsome young fellow with a Spanish accent. He said he and his lady friend arrived here as friends they had become in their home country. It was some time before we mentioned that to her, and you guessed it, we knew both of them separately but kept our secret. They still are unaware of us knowing this interesting fact of theirs. Small world? I vote "Yes!" or "Si!"

Post-Paul Period Begins and Last Visits Remembered

July 2015, New Mexico

A long flight nearly across the US and then a car ride almost as long. We flew to Albuquerque, New Mexico, and drove forever through nowhere, including Cuba, New Mexico, with a resident total of 100(?). Finally, we arrived at the entrance to Chaco Canyon National Park, where we met up with Paul and Delores at a lonesome and isolated gas station/convenient store/rest stop. We drove about three hours Northwest of Bernalillo, New Mexico. Not enough traffic to notice. Two small outposts with *Entering* on one side of the sign and *Leaving* on the backside of the same sign! The most isolated/lonely piece of road I have ever traveled!

Chaco Canyon is at least twenty-five miles back into a remote and historic Indian Antiquity Site from several hundreds of years ago, a thousand years perhaps. We've never been this far from civilization, where there was nothing but scrub vegetation and rocks. There were no buildings, no paved road, no utility poles, not even a random jackrabbit. Solar panels powered the facility we arrived at. Historic. Desolate. Ironically beautiful.

September 2015

We met Paul and his lady-friend/companion Delores Wilson in Pigeon Forge, Tennessee, in the middle of their tour bus trip. We spent two hours visiting. For part of the afternoon, we rode partway toward Mt. LeConte at the peak of the Smoky Mountains. Trees. Scenic views. Then dinner and goodbyes. They were with a tour group, and it would not have been good to join up. A quick visit was all we had! May 2016 Bus Trip

THOMAS E. BYRON

Augusta, Georgia, to New York City

On the next visit with them, we joined up in Brunswick, Georgia, and took an epic multi-day bus trip to New York City.

Paul and his lady friend, Delores, loved to travel with other senior citizens. He talked Sheila and me into a four-day bus adventure to New York City. Paul and I had been there many times before, but Sheila and Delores hadn't seen the sights. We visited Ellis Island, then the Statue of Liberty. Very historic places.

Sometime around now, not *on* this trip but at home, I discovered something unique while trying to go to sleep: the theta state, the stage before REM sleep. It is something which I can go into without drugs, and I discovered it by accident! The colors you see are spectacular, and the feeling or sensation of floating up into a cloud seems very real. Deep blue and purple become reds and finally white. The sense of flying is unnerving! The first step is to lie on your back and play slow Mozart, Beethoven, or Liszt. Clear your mind of your inner voice, which takes about fifteen minutes. Here's a more detailed explanation. https://en.wikipedia.org/wiki/Theta_wave?wprov=sfti1

> Theta state is a state of intense relaxation; it is used in hypnosis and during REM Sleep. The brain waves are slowed down at a frequency of 4–7 cycles per second. For this reason, the People meditate consecutively for hours to achieve this state, to have access to the absolute perfect calm. Theta brain waves can be considered the subconscious; they govern our mind between the conscious and the unconscious and retain memories and feelings. Also, direct your beliefs and your behavior. Theta waves are always creative, characterized by inspiration, and very spiritual. It is believed that this mental state allows you to act below the conscious mind level.

Theta is the first stage of the phase when we dream. To understand this frequency in a simple and comprehensive enough to think about how it feels and what it's like being on top of a mountain absorbed by what's around you and know that you "know" that God is real, know that God "is." At that moment, you are in Theta.

Theta state is a *mighty* state! It can be compared to that kind of trance where children can play video games.

This is a technique that I use on occasions for the sensation of flying and floating in a calm, relaxed state while in "space."

05 September 2016

Paul's condition from his stroke on 30 August 2016, as of 02 September, he's mainly sleeping and still in ICU. He hasn't eaten in five days, and he's on nourishment by an IV route. They put a tube in his nose to go into his stomach. He is probably weak from hunger. He opened his eyes a few times and tried to talk and smile. He hasn't gotten worse since he got into ICU but hasn't gotten out of the stroke results. Time will be the best healer, plus anti-seizure meds. I will keep you up-to-date!

Unknown
Farmington, NM
September 5, 2016 at 23:34

Transcription Beta
"Hi this message is for Tom Byron my name is Carrie I am an RN at San Juan regional medical center in Farmington I'm calling regarding a patient we have here um if we could get a call back that be great you can call his of the patients nurse at 505-609-2747 that's Margie thank you..."

Was this transcription useful or not useful?

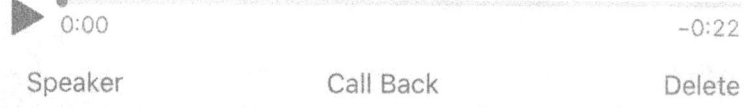

0:00   -0:22

Speaker   Call Back   Delete

 I was shown Paul's brain scans. Typical of how I think, I took it upon myself to grab a few quick iPhone images for future reference. Jumping forward in time, I have a brain MRI scheduled for 29 July 2019. I hope this information will help the doctor compare my brain to his brain for any diagnoses.
 I was present with him when he was on his deathbed, and he never recanted the hatred for, in his words, not mine, the old man. I squeezed

his hand, and he slightly squeezed back and silently left this realm for his eternal rest. He went peacefully and taciturn as he always was in his 76 years on earth. (13 August 1940–05 September 2016). And then there were three of us as a family. My two little sisters were born in 1952 and 1953, and eternity awaits us three.

I had to resolve some questions about *my* brain. My neurological test score was 104. Passed. Dr. Sital Patel conducted it!

Not a happy way to close out my sixty-ninth year, but I am now the oldest member of my immediate family. We were six kids originally, plus a mother and father. Now we are only three, myself and two younger sisters. RIP, my dear dear brother. This is also my step-granddaughter's twentieth birthday, celebrated while at college.

Time adds and subtracts to all of our lives as it sees fit.

Speaking of adding and subtracting, my brother won't get to vote anymore. September 5, 2016, was his last sunrise. I was holding his hand, and he squeezed my hand. Then I knew he had said goodbye quietly to only me. Seventy-six passes/trips around the sun were all he was allowed. He would be thrilled if one Democrat switched their vote this year and voted for Trump, which I will claim that vote as his vote, in his honor.

22 November 2016

One cold autumn morning, at 6:00 a.m., I went outside to get my morning paper. Yes, we still read printed news.

It was my wife's birthday.

I saw my fellow Vietnam veteran who had told me years earlier how he'd been wounded in the jungle there. We often chatted about the mess at the Veterans Administration and the war and his fellow Army buddies he'd meet with regularity. On this occasion, for our chat, he was quietly sitting on the steps. This was a regular occurrence. In a recent conversation a few days earlier, he would tell me he was sorry to hear my brother had died suddenly of a brain aneurism.

"Morning… *Hey!*" I said.

He didn't respond, and I wasn't surprised. This was his usual place. He had probably just dozed off.

I walked down two or three more steps and said, "*Good morning!*" a bit louder. But still no reply.

As I bent down beside him and touched his shoulder, my world stopped suddenly. No movement. *What's going on here?* must have been my thought.

I stepped back up the stairs and went inside to get my cell phone.

The operator replied, "What's your emergency?" Then I knocked on his front door to tell his family.

When they came outside, someone said, "He always does this. He's okay."

The police and ambulance arrived, and I stepped back away. Quietly closing the door, I explained to Ms. Sheila what was going on. It would be a sad next few days.

He wasn't okay. The VA, which had been his major complaint when we chatted, had let him down for the last time.

RIP.

2017 Travel Adventure: Abroad for a Fortnight in the UK

For images for 2017 story on P. 289 click below.

https://byronsblog.quora.com/Abroad-for-a-fortnight-in-the-U-K?ch=17&oid=5656396&share=f46ac840&srid=3JBw&target_type=post

THOMAS E. BYRON

It's great to be home again, Thursday, 20 April 2017. A lot happened between wheels up on our departure flight and spun down upon arrival. There were aches and pains. There were friends to reunite with, and after two weeks, greetings and goodbyes to be said. Again. We all met in 2012, again in 2014, and now!

Note: see Quora link for photos referenced: https://byronsblog.quora.com/The-digital-world-knows-where-Ive-been?ch=17&oid=5706649&share=2b581bff&srid=3JBw&target_type=post

Then: Click on link in lower right side, second paragraph, that says "Abroad for a fortnight in the U.K."

William McQuillan

In the summer of 2016, the plans for our 2017 reunion were discussed. This would be our third *Titanic* reunion after meeting in the middle of the North Atlantic in April 2012. The focal point that created this meeting began in 1909 in Belfast. Harland and Wolff decided they needed to compete with the Cunard Line shipbuilders. Traffic across the North Atlantic was busy and profitable, with commerce between London and New York, specifically the Southampton docks, where people and goods shipped out traveling along this route. It was a proverbial expressway of traffic. Many ships passed eastbound liners going westbound and westward going eastward. There was money to be made. The competition was keen. Thus, it was imagined that *Titanic* could capture some of this business, so the largest ever moving object on earth was conceived. At the Thompson Dry Dock in Belfast, the colossus began.

The legendary liner *Titanic* was unsinkable and luxurious at an enormous size of 882.5 feet in length. Her less famous sister ship, the *Olympic*, was a twin with only minor details to the trained eye to tell them apart. Like identical twin children, only the parents can tell one from another. The *Olympic* (more later about this ship my Great-grandfather, Joseph Byron photography) survived her twin by many decades since the largest liner ever launched, at that time, sank on her maiden voyage in 1912. Then the legend began. Books have been written, survivors have passed down stories, and recently, movies have attempted to create this voyage. Some movies are better than others, but the details are impossible to capture. Our small group of Titanoraks carries this event along with their connections and their interests. We meet every few years. We also get to meet those who have personal stories of their relatives who went down with the *Titanic*. Ceremonies are held annually on April 15 (the date of the sinking).

William McQuillan, a stoker on the *Titanic*, his photo seen here tenderly held by my sweet wife, Sheila Byron, as his granddaughter paused by his name on the memorial wall. This photo and the memorial service will have more details when we get to next week's adventures in Ireland.

Our meeting in Alnwick (pronounced Ah-nick), England, on Friday, 07 April 2017, was the start of our reunion for the 2012 North Atlantic meetup. We were tired since we had left Atlanta at 11:00 p.m. the evening before (Thursday, 06 April 2017), and it was now 5:30 p.m. on Friday, 07 April 2017. The real adventure begins on day 2.

We were talking and hugging, shaking hands, and reuniting at the White Swan Hotel. So many things to catch up on, and time would accelerate, or seem to, for the next two weeks. People arrived from Australia, Germany, Denmark, the Netherlands, Canada, across America, Scotland, Ireland, and Northern Ireland. Thirty-eight different stories and news bits to catch up on. Some of those who arrived earlier visited an antique bookstore. They were the group who lived in the UK. Our travel from the colonies, as I refer to America, didn't allow us to spend the day in Alnwick.

We were now back down from our room and checked in for several days. It was time to meet up to lay out our evening and outline the next several days' outings. Our co-leaders were both doctors (PhDs) and highly organized retirees. (We raised a few glasses and toast you now for all of your hard work!)

We had already received several detailed emails, but our guides wanted to ensure everyone was on the same page. You will see what I mean once we get into day 2 of our journey, when our first excursion was underway! Looking back now, two weeks later, I don't know how we kept up. He was like a former drill instructor. We were told, "Muster in the meeting room by the dining room at five thirty sharp!" What have we booked, an exercise routine or a fun time sightseeing? We shall see.

Dinner was at 7:30 p.m., and with my tux on and my lovely wife, dressed to the nines, we hit the hotel bar first for some aperitifs—whiskey and beer. Sitting down would be a welcomed event tomorrow, and this evening was a grand time. We had no clue how much walking was in store, but there was a well-planned and tightly scheduled agenda. Tomorrow would be a castle and gardens tour.

Day Two of Our Adventure

We had a tour (walkabout) of Alnwick, after a French-themed breakfast at 8:30 a.m. on Saturday, 08 April 2017. I was no longer hungry but far from complete. We wanted to sleep in. We got very little sleep on the eight-hour flight over the pond. Plus, we lost five hours traveling eastbound. C'est la vie!

I put on my old reliable walking shoes and met with my smoking pals out front of our hotel. I even met a few other vapers out front. We were glad we quit the cigs! One of my smoking pals vaped *and* rolled his own. Impressive.

After a brief time, our guide and his wife came out front with iPad in hand and mustered us out, and our adventure began. We went to the left of the hotel. Thirty-eight of us, the senior members, are trailing at the end of the parade. There were townspeople around walking dogs and shopping. It was a lovely Saturday morning. A bit brisk, but the walking did keep us warm.

Our first stop was an open-air market. Very busy. I noticed one vendor was selling a large variety of nice boots, and not being too clever at converting pounds to dollars, I decided to pass up making any purchases. My suitcase and Sheila's were loaded to British Airways's weight limit. No room for an extra sock! We decided before we left home not to bring back trinkets.

The fresh air was excellent, and the old shops and narrow streets being left-hand drives were a constant source of amusement and interest. I can't imagine what the locals thought of this troupe going about their quiet village early in the morning.

Our first planned stop was several blocks away, but we still managed to have several people on either side of the narrow streets, looking in store windows and taking photos. Only one "real" camera was used. The rest were smartphones.

Did I mention there were many planters along the streets with beautiful flowers? Quite a lovely town or village, not sure which. Turning the last corner, several blocks later, we arrived at a fantastic castle! Everything in the area is old, but this place is ancient. Alnwick Castle, home to Harry Potter films and the *Downton Abbey* television series. Wow!

> My wife and I are delighted to offer you a warm welcome to Alnwick Castle, my family's home for over seven hundred years. It is an important part of British heritage. Its walls are steeped in history and filled with tales of warfare, romance, and chivalry. We hope you enjoy visiting our special home.
> (Ralph Percy, twelfth Duke of Northumberland, Alnwick Castle)

No photos are allowed inside. The luncheon served in the castle café was a pleasant time to sit down briefly. Then outside the courtyard and a vaping break combined with chatting up an elderly local chap and meeting a fascinating tour guide. During all of this, there was a lovely wedding party with their family collecting up to go into the outside courtyard area of the castle grounds. Beautiful!

Our castle guide, Leslie Enos, met Frederick Fleet in 1961, four years before this *Titanic* survivor would die. He was so amazed and lucky for this unique experience. He was so excited to tell us about his *Titanic* experience. He had never met one group of dozens of Titanoraks! Knowing that he met a surviving ship member in the crow's nest on the lookout on 14 April 1912, was stunning!

To cap off this day, we spent an hour just sitting in café chairs waiting on the younger members of our entourage to visit the Alnwick Gardens. I enjoyed watching families with their children walking around as they did, many eating ice cream cones from the outdoor restaurant. We were exhausted and knew it was still a hike to get back to our hotel! We were in an energy-saving mode.

By 5:30 p.m., we were back at the hotel worn out, and in yet another meeting. Our leader was laying out the next day's activities and our evening dinner plans and sampling a local distiller's wide variety of tasty products. The best gin you ever tasted is my only memory, but I needed a Guinness or whiskey. Off to the bar! Another lovely dinner at 7:30 p.m., constantly visiting tables and discussing our day and reunion. Then as customary, back to the bar for dessert and then off to bed, perchance to dream? A five-hour time change does strange things to one's biorhythms.

Day Three of Our Adventure

Sunday, 09 April 2017

We are not ever going to get any sleep! Sheila requires more than eight hours of sleep, but I don't. I feel her pain, but she's having a good time despite the routine and sore feet. We will learn when we get home that we lost a few pounds after all of this. The walking has been beneficial, and my feet are holding up wearing dress shoes all day. On day 1, of the many miles we would walk, my comfortable shoes came unglued. I got a little unglued. I looked down at my left shoe and thought a leaf was stuck between the sole and the shoe. That would not be the case. My shoe broke, and I thought I had not tied my leather shoe string. Later, I looked down, and my entire shoe was nearly blown up, and I was a mile from the hotel. Why did I decide not to buy those boots I saw earlier? I had to wear my formal dress shoes for the rest of the two weeks.

It is too early to get down to the dining room and eat and then be on tour. The bus is ready to depart Sunday morning at 0830 hours. Sharp! No room service meal in this joint. They are very polite, and the service is very British and proper. The accents and phrases are quirky, and so is their food. No American fried bacon with your eggs. Just beans, sausages, and ham-like bacon is their staple. A fry-up full British breakfast includes potatoes and toast, eggs, and I don't know what all! We are on the bus and ready promptly. We depart at 8:30 a.m. for a ninety-minute ride to the open-air museum. The countryside in eastern England is quite lovely, with many farms, sheep, and primarily small farmhouses. Not one trailer (mobile homes) like you see in farm areas of America.

Our bus trip to the River Tyne for our next stop is not too far away. This will be a treat. No walking (or swimming), just a three-hour boat ride with lunch and beer or wine.

After parking the bus, it is a short walk to cross this unusual bridge. It raises for taller ships and blinks like an eye. It is in the up position in this photo on Quora. Here's a short video: https://www.youtube.com/embed/vrZ5IE-1GJ4. After another short bus ride, we are at Trinity House. This beautiful building dates to 1803, but the guild which occupied it dates back to 1514 under King Henry VIII. I told you everything around here was ancient. Back to Alnwick for dinner and visiting the bar. Again. Tonight we get to relax; we didn't walk all day! We don't even need to wear formal clothes for dinner. Our tablemates have varied from night to night, and the day's adventures plus discussions about *Titanic* are ever present. The dining room is significant, and every night, the entire dining room is reserved for our group. Why is this dining room so special to us? It is identical to the first-class dining room on the Titanic. It is the actual wood and fixtures rebuilt when the *Olympic* was scrapped in 1936. When this paneling was in the Olympic, my great-grandfather was in that room photographing the same place I'm in now! That gives me a very *strange* feeling! After dinner, we regroup in the bar for more visiting and yet another round of libations to ease the aches and pains of our day.

Day Four of Our Adventure

10 April 2017

This is the fifth anniversary of our group sailing out of Southampton on our Titanic Memorial Cruise. Our last day has arrived. We are settled into a routine. We've gotten to know our driver, Brian. We are a tight-knit group, but at the end of today, I will come unwound. Profoundly! Another bus trip and we have a 0730 Monday muster in the front lobby. Everyone is ready for a great day. (See Quora. On my Facebook page there are several photos.) Shown below is the oldest wooden warship in the British Navy. The HMS *Trincomalee* was launched in 1817. Still afloat but permanently docked here for visitors, it is our first stop after an hour ride traveling south from Alnwick. I can't imagine any crew members over five two being below deck; that's about the total headroom. I got tired of bending down once our tour guide led us down there and, indeed, back in time. The cannon was interesting, but I can't imagine firing those guns in such a small place. I probably ruined my hearing while in the military. I can't imagine hearing after a sea battle!

The living conditions for a long time under sail must have been brutal. I can see why sailors drank so much and swore when seen at port! We all get loaded onto our traveling home and a short jaunt to an inn for lunch: sandwiches and tea. Beer or other spirits for those who wish to take a wee nip and sit outside to smoke or vape. The story of the Shepherd and Shepherdess is quite historic. The Shepherd and Shepherdess Pub and Holly House were built in the eighteenth century but were altered in the late nineteenth century. The pub is decorated with two life-sized painted lead figures of a shepherd and a shepherdess.

The figures were from the Napoleonic wars (1796–1815) when a French blockade restricted England's armaments and munitions capability. As part of clandestine measures to import the metal without detection, lead works of art were commissioned abroad. One of ten pairs of figures brought from the continent to be melted down for weaponry, the Shepherd and Shepherdess, escaped their intended fate when the squire of Beamish Hall purchased them. First, they were installed above the entrance to the hall. They were later moved to the lawn when a storm destroyed the accompanying figures of a dog. Sometime in 1870, according to local legend, the squire returned home after a night's drinking and stumbled on the figures in the dark. The experience was such a shock that he gave the pair away to the inn at Beamish. After that, the pub was known as the Shepherd and Shepherdess Inn.

Having finished my lunch and a chat outside with fellow Titanoraks, I took my empty Shepherd and Shepherdess glass back. I asked the owner/barkeep, "Do you have a website?" He replied, and I inquired, "Might I purchase a glass like this?" I held up my empty pint.

"No," he replied. "Let me give you this clean one to take home."

I was gobsmacked, as they say!

Footnote: The clean one made it safely home to the colonies!

The Beamish Village was our afternoon stop before heading back to Alnwick. This village recreates life as it used to be. A trolley ride. Beer stop at period pub complete with an off-tuned piano. Quaint. Cold beer. After an hour ride and some closing remarks about the past few days' travel, we would be ending our fun and primarily uneventful well-planned trip to Alnwick. As we arrive at the parking lot behind the hotel, we thank our excellent tour guide, Brian. He was prompt in getting us to our places, and we were delighted. We trek back to our hotel, a bit sad that this part of our trip is over so soon but excited about the gala dinner planned for our closing day at the White Swan.

I enter our wee bar for a pint with the group. As I am slowly sagging into my lounge chair, I look at the table. "*Where's my* iPhone!" It was not in my jacket pocket zipped up! "Do you have my iPhone, Sheila?"

My eyes dart about the table for my phone and the others with me. My heart races, and my face goes ashen.

"I need to call *Brian*!" I bolt out of my chair and run to the parking lot to find the bus gone. The only thing I can hear in my head is *I left my —— phone on the bus!* I arrive at the front desk in shock and panting, and after calling Dr. Telford in his room from the front desk to get Brian's cell number, I leave him a hasty voice message pleading my case when he didn't pick up. The taxi the desk clerk called for me arrived after an eternity. The five-minute trip to the bus barn took an hour, so it seemed. Arriving at the bus location, I confirm the bus was there. Locked! My mind is now in complete turmoil! I see a sign next to the bus, Office. After entering the door, I see another character with an arrow pointing up which says Office, and I read as I run past it and take two steps at a time!

"Hello? *Hello?*" No one there, so I go loping down the stairs and outside, confused and having no idea of what's next. I look over at my taxi waiting, and I see Brian coming around the corner! My iPhone is in his extended hand. My ears went deaf. My mind was overloaded! What did he say? I guess he got my voice message before I arrived at the bus barn. I am now aware and explain to Brian, "Tomorrow, early, we fly to Belfast! Our e-tickets are on that phone. My credit card is in the wallet case with the phone. Thousands of photos, documents, etc., my electronic life lives there! "You are a saint, Brian!" I think that's what I said. My mind collapses as I climb back into the taxi. "I got it!" I exclaim as I enter the bar with the trophy held over my head to win an Olympic event. (Irony intended.)

My pint of Guinness is still as I left it. *Gulp, gulp,* I down my pint. That is also another first. I usually savor my Guinness. I calm down. I once was unwound, but my phone was found, and now I'm hanging around.

"Another wee pint, please!" Tonight is our grand finale, formal, with live music, singers, and a wonderful dinner. To cap off the evening, there is a quiz to work on. Each table gets a forty-question test to answer. The correct group answers entry wins a prize. Our group missed about twelve answers wrong! It was not a very easy test. The evening just flew by. We all agreed, "We need to begin planning for our 2019 reunion. Liverpool to Southampton, then across to Cherbourg, France. The days of the week in 1912 and 2019 match up. The dates in April will be even more significant."

Once the goodbyes were said, it was one last trip back to our room. Up the stairs, through a small hallway and then through a door, a right turn down a short hallway, another door and a short flight of stairs, then a final door and right turn to our room on the left. Nothing like a very very old-fashioned but very quaint and charming hotel.

THOMAS E. BYRON

Day Five of Our Adventure

Tuesday, 11 April 2017

    This morning is bright and crisp as we gather out front where we met on Friday. It seemed like yesterday, but the memories we packed into this lovely area in and around Newcastle, England, will be reviewed. Taxi with Claire, Denis, Sheila, Maureen, and me to the airport. We will be in Ireland in a few hours. The flight to Belfast was a nonevent; no tour guide was needed. They were relaxing. A routine flight across the Irish Sea and an invitation to visit the Nightingales in their home. A change of pace to kick back and watch TV and chat. Sleep in and/or stay up late. They were refreshing our bodies!

Day Six of Our Adventure

Tuesday, 12 April 2017

    A tour of the Dark Hedges, *Game of Thrones* television series. We also drove through several very typical Irish seaside villages.

Day Seven of Our Adventure

Thursday, 13 April 2017

    We leave for Cobh, Ireland, early today, but our only schedule is… no schedule. We arrive in the coastal city at the southern end of Ireland. Lovely country, all motorway or dual carriageway. The direction signs are in Gaelic, unpronounceable for my wife and me, and English. We met for lunch with those who were already in Cobh. The choice of the Bunnyconnellan was a perfect relaxing spot overlooking the Atlantic Ocean on Cork Island near the *Titanic's* last port of call. It was not always easy to keep as many diverse agendas in sync, but the view from the restaurant was lovely. You may have noticed by now, not a lot of clear blue sunshiny weather, but it keeps Ireland green! We found our hotel in the heart of Cobh, Gilbert's Bistro in the Square, walking distance from our other gathering place, the Titanic Bar and Grill. It was next to the sea, intimate and cozy. There were about fifteen of us sitting at two tables set at ninety degrees to each other. It was not easy to talk around the table sitting this way. While out on the deck vaping, I met a fan of a Fox News show, *The Tucker Carlson Show*. This is definitive proof that the world is small! The spectacular sunset seen above was my favorite photograph of the two hundred plus I took! The old Titanic pier, long ago abandoned, was also right here at the restaurant.

Day Eight of Our Adventure

Friday, 14 April 2017

Outdoor café breakfast. Good Friday found nearly nothing open. On our way back to Belfast, we stopped at a small inn for a toilet break, which was unusual. The display in the lobby area indicated this was a fun place after dark.

Day Nine of Our Adventure

Saturday, 15 April 2017

A memorial service at Belfast City Hall. A visit to a local pub, Claire, Sheila and me. So much fun to be in Belfast, our second visit to this city. The memorial service was very moving, as it was in 2014. We met two relatives of stokers who died in the sinking of the *Titanic*. So sad to be so near to the real people who lost relatives. The movies about that disaster can never connect you personally to the ordinary citizens whose lives were torn apart. May they rest in peace.

Dander (a short walk, Scottish) found us at a wee pub.

Day Ten of Our Adventure

Sunday, 16 April 2017

A day off, but it is Easter Sunday.

Day Eleven of Our Adventure

Monday, 17 April 2017

Easter egg hunt with the Nightingale family. What an honor! Dinner at Del Toro Steak House.

Day Twelve of Our Adventure

Tuesday, 18 April 2017

Claire drives us a short distance to Belfast International Airport. Goodbyes are said, and we will not see anyone we know until we arrive in Atlanta two days later. Always sad to look back on an adventure after looking forward to it for over a year! The airport isn't busy in the middle of the week. It sure is relaxing to know that our next flight in England isn't until tomorrow. Phew. We remember trying to maintain a running pace while getting to our next (connecting) flight!

Day Thirteen of Our Adventure

Wednesday, 19 April 2017

A day relaxing at our hotel, breakfast, and a five-minute walk to the Newcastle airport for lunch. We flew to London and checked in to yet another hotel. A bit expensive, but time for a light snack and relaxation.

Day Fourteen of Our Adventure

Thursday, 20 April 2017

We had time for lunch at the airport. We had time to watch people. We read the newspaper. We leisurely got to the gate and were ready to be home!

Back in America. What a trip! The leisurely trip home with two overnights and a lot of relaxed time in two airports (Newcastle and

London) made our journey stress-free. No rushing about through security lines, no time stresses. This pace made for a time to reflect, eat, and enjoy adult beverages and watch. Our British Airways flight was fun. Coach seats weren't that bad, even though we were in the back of the plane with some colorful hoi polloi. The flight was smooth and relaxing until about five hours into the eight-hour conclusion of our trip. Clear air turbulence. CAT can be as scary as flying through dark and menacing thunder clouds. We were buffeted for an hour. Not severe, but continuous. In front of us was an older couple, and the missus was very religious, three seats abaft. During the shaking and banging of the plane (a 777-300), she began to raise her hand and point heavenward with highly animated gestures. Her pleadings with the Lord finally prevailed, and her warnings were granted! The flight continued smoothly... finally. Sometime later, I decided to use the toilet, and it looked like a goat had been sacrificed there! What a friggin' mess. Different folk reacts differently to crises. Some pray, and some destroy the toilets! Great journey. It will take weeks to unwind! I hated to leave you all but loved to be home. Life is always about living in the middle—between the peace and love of friends and the great unwashed masses on the other extreme.

From the middle, a very serene place. Thanks for reading to the end of this reunion. The year 2019 is getting closer every day! See you all then. It's great to be home again!

2018

From an email I sent:

On Friday, 6 July 2018, 4:21:43 PM CDT, Tom Byron xxxxxx@att.net wrote:

I just saw an old email I had replied to on 15 February 2015. I decided to inquire again:
No. I'm not dead! But I do remember those walks at lunchtime with ??? Allen around the office in Lake Charles. I'm retired many years now and still kicking. We have lots to catch up on—hopefully, it won't take another three years to start a chat.

Tom Byron's photo below is from 1986, I think.
Here's the reply:

Hello, Mr. Byron, This is Doug's wife, Carrie. Sorry to tell you, but Doug passed away on 21 January 2018. He died after an accident on the Vespa. He had massive brain injuries.

You could have knocked me over with a feather!

2019 Southampton Adventure with Three Germans, Two Frenchies, a Drunken Norwegian, and Two Yanks

Sheila's son Blake picked us up at 3:05 p.m., and our year-long planning and preparation for our fourth reunion had begun. These were our passes, actually our plane tickets, to begin our journey of one week. The waiting was long, and now it seemed the clock went into fast-forward. Tom was nervous as each step unfolded. "Did I miss or forget something?" The thought stayed and dominated his thoughts. All was smooth so far, but we hadn't traveled twenty miles from our home. We had our tickets, and we were very excited. The day was upon us. Actually, a long night with little sleep was more accurate.

After a relaxing Guinness and Bud Light, we left our two new and somewhat inebriated lady friends at the airport bar. They were going on a girl holiday and were a bit too friendly, according to Sheila, but c'est la vie! We bought two lovely ATL coffee mugs for our English Titanic Reunion organizer friends at the next souvenir shop. We also packed our two slanted Titanic Funnel coffee mugs to be raffled off for an eventual £200 gift to the Titanic Maritime Memorial Fund. We raised money every time we met up in 2014, 2017, 2019, and subsequent reunion in 2022. The '22 visit had to be canceled due to COVID.

The Atlanta International terminal was new and beautiful and easy to get around. Of course, when your gate is at the far end, your walk is the most extended option. The farther your destination is, the farther it is to your gate. It's the rule.

Tom had booked and reserved our seats in the economy plus section with a bulkhead in front of us and only a few feet from the entry to the plane. I was a temporary hero for being so lucky to get these excellent seats. Nothing in front of us except a bulkhead. There is no one in front of us to lean back into our space! The flight was uneventful. This is not a selfie of our trip to the Atlantic, but it will serve as one.

About two-thirds of the way across the pond, we were shaken but not stirred, quote James Bond. Sleep came and went in fits and starts, but it would suffice until the following night!

Friday, 12 April 2019. We arrived at LHR (London Heathrow), and with some questions and a lot of training for a 10K marathon, we found two hundred to three hundred other passengers with the same purpose. Customs. We had promised ourselves to avoid this airport for customs. Half of the UK was arriving home when we were visiting. *Ugh*!

The more accessible part was getting to the National Express bus service to carry us and our seventy pounds of luggage. An easy ride, a lovely ride. We passed through Winchester and later found that this was the place the Beatles sang about "Winchester Cathedral." Then to the Central bus station in "So-Ton", as the locals call it, Southampton. A short cab ride and we were deposited at the front door of the Dolphin Hotel. This place was old, as in very old.

To unpack or head to Nelson's bar. Decisions, but first, we felt compelled to find our room. Our broom closet-sized room had just enough space for our luggage since the bed nearly filled the room. It would soon be our refuge and comfort for a much-needed lie down. It wasn't long before our *Titanic* comrades "sailed in." It was as much about our friendships as the tours we were about to take. We stayed behind for the walk to the town quay. In 2012, we were among all these Titanoraks but hadn't met them until our first reunion in 2014 in Belfast.

Saturday would be our first outing and fellowship via a Dutch. More about him later. A fine chap nearly as old as us. We spent some good hours in the bar. I didn't know it at the time, but I was quickly depleting the bar of its Guinness stock. Sheila was able to have all the Bud Light she cared to drink. They had plenty of her beer. A good night's sleep after it got to around 6:00 p.m. at home, or 11:00 p.m. in our seaport home of Southampton, was simply divine.

13 April 2019

We awoke and found our way into the dining area. A full-English breakfast was the fare.

Our group of eight or so all walked over to the Grand Harbour Hotel. Sheila and I had stayed at this hotel as the starting point of our excellent Titanic Memorial Cruise. There were a few notable landmarks along the way. This city is many, many hundreds of years old!

We met, purely by random luck, John Siggins, a retired engineer, pro-Trump, anti-Corbin, pro-BREXIT, and a fascinating chap. He was about sixty-five, and he wore a British Naval uniform. We chatted him up, and the British Titanic Society was meeting. Bill Willard was there, and Christine Kuchler and her partner, Ed, whom we know from our yearly summer *Titanic* meetings in Tennessee where there, we are officially global travelers!

We learned about the recovery operation when "the big piece" was recovered. Interesting video, but a rehash. The takeaway was the people and the displays to look over.

The next part of our day was a short bus trip. We went to a large city cemetery and saw many graves of crew members who perished on the *Titanic*. More walking. Still, more walking, and Sheila's poor wee legs weren't used to this. We were groaning but soldiering on. Sheila asked me which path we could take to get to the bus, a seat, and warmth from the fresh air.

The bus was there before us! Was it unlocked? We needed a rest. We were glad Dutch was comfy there, reading a book on his iPad. It wasn't long before we were engaged in some of his tales of mannerless hooligans and schoolchildren. Dutch and Tom were simpatico and close political allies. As I mentioned, I watched PMQs every Wednesday at noon from the Commons in Westminster. The time passed quickly, and we were off to Cap'n. Rostron's grave. This grave of the captain of the *Carpathia* was a brief second stop on our route back to the hotel.

We arrived back at Nelson's Bar, better known as the Dolphin Hotel. It was a warm watering hole since the Spring air was a wee bit brisk! Chatting was convivial before our lively evening repast at 1900 hours. (Sheila doesn't care much for military time.) Our evening gala dinner was a semiformal affair. The camaraderie was great fun, and it was a lively dinner. A raffle concluded the dinner to raise £200 for charity. I ended up with two new *Titanic* books. The one that I prize is my autographed book.

My comment triggered a wonderful two-hour conversation. Right now, I'm torn between writing this and reading my autographed Nazi *Titanic* book. This week is a series of "do this and miss that!"

Sunday morning, 14 April 2019

Our final day began with a taxi ride after breakfast. We met up at the Southampton Sea Museum. *Titanic*-era photos and life back many years in this busy seaport town. We managed to see the main areas of the museum, but poor wee Sheila wasn't herself. Not quite. We took a taxi back to the hotel. After a nice nap, she was right as rain.

Sunday evening, 14 April 2019

Back to the intro, and as it would turn out, was our highlight of this visit. We missed seeing *Queen Mary II* embark on a sea voyage but enjoyed a great international perspective on the *Titanic* experience. Three Germans, two French, a Norwegian, and two Americans met in a bar by pure chance.

The beer was flowing, and the conversations were convivial. And to celebrate the evening, I had switched to Old Red Hen beer. We were trying to visit and relax. We succeeded and then some! Our German friends spoke with our French friends in English but went to their mother tongue. We learned about the backstory of this movie and that Herr Goebbels, Reich Minister of Propaganda of Nazi Germany, banned this movie. "He hated it," according to our author friend.

Back to the US of A!

15 July 2019

My first mammogram has been completed just now as I type. Exploratory event to diagnose a slight pain in my breast muscle. I can empathize with the ladies now. Owie! Gynecomastia, who knew? I'm on my way to reversing this condition. My doctor's opinion is that it's the result of a drug prescription I'm taking that has caused this. I've ended my daily dose of Myrbetriq (required from my bladder cancer surgery). Getting old is not for sissies!

20 July 2019

As I type these words here, it's the fiftieth anniversary today of man landing on the moon. I distinctly recall being in my G.I. home at 191 Panther, while stationed at KI Sawyer AFB. We were in our living room watching a rabbit-eared black-and-white small screen TV with those fuzzy images broadcast worldwide, and I watched this fantastic feat unfold two hundred thousand plus miles away from the moon's surface in nearly real time!

The world stopped what they were doing and was transfixed and united as one global community, like we've never been before or since!

22 May 2020

I watched my first high school graduation ceremony! Here's a photo of the event we streamed on Instagram. Yes, our TV stand is Sheila's dad's TV!

Last Chapter

Life got pretty darn good. No, actually, it got terrific! Note to self: end on an upbeat note!

What would I have been like if I were to have grown up in a much calmer, a little more normal household? I will never know! Thanks for reading to the end.

"But wait...there's more." This chapter is like where you put stuff when unexpected company shows up.

A Place for an Old Man to Mention Things He Forgot Page

The following items (in no particular order) are detailed events I forgot to weave into my autobiography. Time and, at this point, laziness prevent me from a few days of editing.

- *Visit Elberton.* This small town is a huge source of granite used to build the Georgia Guidestones. Very quaint small-town America off the beaten path.
- *Visit Byron, Georgia.* It was an odd coincidence for a Southern town named Byron. Not too far from Plains, Georgia. Not much else to say about the place.
- *Sandra Terry's dad's funeral in Deep Southern Georgia.* Sheila and I got very lost trying to find this country church. It was not far from Warm Springs, Georgia, and without GPS back then, it was a challenge! We arrived a few minutes before the service for Mr. Terry. We sat quietly near the back of a small but crowded county church. His recent fiftieth wedding anniversary, which I photographed, was one of those photographs on his memorial flyer given out at his funeral. We were the only two White people for miles and miles, and we do not know what may or may not have been said as we took our seats about two rows from the back of the church. The ceremony was beautiful, and the music and the singing were divine. We quietly exited the church about an hour later after first lining up to go upfront and pay our respects. Then we returned to Marietta.
- *Free cruise and overnight visit to Freeport, Bahama.* A free cruise to Freeport and an intense sales pitch to pay a small fortune for a timeshare. "No thanks" was said by Sheila and me at least a hundred times.

- *Sheila B. meets Joe B.* As memorable moments go, this was a topper. We were going on your honeymoon, and Sheila was being introduced to her new in-laws for the first time. Priceless! Sheila's parents were as different as mine were from hers and were as if mine were from another planet. No! Another solar system!
- *Sheila meets Aunt Grace in Flushing, New York.* She was contrasting the above meeting, "When Sheila meets Joe…" His sister, Aunt Grace, "Vive la différence!" Hospitality Plus, and a chain-smoking (Camel nonfiltered cigarettes) sweetheart! Like no one Sheila had ever met. We visited her in her rent-controlled New York City apartment that she was still living in and had raised two children since the late forties (i.e., forever). Her children married and moved away. My uncle George, her husband, passed away before I knew him. The neighborhood looked like something from the hit TV show *The Wire*. But we had a visit that we wished would never end!
- *July Fourth Grand Rivers parties.* What a great memory this was for several summers in a row. Our photo studio was turned into a mini guest house. Just an air mattress and a blanket, but after a day of swimming, drinking, pool, drinking, and some karaoke with fireworks outback, *everyone* was sad to leave after four or five days!
- "His Eye Is on the Sparrow." Hammock Funeral home, Velma Hammock sings a cappella and brings out Speedy to meet the guests. Speedy drowned in the 1935 flood. The funeral director was given some embalming instructions (Egyptian style), and when no one claimed Speedy's body, Mr. Hammock embalmed ole Speedy. Joe B. meets Speedy photo somewhere. My father had to have that tourist-type photo made with this tuxedo-dressed mummy hanging in the funeral home closet! Speedy was his nickname since he was found washed up along the Ohio River bank.
- Wildcat bus trips with Bill Scott to Rupp Arena and other SEC basketball trips.

- Kentucky Moonbow visit.
- St. Louis Arch trip.

Lest I forget, here's a funny but sort of typical memory about my father's ability to do simple jobs around the house—an epic story about a wallpapering job done around 1960s by "my father." It was for the second-floor bathroom used by our parents, Judy, Laura, and Debbie. We three boys had the third-floor bathroom to ourselves. The wallpaper design was an underwater view of corals, sea flora, and bubbles from the fish. I realized that something was amiss—the bubbles were going *down* not *up*! The entire job was screwed up! He also stored his father's handmade camera built in 1940-ish out in his (not dehumidified) storage shed in Florida—not a good idea!

A Few Moments to Remember as My Time to Complete This Story Draws Near

Today, *14 June 2020*, I got a return call from February 2020. I was still trying to find my old scout friend. I got Johnny Pearce's phone number and called him. This was amazing! He was *gobsmacked*! The last time we spoke was probably in 1960, I guess! More later, but for now, I just wanted to time stamp and commemorate this event!

17 August 2020

I sent this note to my son, Mark.

>Just heard from a relative I've never met. To keep you up to speed:
>
>Hi Thomas, I'm your cousin Jill Worthington. Your mother was my Aunt Betty, and your father was Uncle Joe. Mom died in 1986, and my father Val (worked at WHOI) in 1995. I remember Paul but most of all, your sister Judy who was around Woods Hole a lot when I was young. She moved to Arizona many, many years ago, but I don't know more than that. My younger brother is nicknamed Beaver. He and I are both still in Falmouth. My boyfriend gave me the Ancestry DNA kit, and I know all my ethnic backgrounds, but I have not had time to start building a family tree because I work and am moving to Mashpee. I hit the deck running every morning. Glad you got in touch. I have always been unfortunate that I know so little about my mother's side.
>
>Dick McGuinness and Ethel Dobbins were our grandparents. Grandma was the only grandparent still living when I was born. I so wish I'd known our grandfather; he sounds like he was a lovely gentleman. Mom and my Aunt Jay adored him. Years ago, before Ancestry, some genealogy folks tried to help me track down some Irish ancestors with little luck. Grandma's brother and sister were Tom and Addie—and I think our grandmother's mother was Mary (?), and there is also an Agnes in the mix. Do you have some info you can share with me? (Her

email and phone number are only on my iPhone.)
If you call and miss it, I will try to call you back.
Thanks again, Jill.

What a fascinating "bolt from the blue!" She and I will talk soon. My connection with my mother's side of the family is sketchy, as in not much information! I must correct this before death destroys all records of my family.

09 September 2020

As I type this, Sheila just got a phone call from her son Blake and…drum roll…learned that her grandson Ryan and his new bride, Madyson, are having a baby in March 2021! "Great-Granny-Nanny," as I dubbed her, is *over the moon!* They are both enlisted personnel in the United States Navy. Their careers are just beginning, and Ryan speaks Russian he learned in the Navy. Will the newest Adams speak Russian also, just like his daddy?

19 September 2020

As I edit this manuscript, it would be apropos to announce that this day, I found out that my granddaughter is expecting. It is yet unknown when I will be renamed as a great-grandfather or call me that specific name. I never named myself "Grampytom!"

22 March 2021

Welcoming to the family, Magnolia Ann Celeste Adams, Sheila's great-granddaughter! *22 March 2021*

Welcoming to the family, my great-grandson, Chapman Scott Whisenant! *03 May 2021*

Yesterday, while at our favorite place to socialize and enjoy an adult beverage, a story arose that is memorable to the unknown woman in my account and me. I think it's worth sharing.

You may or may not know my lovely Sheila's background and deep Kentucky roots. Her parents were from Logan County, where, like the place I'm going to relate where my story happened, everyone knew everyone. Sheila's parents knew the parents of Sen. Rand Paul's wife. As I said, everyone knew their neighbors! Logan County was typical, but sadly, today, is uncommon. No one knows their neighbor anymore, much less most people within even one mile. The times, oh, how they've changed! But not so with a Kentuckian. You can take *them* out of Kentucky, but you can't take the *Kentucky* out of them! That is what this brief story is about.

We were settling down for a well-deserved break that started the week yesterday at the hospital for Tom's periodic exam involving anesthesia. Even wearing a mask in a surgical setting while knocked out and with all the required vaccines—"WEAR YOUR MASK AT ALL TIMES!"

The person I'm referring to was not wearing a mask, nor were Sheila or your humble correspondent. Why do I mention that factoid? You can see a person's expression of sadness, crying, happiness, or boredom via their mouth! It's why we smile when we see a friend or loved one.

She was visibly upset. She was on her phone, but I couldn't overhear a peep! Sheila couldn't see her since Sheila was facing me. So I continued to see her face show expressions like she just heard someone had died, or her husband called and told her something horrible.

Next, she became seriously distressed and began breathing rapidly and shallowly. Her mouth was moving, but I heard no words. She might have needed medical assistance, but *what* was the matter? Pause again. I refused to butt in!

I asked Sheila eventually, "Do you see what I see?"

She adjusted her chair and saw. "She's saying, 'I can't breathe,'" Sheila quietly told me.

Eventually, over five minutes later, she was no better. She'd stopped eating her lunch or finishing whatever she was drinking. Sheila went above and beyond and asked her if she could be of any help. She soon found out what we couldn't, from the distance, hear her. She said, "I can't breathe… I can't breathe…" repeatedly!

Slowly, Sheila offered help and advice, and she calmed down a little, but would then resume crying and sobbing. Intermittently, she again begin to hyperventilate. I was scared she might pass out and fall over off her chair. The floor was stone!

She talked to Sheila, God's angel sent to help this stranger. I remember Sheila after my biggest battle with a death experience. She's still that angel.

Our brief encounter was finished, and multiple "Thank you, thank you, thank you's" were said to Sheila! Our stranger's cab arrived. The waitress had called.

What an afternoon! I spent the rest of the day with an angel. But I enjoy the presence of an angel *every day*! *Thanks be to God for that*!

Nikki, our cleaning lady, told us that she had written an article for high school about the Byron camera several years before she met us. She was gobsmacked when she realized she had come face-to-face with the owner's descendant! I had the original camera and the carefully typed and assembled patent work-up. My father had kept this leather/ heavy cardboard box-case in his un-air conditioned storage cabinet, outside on his driveway in central Florida's very humid climate! What a %@$&# idiot! Luckily it was in salvageable shape.

ZERO TO SEVENTY-FIVE

27 May 2021

The story to the top of all stories is about to be revealed. Remember my lost Zippo? On 23 July 2012, I told you about my "long-time friend", my Air Force Zippo lighter.

It was found as weirdly as it was lost! Remember, I've been looking for this souvenir of my military lighter off an on since I lost it! Today, 27 May 2021, I was sitting in my favorite "Archie Bunker" recliner chair (look it up), watching the news. As I reached, from habit, inside the nooks and crannies of my seat, I felt something different. Not another loose spring, but as I zeroed in, I felt a sharper edge of something. Was my mind playing tricks on me, probably? Another second later, I felt a corner to this object! I froze and called Sheila. "Bring me my pocket knife from my desk! *Please!*" Immediately, I had a very sharp knife in my hand. Open. Ready! Going in. I took a slow and accurate slash to the left (away from my body, so as not to accidentally slice myself) and I delicately freed my Zippo(TM) from his prison of almost ten years!

Now for a little self-deprecating humor, I fell flat on my face in a stress test on a treadmill. See "1976" about how my leg went numb if you're skim reading (or forgot). I passed the stress test, and before someone turned their "torture machine" off, my right leg had had enough and stopped being *forced* to hold me up! Nothing hurt. My sense of humor saved me—yet again!

And that's my story, thank you for reading this last line. There are a few miscellaneous items to attend to next.

THOMAS E. BYRON

Strange Cigar Shaped Object Seen & Photographed.

Posted on November 23, 2021 by Administrator

Location of Sighting: Marietta, Georgia
Date of Sighting: November 6, 2021
Time of Sighting: 8:55 AM EST

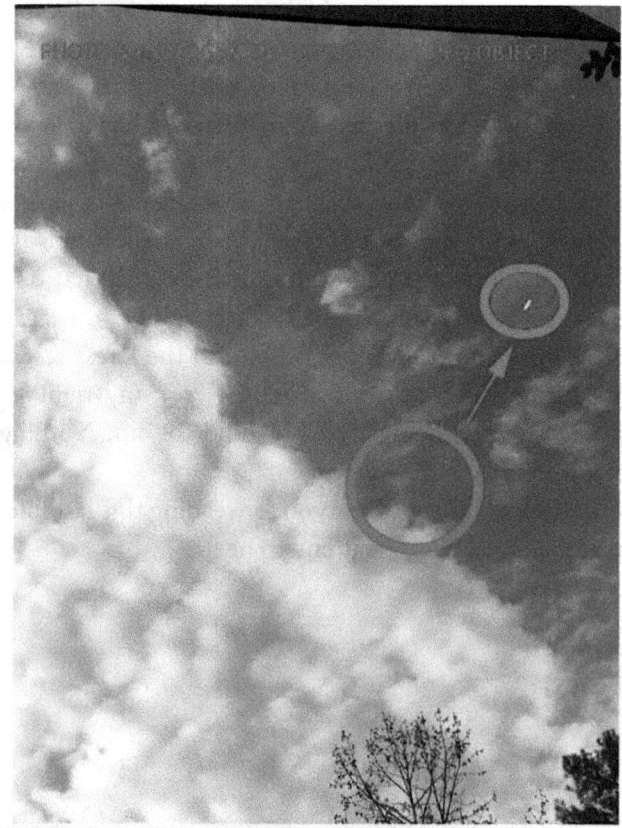

PHOTO & ENLARGEMENT OF CIGAR SHAPED OBJECT.

©Byron

Random Accidental Meetings

My answer to where's the weirdest place you've seen someone you know? I copied this from my Quora account to save me some time.

Strange life coincidences and random encounters that can't be explained:

1. I met my cousin Bart in Times Square on New Year's Eve by accident in 1963–64.
2. Met brother-in-law John from Arizona (1800 miles away) at a five-minute stop in a Tennessee rest area on I-24.
3. Met my hometown Ambler, Pennsylvania, and family doctor in East Tennessee woods in 1978 during an engineering visit for a new telephone service.
4. I met a high school classmate, Ledley, from Ambler, Pennsylvania (815 miles away), at Lifetouch, Georgia. We went to HS in Pennsylvania forty years prior. She's also mentioned on the back cover.
5. Going to Penn Hills HS and Wissahickon HS with my longtime friend Steve Clark, three hundred miles apart. My father and his father got transferred to Pittsburgh, Pennsylvania, from Philadelphia, Pennsylvania. We ended up in the same high school, much to Genevieve's (Steve's mom) dismay. Steve and I were always getting into mischief, according to what Steve told me, his mom thought about me!
6. Neighbor next door, Sheila Brown in Marietta, lives next door to us, and my wife's former name was the same.
7. I saw an F101 (military jet) that I used to work on (same tail number 58-373) from Sawyer AFB, MI, at the Bone Yard in Arizona.
8. Original print of my grandfather Percy's sailboat drawing was returned from New Jersey to Georgia via a stranger. He was seventy when he made it. I was seventy when I received it. The print was given to a stranger before she died. The house's

new owner where the image was located and found traced the family. My son, Mark, was discovered, he led them to me and eventually they hand-delivered it to me (courtesy of the world-wide-web).

9. My wife Sheila's daughter-in-law, Terri, is our neighbor across the road from us in Grand Rivers, Kentucky. Her daughter-in-law never lived in Kentucky.
10. My stepson Jason and I were discussing a lecture in an old economics class. He had heard the same story! Ronnie Hollis and I had the same economics teacher at UAB. Ronnie is forty-five, and I'm seventy. Dr. Johnson told his class the same story as he told me. I was in his evening class as a thirty-nine-year-old, and Ronnie was a twenty-something day student.
11. Commuting GE (Ohio) to and from Erlanger, Kentucky, same person two days in a row, let me merge on I-75 (very congested interstate).
12. I was in Central City, Kentucky, and met a friend who knew my former manager from Cincinnati, Ohio. The customer's name I met was Elvis "somebody." Sadly, I forgot his last name, and he knew Irving Napoleon Howell when I worked in Birmingham, Alabama, at least five years earlier in 1989.
13. While in Hawaii in 1997, at a basketball game, I spotted my wife's cousin in the crowd. We lived in Kentucky, and she resided in Tennessee at the time. We were about six thousand miles away from home and at the same basketball game with two thousand people. We neither knew the other was going to be there. It could not have been more of a surprise to both families!
14. My stepson lives in Smyrna, Georgia. While on our cruise to the *Titanic* wreck in 2012, I was chatting with someone. I was shocked to find out he, too, was from Smyrna, Georgia.
15. I was on a train from Birmingham, Alabama, to New Orleans. I asked a lovely older lady, "Where do you work? I worked for the phone company."

    Her reply to my "little job" at the phone company was interesting but soon took an odd turn. She said dismissively,

"Oh, he had a job there too." I was a peon engineer at the phone company, and this lady's son was the president of BellSouth, Alabama. She never used his title in her reply.

I was in the exact random location in East Tennessee when Anwar Sadat was assassinated (https://en.m.wikipedia.org/wiki/Assassination_of_Anwar_Sadat) (10/81) and the same place five months earlier when the Pope was shot (https://en.m.wikipedia.org/wiki/Pope_John_Paul_II_assassination_attempt) (5/81). I heard both news events on the radio.

In discussing many of these random meetings with my son's lady-friend, I asked her about his last name. It dawned on me that she was from the same city, and I said, "I used to work for someone with that name."

"Oh my," she said. "He was my late husband's uncle." Spence Essell, from Cincinnati Bell in 1971 to 1974. Weird!

16. In Alnwick, UK, we were with our TMC group from 2012 and 2014. It was April 2017, and we were about to tour Alnwick Castle of Harry Potter fame and the *Downton Abbey* TV show. Our tour guide was Leslie Enos, and he told us about his meeting in the early sixties with Frederick Fleet, who spotted the berg that sank the *Titanic*.

17. We were at the *Titanic* restaurant in Cobh, Ireland (formerly Queenstown), where the *Titanic* made her final port. I was out on the porch watching the sunset and puffing on my Vape-pipe, and I had an unusual conversation with a local taking a smoke break. He was a fan of and watched my favorite American TV show, *The Tucker Carlson Show*. Wow. He brought it up when he realized I was a Yank from 3,856 miles away.

18. Very eerie sight early in the morning of 15 April 2012, after being at the *Titanic* wreck site in the North Atlantic. Curtains looked like a cross on the *Balmoral*.

19. Sevierville, Tennessee, 1980. On an engineer visit, I pulled up to a customer's house to get telephone service. As I got ready to leave my car, a song played. I didn't pay much attention

until a moment or two later. There was a black station wagon out front, and as I approached the house, two people came out the front door. A gurney was being moved across the front porch, and the wreath on the front door and the song all made sense. George Jones's "He Stopped Lovin' Her Today" was playing. The customer no longer needs a telephone. The funeral home was taking *him* away.

20. In 1976, I took a job as a telephone engineer in Tennessee. Not long after, I was temporarily transferred to Morristown, Tennessee, where I met Jeff S. In 1982, Jeff and I were selected to go to Louisiana as engineers. Two years later, we were transferred to Alabama as tariff analysts and worked together again. We lived in the same neighborhood, and carpooled.

21. I've known nine people who were murdered (M) or who committed suicide (S): Tim Wright (S), Tim's father (S), Rachael Lively (S), Templin's (M, S), Ricky (S), Babysitter (S), Jack (M) from military, our mother (S according to Laura and me).

22. While discussing Hurricane Harvey with a casual acquaintance at our karaoke bar, Louisiana came up. Since I've lived in eight states, I said, "I lived near Lake Charles."

    Our friend said, "My husband from there too!"

    Then it got stranger. "Oh," I said excitedly. "I lived in Moss Bluff." (The population was only about 10,000.) What are the odds of that?

23. My grandfather was born in September in England. I was born in September in Cincinnati. My son was born in September in Cincinnati. My daughter was born in September in Michigan, and my grandson was born in September in Cincinnati.

24. I sent an email to an old friend in Louisiana from thirty years past!

    "I just saw a note from 15 February 2015. No. I'm not dead! But I remember those walks at lunchtime with the first name George?? Allen around the office in Lake Charles. I'm retired many years now and still kicking. We have lots to catch up on—hopefully, it won't take another three years to start a chat."

The reply three days later:

"Hello Mr. Byron, Doug's wife, Carrie. I am sorry to tell you, but Doug passed away on 21 January 2018. He died after an accident on his Vespa. He had massive brain injuries." I WAS GOBSMACKED!,

25. The *Titanic* was stamped as 401, and this was her build number. When we sailed to the *Titanic* wreck site, our cabin was 4010. Our hotel room number was 410. Too close for comfort!
26. While in Southampton, UK, I talked with a German fellow in the hotel bar late in the evening. When the subject of the *Titanic* came up, I found out he'd written a book about the *Nazi Titanic* movie. When he handed me my signed copy, he dated it. The date we discussed the *Titanic* is marked in the book, "14/15 April 2019," or the 107th anniversary of her sinking! Both were on the same Sundays/Monday as well!
27. In 2019, as I'm finishing up this autobiography, I can add another unusual coincidence. A random answer/post to one of my sessions on Quora caught my attention! I was stunned! When I saw the name, I said, "I remember that name...mmm!" So I posted, "Do you know Paul and Odie?" Immediately I saw a reply. "Yes! They are my parents!" My goodness. This was a neighbor I remembered from 1982. We moved to Tennessee. She and her parents moved to Florida. She was a twenty-year-old then, and she's fifty-seven now. That was a long, long time. We have been chatting and keeping up. She used to babysit my three young kids back then.
28. My story about my first flying experience had a dramatic twist this year—2020. I encountered a random first contact

with a Quoran from the same tiny village in Pennsylvania. The event I was talking about was from an experience sixty-eight years ago—**_sixty-eight years_**!

Tom, we must be near neighbors. I'm in Skippack Township and maybe went up in the same plane—a 1929 WACO mail plane with teardrop wheel covers out of Perkiomen airport. Small world, eh? (Paul Metsch)

29. I met someone in April of 2021, editing and reviewing this tome. A young lady wrote a high school report about Percy Byron's camera. (He wanted to secure a patent!)! When she saw the copy of his booklet on his camera in our library, she was flabbergasted! *So was I!* She reported on *the Byron camera* in 2011. My grandfather had applied for a patent for a view camera. She was stunned while cleaning our apartment when she saw the patent book showing that camera. Then I showed her the actual physical camera. *She looked as if she'd seen a ghost!* Will this list never end?

This entire autobiography you have just read was typed with only my left index finger on my iPhone 6C and finished on my new iPad mini!

Pithy Byronisms

My adage applies: "Learning about the past is the best way to improve the future."

"Keep your keyboard close and your thesaurus even closer" (04 January 2017).

"I'm just struggling along life's path—uphill through a very mosquito-infested woods" (30 November 2016).

"Terrorism or not? Ever been attacked by bees that didn't come from a hive?"

"Destroy terrorists at their home base!"

"Political correctness is slavery to the tongue!"

"He [she] has too much slack in his/her leash!"

"Is digital racing "erasing" (phonics trick)?

"I'm a rebel without applause!"

"I have lived a half century in the last millennium."

"Some of my enemies will outlive me, but the whole truth, and nothing but the truth will outlive *them all!*"

"The trouble with getting older? Running out of *yet.*"

To quote me, "Don't chicken out while you're counting!"

"I'll take all the yesterdays I can get!"

"If I were any sharper, I'd probably cut myself!"

The division is the common core of the democrat party. Keep a victim base and elect the uninformed masses to be imprisoned in poverty and violence. The lucky ones are safer in jail than at home with their families. Import low-wage replacement workers to keep the base replenished. What a sad, sorry mess!

Don't keep pissing in your shoe and expect to pour champagne one day!

There is no ultimate truth, and those who spend their life looking for it never live a life of satisfaction. Searching for an illusion, someone else's dream, or hope prevents one from adding meaning to life.

This is the truth: adding meaning to one's life, not looking for life. It is just too easy.

Today is the only day in our lives we can use.

We have thousands of days to live if we are fortunate. We only have one "today" at a time. Our life is all "tomorrow" for *now*! The future is forward, not backward. One day we will have a lot of missed opportunities called "yesterdays."

He doesn't have just a few issues (i.e. problems); he has a lifetime subscription.

I didn't get this old to be stupid!

I hope I never master ignorance because then I will stop learning. Once you know everything, you indeed must then grapple with arrogance. I prefer the journey of growing in understanding.

"I am only concerned with politically correct speech trumping the truth!" You may quote me on that. No more, no less. This includes the left, the right, and the independent and uninformed viewpoint.

If you can't heat the kitchen, *stay out of it*!

"If he were turned into a watch, he wouldn't ever be on time!"

"If it weren't for *ifs*, many people would have no hope!"

"Life is the luck of the draw, played in a time-sensitive environment, with no agreed to rules."

"Consensus can occur anywhere between two sides of a debate, whereas the truth is a single point between those same two sides."

A lot of things fall under the category of "stooopid!"

"Winners make choices. Losers make excuses."

"Old age is like ill-fitting underwear. It eventually sneaks up on you, and it does not make you feel *more* comfortable."

"That is just your opinion, but it depends on how you look at it. After all, it depends on your prescription!"

"The more you know, the more you have to get confused."

"You *can* be too dumb, but you *can't* be too smart."

"In the long run, the only thing [in life] that matters is the total of every little thing that is presumed to have had no consequences."

"A lot can fall off the lip before it turns into a sip!" (21 September 2014).

"The *worst* person to take advice from is yourself!" (19 September 2014).

"This is stupid, obviously designed by morons!"

The "Genesis" of what the Bible says ends with an interesting "Revelation."

Those politicians are "the dumb and the restless!"

Some of us find the truth, but not until after it has been beaten and robbed and left for dead on the side of the road!

History will decide, as it does, who is famous, who is liked. The facts will determine the truth.

I am a conservative orphan stranded on a deserted island surrounded by liberal sharks.

My mind is gone, and the best I can remember, it left without saying goodbye!

"Facts in politics are like tumbleweeds driven by the winds of public opinion" (Tom Byron).

She's not stubborn; she's just wrong!

When everyone is treated equally, not everyone is treated fairly.

I was asked, "Class action lawsuit?" Tom Byron replied, "You take the 'action,' as I have 'no class.'"

Is it better to die for what you believe in than live a life you don't believe in? The word *l-i-f-e* is separated from an *f* from an *l-i-e*. Does this *f* stand for faith or failure to this man? (You may quote *me* on that.)

Everything that it was, but just in a different form. Everything that isn't may or may not ever be in any form.

"Am I my own keeper and my brother's? For if I can't help myself, how can I help him?"

I wouldn't trust _____ to tell me what time it is!

She said, "It is taking a while to get to the meat of this newspaper." (Large holiday issue.) I immediately replied, "That's because *that* newspaper is full of baloney!"

"In the end, some of us find the truth, but not until after it has been beaten and robbed and left for dead on the road!"

You don't win by being safe. You win by being bold.

Why do people who play and practice make a lot more than those who *work*!

"Government's primary duty is to protect itself from an informed populace!"

Does the prettiest lion eat the most, or is it the brightest hunter who gets fat?

"My sand is getting into the neck of the hourglass."

"In practice, there is sweat from accomplishment. In theory, there is sweat from worrying."

Rainy weather brings out the lost drivers!

If I *did* care, I would have empathy!

"Yesterday's now gone. It has belonged to the past for as long as we remember it.

Then it is gone when we are gone."

"You have two rights: the right to your opinion. Your right to be wrong!"

I've slept more years than you have lived!

Those offended with having to cope with reading big words have escaped the learning environment, as it were! You may quote me on that closing bit of irony (http://qr.ae/T20mH).

"Winners never win with points from the *other* team."

How are you? "I'm only one heartbeat away from death, thank you!"

"Carpe rectum. If you can't do that, seize the day!"

"I am not lazy. I'm just efficient."

"Life is a chain of events. Causes. Reactions. Decisions. Results.

They are intertwined, intentionally and unintentionally."

"He just ran outta IQ."

"Acting stupid and crazy with a deadly weapon can never be stopped by law, only a bullet!

Even firefighters do stop the fire with fire [backfires to burn up the fuel to stop the wild advance (read shooter), and stop out of control fires!]."

"Teach people to expect nothing, and they will do nothing."

"Children are our brush with immortality."

"Learning every day."

"On Romney losing, 'The MSM's mantra stepped on his dogma!'"

"You never know if you don't ask."

"Allow a poor person to earn an education and teach them responsibility, and you have raised *one* Republican. Teach a poor person to live off the government and expect conception-to-death assistance to be provided, and you have raised an entire *family* of Democrats" (Tom Byron). You may quote me if you like.

The truth is a statement that is bookended by confusion.

So close you can't put a piece of paper, not even a *thought*, between those two places!

If I knew life would be this much fun, I would've asked my parents to have me sooner!

When some people are challenged, their tolerance of an objective disagreement with their position flies out of the window faster than sunlight comes in a window!

I am just trying to get along with life.

"The more I learn, the more I realize that what I thought I knew, I never *really* understood. That makes the next learning event more valuable when it corrects my past ignorance."

"Small people see the riches of this world in a small way."

"Someone's gonna play the stupid card!"

"It wasn't a kiss of death, just a *big* hug!"

"Fame is a cruel master."

"If I were doing any better, you'd see me on the evening news!"

My Last Thought

"He tried, sometimes he succeeded, sometimes he did not, but trying is about all one can do—since life was, as he oft said, 'not a dress rehearsal but the final [and only] performance. You do what you can."

Someone heard me off in the distance say, "Mom, now I'm glad you never drove a car your entire life, or else you would have traveled even farther away from me!"

Now imagine with me, if you will. What would I have had to say *had I kept a written diary?*

Postscript

Thomas Edward Byron (1946–20xx). This is a preview only. One of you needs to edit (xx) at the date at the "end of the dash" and a brief cause of my demise.

I am now referred to in the past tense. My time has come and gone. "I am" has become officially "He was."

I was born to Elizabeth McGuinness Byron and Joseph Marrin Byron. They were not wealthy and had no telephone. I was not "the obvious child" but the third child. My neighbor Bill Wesling was called and knew about me before my father. He walked next door and told my father he had a second son. My brother Paul and sister Judy were my older siblings. Ricky, Laura, and Debbie followed my birth. My two young sisters presumably survive me. My three children from my first wife, Julie. Lisa and her children, Lauren and her son, my great-grandson Chapman, and her younger brother Alex, and my son, Mark, and his son Zachary all survive me, I hope. I also leave to take care of their mother and my dear sweet Sheila, her three children Blake (children: Ryan, Belle, and Tess); Jason (children: Macy and Sully); and Craig Adams (children: Tatum and Vivienne), Sheila's children and grands by her first marriage. Until those who knew me are "They were," I will become a "they" and then forgotten.

I have a few years while this obit floats around to explain here what "I am" to "he was" was all about. I assume this will be found if I remember to tell anyone I wrote it.

> He apologizes if he was moved late in life and either didn't care to edit the above list of states or forgot to edit this. He was like that. He tried several career-type adventures, which he found out never led to riches. He was a bagman for the mob at age nine, then delivering newspapers legally was his part-time job until high school graduation.

THOMAS E. BYRON

USAF aircraft mechanic until 1970, then a civilian again with jobs ranging from telephone engineering, jet engine assembler at GE, McDonald's manager, wedding and portrait photographer, school photographer, and for his finale, a top writer on Quora.com for over five years, well into his seventies.

You just read the highlights. Death came from a long and unsuccessful struggle with "being agreeable." He fought to be a curmudgeon for many decades all over the United States, from his birthplace, Cincinnati, Ohio, to other states he adopted and loved as home: Ohio, Pennsylvania, Texas and Illinois USAF (briefly), Michigan, Kentucky, Tennessee, Louisiana, Alabama, Georgia.

As you read this and know that I'm dead, I am writing this as (if) I'm alive...ha. We are both wondering where I am now. Maybe not. I won't tell you, and you can assume you know, or you will have to wait. I now possess the answer you and humanity all seek to understand. Cue up his selections of funeral music on his iPhone.

On My iPhone / Funeralmusic.jpeg

Ledley 1960s classmate

"My, my, my! What a life! You had to have made lots of notes over the years! I enjoyed your life! I love reading, autobiography usually is not my preference, but you held my attention for real! One thing. If you were a Black man, you would not be here to one finger type your first seventy-five! Not with your encounters with the police! Good Job, Tom! Good!" She's mentioned on Pg. 321 item 4 when I relate how we randomly met fifty (Ledley).

Ian, my nephew,

"It's a real roller coaster for sure. I've learned a lot I didn't know [obviously], but that also makes me realize how disconnected we all are from each other. Growing up with it as a norm never really seemed off or unfortunate, but now it's a bummer. I love all you guys and honestly don't know you all." (He's mentioned in a Vermont meeting of ours in 2013 on Pg. 247 (Ian))

I'm coming to join you… ELIZABETH!!
This was a TV show reference. My mother's name is Elizabeth. This is not a Royal reference!

THOMAS E. BYRON

Funeral music

▶ Play   ⤭ Shuffle

Amazing Grace
Combined Bands

He Stopped Loving Her To...
George Jones

Méditation from Thaïs
Joshua Bell, Nigel Hess & Royal P...

Somewhere Over the Rain...
Israel Kamakawiwo'ole

Time to Say Goodbye
By Francesco Sartori & Lucio Qua...

The Emperor's Adagio
Michael Dulin

Agnus Dei (From "Platoon")
Crouch End Festival Chorus

Angel
Sarah McLachlan

About the Author

Thomas E. Byron is/was the only sixth-generation photographer, and his great-grandfather created the first selfie in 1909 (see intro to *this* autobiography). His son is/was a sixth-generation professional photographer.

I was raised in a raucous household, and I did not use the term *home* on purpose. All of my nearly twenty years living with my parents was unharmonious and rarely calm. My older brother left home upon graduating in '58. My older sister got married in our hometown the same day in '66 that I got married in Chicago—775 miles away!

After four years (actually three years, nine months, and twenty-seven days) of military service, we moved to Kentucky. My parents were still living in Ambler, Pennsylvania, where I grew up. I also started a four-year pursuit of two degrees. An epic odyssey. In 1974, I earned an associate's degree, and then I would receive my bachelor's degree and then continue my engineering career.

At some point, my parents moved to Florida. One of my two sisters moved to Vermont and the other sister to California. I was working in Ohio as a clerk for Cinti. Bell. I got transferred to Tennessee, then Louisiana. Next, it was Alabama and finally/lastly (phew), in 1989, to Kentucky. You get the drift—I had a career that enjoyed moving employees all over their territory. Correct! I moved to Georgia and retired, after a six-year stint as a school photographer.

My two younger sisters and I are the last of our family of eight. I'm now in Georgia, and I won't move! Again! Ever! My second marriage is wonderful! We are close to my great-grandson, and my Sheila has a great-granddaughter in Maryland.

I'm a retired professional photographer, "a soon-to-be" published writer, a degreed economist, a retired telephone engineer, a tariff analyst, a military veteran, a handyman, a father, a husband, an uncle, a brother, also a proud grandfather, and an even prouder great-grandfather!

www.ingramcontent.com/pod-product-compliance
Lightning Source LLC
Chambersburg PA
CBHW071650160426
43195CB00012B/1412